PAUL FAIRFIELD

Moral Selfhood in the Liberal Tradition: The Politics of Individuality

UNIVERSITY OF TORONTO PRESS
Toronto Buffalo London

© University of Toronto Press Incorporated 2000
Toronto Buffalo London
Printed in Canada

ISBN 0-8020-4736-X

Printed on acid-free paper

Toronto Studies in Philosophy
Editors: James R. Brown and Calvin Normore

Canadian Cataloguing in Publication Data

Fairfield, Paul, 1966–
Moral selfhood in the liberal tradition: the politics of individuality

(Toronto studies in philosophy)
Includes bibliographical references and index.
ISBN 0-8020-4736-X

I. Liberalism. I. Title II. Series.

JC574.F34 2000   320.51'2   C99-931688-5

University of Toronto Press acknowledges the financial assistance to its publishing program of the Canada Council for the Arts and the Ontario Arts Council.

This book has been published with the help of a grant from the Canadian Federation for the Humanities, using funds provided by the Social Sciences and Humanities Research Council of Canada.

University of Toronto Press acknowledges the financial support for its publishing activities of the Government of Canada through the Book Publishing Industry Development Program (BPIDP)

Canadä

Contents

Acknowledgments

I would like to express my gratitude to Gary B. Madison for his counsel through the years, which had a profound influence on both this work and my development as a philosopher. I would like to thank Lawrence Haworth, who generously supervised and commented on the manuscript. His remarks and suggestions from the preliminary stages to the preparation of the final draft have been consistently beneficial. I would also thank Jeff Mitscherling, Evan Simpson, and Sam Ajzenstat for their insights and suggestions on this manuscript as well as on some of my other endeavours. At the University of Toronto Press, I thank Alex McIntyre and Ron Schoeffel for their scrupulous editing and professionalism. Two anonymous referees generously commented on the manuscript and contributed to its improvement. Finally, I am grateful to the Social Sciences and Humanities Research Council of Canada for granting me a postdoctoral fellowship.

MORAL SELFHOOD IN THE LIBERAL TRADITION

Introduction

Historically, liberalism is founded upon a gesture of opposition to political conditions at variance with autonomous individuality and to the doctrines that make those conditions possible. From the seventeenth century to contemporary times, liberal and protoliberal writers have sought to identify all that negates the free expression of individual natures and to issue a critique informed by a conception of individual agency and its conditions of possibility. Ancient and medieval doctrines both political and philosophical had given expression to a view of human beings as primarily members of a community dependent in their beliefs, ends, and identity on the social body of which they were a part. Persons were conceived within these doctrines as essentially social beings and as such inheritors of obligations and roles having a basis in tradition, principal among which was the duty of obedience to authority both in the political form of obedience to an absolute monarch and in the semipolitical form of obedience to the Roman church. Rights and obligations were contingent both on one's place in the social order and on the discretion of absolute power. Liberalism in its original manifestation is a critique of conditions at once political, social, economic, and theological which had produced a social order of intolerance, civil and religious strife, political absolutism, and excessive reliance on tradition. In keeping with the general spirit of enlightenment of which it is a part, classical liberalism understands itself as a doctrine of liberation from all that had circumscribed the domain of individual agency and subordinated the capacities of rational reflection to the powers of church and state.

If liberalism in its initial form is a protest against political servility, identifying the multiple obstacles that inhibit the development of the free personality, it also contains an implicit 'positive' moment informed by assumptions of both a political and ethical as well as an ontological and metaphysical nature. In this view there is a part of human existence that lies beyond the legitimate reach of political power, a domain of agency on which authority may not encroach without violating the dignity of persons as rational and individuated beings. Persons must never lack a sphere of action and concern over which they preside freely as individuals, a domain constituted by a set of rights. Political institutions properly serve the requirements of not only civility but individual agency conceived as the capacity for rational self-determination. The basis of political legitimacy is individuality itself and the terms of association to which individual agents prudently consent. Liberalism is accordingly a politics of individuality or a configuration of principles placed at the disposal of the rational and autonomous self.

In liberal terms political power has its source only in the consent of a free citizenry. It being the nature of power both to corrupt and to extend its reach until it encounters a limit, the exercise of power is governed by constraints protective of the individual's freedom and autonomy. The principles of constitutionalism and the separation of powers are to prevent abuses all but guaranteed to occur whenever political power is checked only by the discretion of those who exercise it. The use of power, in the liberal view, must be carefully delimited and philosophically justified in view of the constitution of the individual as a moral and political agent. The rights of the individual serve as constraints on state power and indeed all power, and it is here that political authority has its proper basis. Liberalism distinguishes itself among political philosophies in the emphasis it places on the limits of state power and the rationale for these limits.

The accent on rights reflects a larger shift in modern thought which places the individual at the centre of the moral world and analyses social phenomena from its perspective rather than perspectives of theological origin, tradition, community, class, and so on. Early liberal thought reflects a profound shift in the status of the individual from a subject of absolute and divinely ordained authority to the basis of political legitimacy. It becomes an autonomous self whose obligations are neither inherited nor unchosen but entailed by the rights that it claims for itself. This shift in status of the individual within classical liberal theory is the political counterpart to the shift characteristic of Enlightenment thought in general toward a radical concentration upon subjectivity beginning with Descartes's *cogito*. Political judgments no less than those of an epistemological, scientific, and theological nature have their basis no longer in authority and tradition but in the rational capacity of the individual self. The basis of knowledge, political and otherwise, is the constitution of the reflecting subject, a constitution characterized by rational autonomy. The reason that early liberal thought identifies, following the tradition of the Greeks, as the defining trait of human beings is the reason of Enlightenment philosophy generally – the reason of abstract methodology, rule-governed inference, and prudent instrumentality. As the person is conceived increasingly in terms of its cognitive faculties and sovereign individuality, it is abstracted from the bonds of the communal order more readily associated with premodern thought. The social order is a contingent and fragile structure held together by no unifying element stronger than the shared self-interest of an assortment of individuals with varying ends.

Liberalism's dominant moral passions concern the individual and its freedom, broadly speaking, to live by its own judgment, sentiments that reflect a modern conception of the self as not only the centre and basis of the moral world but a sovereign chooser disposed to social reality in a particular manner. The individual is able to separate itself reflectively from not only its moral ends but its facticity as a whole (its participation within tradition, the customary sentiments, expectations, and practices that make up its way of life, its beliefs, commitments, and particularities of various kinds), all of which are merely accidental properties of the self distinguished from its underlying essence. In its essence the individual of conventional liberalism is an altogether sovereign and rational agent bearing each of its accidental properties and ends by an act of will. Its nature is describable in metaphysical language as either the noumenal self of transcendental idealism, the materialist and mechanistic maximizer of utility, the proprietor of its person and capacities, the free and rational will, or the possessor of an underlying spiritual principle or core of being of one description or another. While accounts of its metaphysical nature vary widely within the liberal tradition, a recurring assumption is that in order for a theory of justice to assert the moral priority of the individual and its rights to the collective – the general welfare, the interests of community life, the claims of tradition, class, church, and so on – it must also assert the individual's ontological priority to all intersubjectivity. The self must be describable in asocial and ahistorical terms as the possessor of a deep human nature hidden within its innermost recesses, an inner citadel of some description upon which no trespass may be allowed and in virtue of which the person is awarded absolute value. Liberal writings on the individual almost invariably accentuate its rational autonomy, its capacities for reflection and choice, and its independence from communal ties. The implication is that without the assumption of a 'true self' or ego substance located in its inner depths, no act of coercion against it could count as an injustice. A relic no doubt of medieval doctrine for which no indignity is possible for a being lacking an eternal soul-substance fashioned by a divine creator, classical liberal theory invariably resorts to a metaphysics of individuality as a foundation for political individualism. As a consequence, liberal individualism from its inception to the present contains a mix of assumptions (ontological, metaphysical, psychological, sociological, anthropological, economic, ethical, and metaethical) regarding the fundamental constitution of the individual, and it is this set of assumptions at the heart of conventional liberalism that must at long last be called into question.

The liberal problematic implicitly rests upon premises concerning the self which are increasingly controversial and problematic. The liberal individual's vaunted independence, its strategic and instrumentally rational mode of comportment, its single-minded and often mechanistic pursuit of gratification in its economic, political, and ethical relations, and its unlimited sovereignty over its existence are assumptions that by contemporary standards appear largely unpersuasive if not evidently false. Fastening upon such assumptions, critics of liberalism often allege that because liberal politics, particularly in its contractarian and utilitarian formulations, presupposes an altogether asocial, ahistorical, and metaphysical conception of the self, a political morality predicated on it must fail. A politics of individuality, as liberal theorists themselves have traditionally assumed, rests upon a metaphysics of individuality, which by most contemporary accounts is a bankrupt enterprise. Metaphysical essentialism and social atomism likewise appear hopelessly inadequate premises on which to erect a conception of justice. Conventional liberal assumptions that regard persons as mutually indifferent, strategic, instrumentally rational, socially unconditioned, sovereign, hedonistic, and often egoistic seekers of gratification present a phenomenologically inadequate interpretation of moral agency. There is no reason to suppose that the self contains any deep essence removed from the vicissitudes of history and culture, nor is it correct to model ethical and political relations on economic practice after the fashion of contractarian and utilitarian theory.

Liberal individualism necessarily relies on a strong conception of personal agency, yet the ways in which this conception has been articulated since the seventeenth century present contemporary liberals with a troubling legacy of assumptions from which liberalism itself must be liberated. The legacy of Hobbesian atomism, Kantian metaphysics, Benthamite rationalism, and a host of other assumptions often viewed as fundamental to liberal discourse must at long last be renounced. Critiques of the foundations of liberalism from Hegelian, Marxist, socialist, communitarian, conservative, feminist, postmodern, and other circles have largely succeeded in demonstrating the inadequacy of the foundations of conventional liberalism and compel its contemporary proponents to undertake a thorough re-examination of the basis of liberal politics. The (partial) success of (some of) these critiques necessitates a fundamental reconsideration of not only the argumentation traditionally offered in support of liberal principles but the underlying assumptions concerning the constitution of the self as a moral and rational agent. The need for reconsideration is especially pressing in light of the suggestion implicit to such critiques that liberal principles of justice are to be rejected since they are premised on a false ontology, one that fails altogether to comprehend the reality of human embeddedness and intersubjectivity. It is now a virtual commonplace, even among many liberals themselves, that the classical formulations of liberalism err in presupposing a view of the individual as a sovereign moral whole possessing a fully formed constitution prior to or apart from social involvements. Subjectivity is never merely given but is contingent on the self-understandings, traditions, practices, language, institutions, and a variety of other particularities which situate us within history and culture, as numerous philosophical schools of thought have brought to our attention. Political philosophies premised on asocial and ahistorical conceptions of agency distort our understanding of justice and can fatally weaken the very conditions of intersubjectivity that make individual agency possible. Indeed, much of the persuasive force of nonliberal politics stems from the premise that individuals are not asocial atoms but are constituted by particularities stemming from the communal order to which they belong, and accordingly that political institutions must accord with and do justice to persons thus constituted.

The communitarian challenge to liberalism represents perhaps the most incisive of the contemporary critiques and it is particularly with this challenge in mind that I undertake a reconsideration of some fundamental assumptions of liberal politics. This critique in particular has served to remind political philosophers of important lessons of largely Aristotelian and Hegelian origin which are too often forgotten within political cultures and philosophies committed to individual rights, and which frequently force liberals into a defensive posture on the assumption – the mistaken assumption, I shall argue – that a comprehensive recognition of human sociability carries troubling implications for political individualism. That the self is indeed embedded within communal practices, that it is formed by an array of social conditions that precede it, and that its fundamental mode of comportment and identity are its inheritance as a social and historical being are premises whose truth value is no longer in question. Nor are such hypotheses merely trivially true, as one contemporary liberal response has it. There is nothing trivial in the premise that a conception of justice must accord with who we ourselves are. No adequate conception of politics fails to be mindful of the basic manner in which persons are constituted as moral and rational beings, nor may it bracket this matter from consideration. Political philosophies invariably contain assumptions about the self which are imported into their methodology and basic problematic in a fashion that is not always apparent on first inspection but that is of paramount importance. It is therefore imperative to pose anew the basic problematic of liberal politics by liberating it from the standard premises of contractarian and utilitarian methodology and moving toward a formulation which incorporates a phenomenologically adequate conception of moral selfhood.

Liberal principles neither need nor ought to be defended on the ground that they represent the terms of political association to which all strategically inclined, utility maximizing, and mutually indifferent individuals would consent were they in a state of nature, or behind a veil of ignorance, or occupying some other purportedly objective and impartial standpoint. The myth of ahistorical and atomistic individuality which has plagued liberal doctrine from its inception has run its course, as have the methodologies that have depended on it, and must make way for a theory of individuality that fully comprehends its social embeddedness. Liberalism should be articulated in a manner that comprehends both the conditions and limits of individual agency. It can neither take the individual as a moral and metaphysical given after the fashion of classical liberalism nor abstract it entirely from the social circumstances in which it is situated. It must relearn the Aristotelian maxim that the human being is a social as well as a rational agent and inquire into the conditions that make such agency possible.

With this in view, the study that follows has a twofold aim. First, it discusses and critically examines conceptions of moral selfhood operative within liberal doctrine from the seventeenth century to the present. It describes the manner in which assumptions regarding the constitution of moral agency have informed the liberal problematic in the writings of such figures as Thomas Hobbes, John Locke, Jean-Jacques Rousseau, and Immanuel Kant to such contemporary writers as John Rawls and Robert Nozick. Second, it proposes to overhaul the liberal understanding of rational moral agency. The overhauled conception that I advance accommodates elements of the contemporary critiques, particularly the communitarian critique, without abandoning principles of liberal individualism and endeavours to provide a more defensible philosophical basis for such principles. The study is divided into two parts corresponding to these two aims. The three chapters comprising Part I, 'The Metaphysics of Individuality,' provide separate discussions of several key figures within the liberal tradition, discussions that focus on premises regarding the self, community, and rationality upon which liberal politics has traditionally relied. The general conclusion of Part I is that communitarian and other recent critiques have been largely successful in unseating many of liberalism's standard assumptions and that in view of this a fundamental overhaul of the liberal conception of the self is urgently required if liberalism is to survive these critiques. The three chapters comprising Part II, 'The Politics of Individuality,' provide this alternative conception. The first of these defends a narrative conception of the self following in the tradition of phenomenological hermeneutics while incorporating premises derived from certain twentieth-century philosophies of existence and from the pragmatism of John Dewey. The conception of moral selfhood that liberalism requires, I maintain, is a narrative conception that includes a central place for the categories of lifeworld, practice, and self-interpretation. The account that emerges is one of situated agency – a socially, historically, and linguistically constituted being, yet one that is never without the capacity for individuated and autonomous agency. Part II also provides a discussion of reason and rational agency to complete the characterization of the self as a situated agent. The final chapter pursues some political implications of the theses defended in Chapters 3 through 5. I argue that the account of the self defended in these chapters affords a proper vantage point from which to support and interpret liberal principles. The eminently contestable notion of a liberal order or a free society is given a particular interpretation in this chapter, one largely critical of egalitarian, social democratic accounts and inclined toward a more limited conception of government than most contemporary liberals recommend. The principal function of the state within a liberal order, I argue, is to identify and secure the political conditions that make autonomous agency possible, a policy that requires significant modification of the massive welfare states of present-day liberal societies.

Readers familiar with the history of liberal doctrine may wish to proceed ahead to the latter sections of Chapter 3, where my 'positive' argument begins. I include the initial two chapters on the premise that liberalism is best understood historically (indeed that it cannot be understood otherwise) and also as a reminder to contemporary liberals of the rich yet troubling legacy with which we are obliged in one fashion or another to come to terms. These chapters also serve to remind liberalism's critics of the internal diversity of this tradition, something often overlooked in critiques of 'atomistic individualism' or the 'unencumbered self,' which too often presuppose a unified philosophy of the self underlying all important articulations of liberalism. Part I attempts to demonstrate that there is no such unified conception neatly fitting either of these epithets, both of which oversimplify a long and internally contested tradition of thought. What the various historical and contemporary articulations of liberalism express is not a unified body of doctrine but a set of differing and overlapping assumptions regarding the constitution of the self as a moral and political agent, premises that are ontological, metaphysical, psychological, economic, and moral. In differing ways such premises give expression to notions of individuality that accentuate the capacity for autonomous and individuated agency, yet too often in ahistorical and metaphysical vocabularies. The position defended here is that while it is untenable to conceive of the self as an asocial and sovereign chooser in the sense dear to many classical and neoclassical liberals, it can still be regarded as possessing both a capacity and right of self-authorship which political institutions must take seriously.

A political morality that eludes easy description, liberalism is best understood in historical terms as a conception of justice that would safeguard the liberty of the individual from a succession of historical circumstances that tend toward its negation, whether these be the forces of absolutism, religious authoritarianism, civil strife, economic hegemony, totalitarianism, ethnic intolerance, or other conditions. As the major obstacles to liberty have succeeded one another in modern history, liberal discourse has modified itself so as to provide an effective opposition against tyranny in its several forms. It has upheld the rights of individual agency against a succession of historical conditions that breed servility in both our public and private lives. At the present moment in history, amid the decline of totalitarianism, one major obstacle to liberty too often overlooked in liberal discourse is the hegemony within virtually all areas of contemporary culture of the paradigm of science-technology and instrumental rationality. The main political expression of this is the calculus of social utility which with seeming impartiality and quasi-scientific exactitude sets about tallying individual rights and freedoms, placing these alongside other ends with the aim of maximizing what is ambiguously termed 'the general welfare.' No longer inviolable constraints, rights too frequently are subordinated within contemporary political culture to the calculus of social utility and placed alongside other competing 'preferences' in the interest of collective expediency. A refashioned liberalism must find the resources with which to counter the reigning paradigm of instrumentality and offer an alternative political morality committed to 'taking rights seriously' by identifying and securing the political conditions of individual agency.

PART ONE:

THE METAPHYSICS OF INDIVIDUALITY

1

The Classical Liberals

From its inception, liberalism's principal aim has been to identify the conditions of the possibility of individuality. There is a part of human existence, liberalism maintains, that properly lies beyond the rule of collective opinion, beyond custom, authority, tradition, and above all beyond the legitimate reach of state power. Liberalism holds that an individual's life ought never lack a certain sphere or jurisdiction in which one is at liberty to determine one's own manner of living and choice of values. It was above all the values of individual freedom, autonomy, self-creation, self-expression, and civility that found expression in classical liberal principles of justice and human rights, principles whose primary *raison d'être* was to safeguard the dignity and inviolability of the individual. Under no circumstances were persons to be reduced to the status of mere instruments of another's will, but must be treated in a manner befitting rational and self-respecting agents.

If classical liberal politics placed itself at the disposal of the individual, seeking both to identify and to secure the conditions of the possibility of autonomous selfhood through the establishment of political and legal institutions, the task fell to liberal anthropology and metaphysics to describe the constitution of this individual. In order for this much-celebrated notion – the individual – to capture the imagination of early modern Europe, it was imperative that it be given philosophical expression and dressed up in modern metaphysical guise. This was accomplished by appropriating and modernizing the classical notion of the human being as a rational animal, the being that is possessed of the *logos*. It is on account of the subject's rational faculties – conceived both in epistemological terms as the capacity to ascertain the truth about the world and in practical terms as the capacity to realize whatever ends it may happen to hold in an efficient manner – that it is elevated above the order of nature and declared a being of intrinsic worth. The possibility of human dignity squarely rests on the constitution of the individual as a rational being. This is a constitution that is capable in principle of employing its own understanding and liberating itself thereby from man's 'self-incurred tutelage.'

For classical liberalism, the individual is a rational agent in a rather strong sense. It is a fundamentally self-interested and self-determining being capable of fashioning its existence with conscious will and purpose and of being the cause of its own actions. In its essence, the liberal self is a sovereign chooser which assigns to itself its own plan of life together with a set of values, principles, and beliefs without having to take direction from any higher authority. The individual possesses an underlying identity – a deep core of being – with a determinate nature describable in the language of metaphysics. Whether conceived as the materialistic maximizer of utility or the transcendental subject, the liberal self is the possessor of an essential nature which remains unchanged through all the vicissitudes of history and culture, which is determined in its being quite apart from such accidental circumstances as the language, social practices, forms of community and interpersonal relationships in which it becomes involved. It is, as well, a self that is given prior to its choice of ends. The individual always remains at some remove from its own values and preferences, as well as from the conduct in which it engages, all of which factors are mere contingencies and accidents which may be added or subtracted without affecting the fundamental constitution of the self. Underlying and persisting throughout the individual's various choices and courses of action is a stable substance that remains fixed apart from its involvements in practical affairs. The actions that it performs, the ends that it chooses, and the social ties that it forms are likewise peripheral to the core of selfhood that is the basis of moral identity.[1]

A condition of the individual's proper existence and 'felicity,' according to classical liberalism, is the liberty to make choices affecting its own life. It is here that we find the source of all political legitimacy in a liberal order. Institutions must be arranged in a manner that will make possible the free expression of individual natures. They must create a sphere or jurisdiction within which one may practise self-creation in freedom from other persons and the state. The sovereign and rational individual became the basis of the just state, the rights of the individual taking priority over all other kinds of ethical and political considerations. This fundamental principle of classical liberalism – the primacy of individual rights and freedoms – needed, it was believed, not only to be theoretically grounded on a firm, rational foundation,[2] it was also in need of the services of the metaphysician in order for its notion of the individual to be considered philosophically estimable. Who was this individual – that all-important invention of seventeenth-century liberalism – and how was it constituted? A politics of individuality, so it seemed, presupposed a metaphysics of individuality.

Before discussing individually several of classical liberalism's principal figures and their respective accounts of moral selfhood, I shall begin with a brief overview of several themes common to these and other figures associated with classical liberal thought. Understanding liberalism's history will ultimately shed light on what an adequate formulation of liberal politics will look like.

A Classical Fable

In the beginning there was the individual. Sovereign, independent, free, rational, the natural proprietor of its person and capacities,[3] this much-celebrated individual of classical liberalism represented the true state of human beings in their natural condition. Living a life of splendid isolation in the fabled state of nature, the individual was an autonomous and solitary being. It led a rather mean and lonely existence in this pre- or, on some accounts, semi-social condition. An egoist by nature, its relations with other individuals were decidedly strategic, sporadic, and frequently troubled owing to its fundamentally antithetical constitution. Above all, such relations were contingent. Interaction with other individuals was an occasionally useful means of acquiring goods or of satisfying certain natural desires, but it was far from being a necessary element of human life, nor did such involvements alter in any way the individual's fundamental nature and identity. This asocial atom was without aims that extended beyond the bounds of self-interest. It valued its own happiness, peace, security, the satisfaction of its given needs, and, above all else, power. Interaction with other selves was a practice fraught with danger, given the universal desire of human beings in the state of nature to achieve domination over others by any available means.

The state of nature – in some accounts a historical hypothesis concerning the actual condition of human beings in a presocial state, on others a conceptual device or a piece of moral fiction – represented a moral description of the natural human condition as well as a logical starting point for political theorizing. Fictional or otherwise, the state of nature was taken in classical liberalism to represent a condition of perfect freedom. Prior to the formation of social bonds, institutions, and practices, the isolated and amoral self was continually preoccupied with its own preservation and gratification. With neither justice nor injustice in this original condition, prudence alone governed human nature. The individual was sole judge of its interests, all of which were strictly subordinate to its continued existence and happiness.

Among the principal founders of the liberal tradition – including Thomas Hobbes, John Locke, Jean-Jacques Rousseau, and Immanuel Kant – accounts varied over the exact condition of the state of nature, differences that deserve to be noted briefly. While it was agreed that the state of nature served as a useful starting point for political theorizing (since this state, it was believed, provided an accurate depiction of the natural moral condition of human beings), interpretations of this natural state differed in some important particulars. For Hobbes, the state of nature is a state of unending conflict owing to the natural desire of human beings to seek power over others. Human life in the state of nature, as Hobbes so famously put it, is an unbearable state of war between individuals who are by nature enemies – a life that is 'solitary, poor, nasty, brutish, and short.'⁴ Civil war, the unending war of all against all, constitutes the truth of the human condition. It is a truth that is discoverable by observing the condition of contemporary social relations, a condition in which a thin veneer of civility masks a universal appetite for power and domination. It is only the relative intensity, not the presence, of this appetite that varies among individuals. Its utter predominance in the human heart, together with its universality, combined to produce an unbearable condition for all alike. The threat of violent death was an omnipresent feature of human experience, and it was the fear of this that provided the original motivation for individuals to enter into social relations under the rule of law.

For Locke, the state of nature was not a warlike condition for the reason that rational individuals possessed the capacity to understand and obey the laws of nature, a belief founded on Locke's theological conception of human beings as created by God. As created beings, individuals in their natural state must be capable of observing God-given laws of nature (assuming that the deity would not set down rules that human beings were incapable of following). Locke's state of nature was not an altogether amoral condition, but instead was governed – albeit far from perfectly –

by natural law. It did tend, however, gradually to approximate a state of war as conflicts arose between individuals, each of whom took itself as sole judge of its actions and interests, resulting in a steady erosion of the original state of peace. While the state of nature was not in its essence a condition of civil war, it did nonetheless tend to become this over time.

Rousseau's depiction differed more radically from Hobbes's account. For Rousseau, human beings originally were a gentle and solitary race. The individual led a completely independent and isolated existence free from all social conventions and artifice. Here was the fabled noble savage – the atomistic individual par excellence – living in perfect freedom and splendid isolation. While a solitary being, it did possess – unlike Hobbes's embattled egoists – a natural compassion which rendered the state of nature generally peaceful. Hobbes's error, according to Rousseau, was to view human beings ahistorically, or to assume that they possess an immutable nature which would make it possible to read back into the state of nature traits that characterize the present constitution of human beings. To understand their original constitution, it is necessary to abstract from all traits acquired in subsequent stages of development, including the appetite for power and the inclination toward sociability.

Closer to Hobbes on this matter was Kant, who also viewed the state of nature as one of perpetual uncertainty and conflict. While for Kant violent struggle was not a permanent feature of human existence, the absence of rules governing relationships produced a permanent threat. The state of nature, having no guarantees that anyone's autonomy would be respected and no agreed-upon method of resolving disputes, was a condition of perpetual insecurity for all and was very far from the state of innocence spoken of by Rousseau.

If human beings in their natural condition did not enjoy the protection of legal rights, they did (by most accounts) enjoy natural rights. These were natural endowments intrinsic to the individual and therefore not dependent on social recognition. Classical liberals frequently maintained that individuals, prior to any involvement in civil society, possess rights which no state may justifiably override.[5] These rights typically included life and liberty as well as the means that would ensure their continued existence, including the right to property. Individuals possessed an unlimited right to perform any action they desired and to accumulate any goods that were within their power to obtain. This was Hobbes's *jus in omnia* – the right over everything – which was universally held in the state of nature and rooted in the need for self-preservation. Being the first need of all human beings, self-preservation was also their most fundamental right. Since the end cannot be had without the means, anything that contributed to this end and ensured the individual's continued existence also fell within its natural rights. Locke provided the liberal tradition with its classic justification of private property. Since all persons were the owners both of themselves and of their labour, they enjoyed a natural right to the possession and enjoyment of those goods that they happened upon in nature and with which they 'mixed their labour.' Property enters the scene through the activity of labouring on some good or resource formerly held in common (or not held at all) in the state of nature, and does not depend on the consent of others or on the rule of law.[6] One important dissenter from early liberalism's doctrine of natural rights was Kant. Arguing that all rights were dependent on the establishment of a civil constitution, the state of nature was accordingly devoid of human rights of any sort. Although Kant did on occasion make reference to the notion of natural rights, these were understood to be so only from the vantage point of civil society, and were based on the presumption that individuals in the state of nature would subsequently band together to form a state. Rights, in Kant's view, were strictly contingent – neither innate possessions nor intrinsic to the person.

Individuals in the state of nature were typically characterized in classical liberalism not only as rational beings but as free and equal by nature. There existed no naturally given hierarchies between persons as all were said to possess identical capacities both to know and to follow the law of nature. All shared the same rational faculties, not in the sense that all possessed an equal understanding or level of intelligence, but that they shared an identical capacity for acquiring such understanding. The natural human condition was without inequalities or power relations of any significant kind. No one, above all, possessed a natural right of jurisdiction over another, 'there being nothing more evident, [as Locke expresses it] than that Creatures of the same species and rank promiscuously born to all the same advantages of Nature, and the use of the same faculties, should also be equal one amongst another without Subordination or Subjection.'[7] Because individuals by nature were independent, free, and equal, all relations of inequality within civil society stand in need of moral justification, as did the very existence of civil society and, of course, government.

It was by conceiving of the self and its original condition in this manner that classical liberalism was sent on its course of having to explain why such a being would choose to enter into social relations, erect political and legal institutions, and submit itself to the rule of law. Why would individuals who are already free, autonomous, equal, and rational in their nature desire to enter into a social contract when doing so would involve surrendering a considerable portion of their liberty to a sovereign over whom one (as an individual) had very little control? Liberal theorists, on account of their essentialist and atomistic assumptions about the self, thus became embroiled in attempts to provide a theoretical reconciliation between two fundamentally separate if not altogether antagonistic notions: individuality (the personal sovereignty thought to be essential to human nature and moral agency) and sociability (the contingent motivation to enter into civil society and to observe the terms of a social contract). Since the liberal self was an egoist by nature, it was only on grounds of individual prudence that any such reconciliation could succeed.

This was accomplished by means of the social contract, the (usually hypothetical) agreement struck between persons in the state of nature to set up lasting communities and institutions for purposes of self-protection. Individuals entered civil society and submitted to the rule of law solely for prudential reasons: primarily as a means of preserving one's life from the violence, actual or potential, of the state of nature. They entered into society, as Locke wrote, 'for the mutual *Preservation* of their Lives, Liberties and Estates.'[8] The principal aim of the state was therefore to secure conditions that would make for peaceful coexistence between citizens. In addition to property rights, these included a broad range of political and civil liberties. The liberty of each could be secured or guaranteed by constraining the conduct of all persons alike in an identical manner.[9] All were to be equal before the law and allowed an equal say in matters of public concern. Disputes between persons were to receive an impartial hearing by the state and be resolved according to the rule of law.

The autonomous individual thus became the foundation of political legitimacy. Since it was only to secure the conditions that would make the free expression of their individual natures possible that contracting parties agreed to the formation of the state, the legitimacy of its institutions was strictly contingent on the continued consent of the governed. Individuals had entered into civil society on a strictly contingent and voluntary basis, and had done so solely on grounds of prudence. They were therefore at liberty to withdraw their consent whenever political institutions failed to satisfy the conditions that had motivated them to agree to the terms of the original contract. Civil society was an artefact – a contingent and wilful union of individual contracting parties – which could be disassembled as readily as it had been assembled. Political legitimacy therefore depended not on any imagined natural hierarchy among persons or divine right of kings, but on the consent of the people. The moral authority of government rested on a new and decidedly terrestrial basis. Political and legal institutions were placed in the service of the general will, and it was to this that such institutions were ultimately responsible.

If the original founders of liberalism shared (to a degree) certain assumptions about the constitution of the self and its original condition in the state of nature (as well as a variety of other premises and methods of argumentation), they differed markedly over the terms of the social contract. What institutions, rights, and forms of association would be agreed upon by rational egoists entering civil society was the subject of considerable controversy. Opinions ranged from Hobbes's and Rousseau's defence of absolute power, and the view of the sovereign as above the law, to the view (more properly identified with liberal doctrine) that the power of the state must be strictly curtailed and limited primarily to the protection of individual rights. While classical liberals and near-liberals agreed that the foundation of political obligation was the constitution of a rational being, they parted company over both the precise nature of this being and the obligations that derived from it.

Hobbes held the notorious view that the only escape from the violence of the state of nature involves a total surrender of the individual's natural rights to an absolute sovereign. The Leviathan was as unlimited in its sovereignty as the individual had been in the state of nature. Rousseau also took the view that rational agents would transfer all rights to the community and that the sovereign must have unlimited power. The rights of individuals were to be placed at the disposal of the general will. Since it was as inconceivable that the sovereign could wish to harm any of its subjects as that an individual could wish to harm any of its limbs, it was unnecessary to place limits on state power.

While Hobbes, Rousseau, Locke, and Kant each set out from the premises of liberal individualism, (arguably) it is only the latter two whose political philosophies are properly described as liberal. The principles that Locke and Kant derived from the theory of the social contract emphasize the primacy of individual rights and the limits of state power, and accordingly both their premises and conclusions fall clearly within the parameters of liberal thought. Human rights, they held, may not be overridden by positive laws, even when these meet with general approval or reflect the general will. In Locke's account, individual interests were to be self-chosen both because they possessed all the competence and rationality needed for this purpose and because governments had no special insight into the nature of the good. The state was to be a party to the social contract and subject to the law. Its chief end was to protect the freedom of the individual to the greatest extent compatible with respecting the freedom of all. This was Kant's view as well – that liberty was the first principle of justice in a liberal republic and that this was entailed by the rational nature of moral agents. As Kant formulated it:

> No-one can compel me to be happy in accordance with his conception of the welfare of others, for each may seek his happiness in whatever way he sees fit, so long as he does not infringe upon the freedom of others to pursue a similar end which can be reconciled with the freedom of everyone else within a workable general law – i.e. he must accord to others the same right as he enjoys himself.[10]

This principle explicitly ruled out state paternalism and the forms of despotism that Hobbes and Rousseau had each allowed for – at least as a possibility. Both Locke and Kant defended the doctrine of the separation of powers as a means of limiting the powers of the state. Separating the functions of government (legislative, executive, and judicial) and using each as a constraint on the others was a measure designed to defuse the threat of tyranny, something which Hobbes's and Rousseau's formulations of the social contract had not properly achieved. A central principle of classical liberal thought (as represented not only by Locke and Kant, but by such notable figures as Montesquieu and Benjamin Constant, among others) thus became that power must limit power. Since it was as a strategy in self-protection that rational egoists would agree to enter into the social contract, they would only do so on the condition that there be legal guarantees against the abuse of power by the very institutions the social contract brought into being.

While the founders of the liberal tradition disagreed sharply over the terms of the social contract and the nature and extent of the citizen's political obligations, it was by virtue of the premises they shared – concerning above all the self, the rugged individualist, and its original presocial condition – that this disparate group of thinkers is classified under the heading of liberal (or near- or proto-liberal) thought. Their main political differences were variations on a set of common themes, conflicting conclusions from largely shared premises. Although their differences, both political and metaphysical, must not be underestimated, what is more philosophically interesting is their shared attempt to ground political principles on the constitution of the self. Liberal politics represented, and continues to represent, an attempt to identify and secure the conditions of the possibility of individuality. It is a politics of individuality, and one that according to its classical founders presupposes a metaphysics of individuality. It is to a more detailed discussion of the differences in their respective accounts of the self that I now turn.

Hobbes: The Appetitive Machine

Nowhere in modern philosophical thought has the metaphysical imagination ventured further in its flights of fancy than in the depiction of the state of nature as it is originally spoken of by Thomas Hobbes. Here is the metaphysical quest for origins par excellence. Here the quest for 'natural man,' the original condition of human beings prior to all sociality, assumes mythical proportions. Inspired by the revolutionary shift in the scientific thought of seventeenth-century Europe, Hobbes set out to provide a metaphysics of human nature that was entirely reducible to materialistic premises. The content of political obligation was to rest securely on the basis of a self whose constitution was properly captured in the language of materialism. Human nature was understood in ahistorical fashion as something that is fixed, immutable, and above all asocial. It was something that the self brought, in fully constituted form, to its interactions with others, and consisted of a set of fixed psychological traits. In its essence, the individual self in Hobbesian individualism was a system of matter in motion which possessed the capacity for self-direction. As a self-moving mechanism, any moral and political considerations that applied to it had ultimately to be rendered in a vocabulary of mechanisms and their associated motions. Morality was understood in terms of rights and obligations, the ultimate purpose of which was to continue the motion of the individual self. Morality, conceived solely in terms of prudence, served to further the overriding goal that was built into the mechanism – the continuation of its own motion. This being the ultimate end of the human machine, all of its varied endeavours were reduced to the order of automated responses to appetite and aversion.

The human being, in Hobbes's view, is an appetitive machine. Its actions (more accurately spoken of as behaviours) are strictly reactions to the motions of external objects acting upon it. Through a complex series of intermediate causes and motions internal to the mechanism, human behaviour is an indirect physical response to external matter in motion.

Objects in the external environment continuously impact on the senses and transmit motion via the nerves to the heart and brain. There a countermotion is produced, one that with the aid of memory, language, and reason constitutes the individual's response to the external stimuli. A conception in the brain is generated which in turn produces either appetite or aversion, what Hobbes speaks of as 'the first unperceived beginnings of our actions.'[11] Behaviour is prompted by either appetite or aversion, the former being a type of internal motion that is toward a certain object (an object that accordingly is registered as good), and the latter being a motion away from an object (thereby registered as evil). That for which the machine has an appetite or desire is judged to be conducive to its continued motion and is sought for this reason, while the reverse holds in the case of its aversions. The majority of its appetites and aversions are acquired in the course of the individual's experience, with relatively few being present from birth. Within the categories of desires and aversions Hobbes includes everything from basic physiological urges to the emotions and states of mind. Joy, sadness, love, hate, admiration, envy, anger, ambition, and the full range of human mental states are understood as internal motions either toward or away from certain objects in the environment.

The dominant appetite governing all human behaviour and interaction is of course the desire for power. It is the desire to be first, to dominate one's fellows, that underlies human endeavour in general, as it is this that guarantees that the motion of the machine shall continue on indefinitely. Human interaction, reduced to its most fundamental (physiological) level, is a struggle between individual contestants, each of whom desires the subordination of all others to its own will. All other appetites are mere instrumentalities and strategies designed to bring about this ultimate end, and thus are reducible to it. The truth about human relations, according to Hobbes, is the struggle for power. Physiologically, this is explained by means of the principle of opposed motion. The motion of each individual, in addition to being self-directed, is said by Hobbes to be necessarily opposed to that of all other individuals. The individual is in the first instance a competitor for goods that will appease its appetites, many of which goods are scarce and difficult to come by in the state of nature. Other selves represent either useful means of satisfying one's desires or else, and more likely, they are obstacles in one's path. Interaction between Hobbesian individuals is never without prudent calculations from all parties as to the probable consequences for their appetites of association. Cooperation with others invariably constitutes a means to an end between persons inclined to defection and, when it suits their purpose, violence.

The motion of the individual being by nature opposed to that of every other, this produces a permanent condition of struggle both in the state of nature and in civil society (wherein it is more concealed, more subtle, and more managed, but no less real). All persons live an embattled existence in a condition of perpetual and shared insecurity. Insecurity, Hobbes believes, is universal for the reason that the power individuals have to achieve their ends (most especially domination) are roughly equal. All may kill or be killed at any moment in the state of nature. Accordingly, the first law of human nature is to seek peace. Obeying this most fundamental law is the rational course for all alike since it is only in a state of relative peace that the individual may go about satisfying its appetites with a measure of security. One ought to seek peace insofar as this is attainable by means of the social contract. Insofar as this is unattainable – if others in the state of nature opt not to renounce their rights in the interests of peace – then the rational course is to prepare for war. The second law of nature, accordingly, is to defend oneself using all available means against any who would seek to gain power over oneself. When conditions are unsuited for peace, one must protect oneself in the war of all against all.

A theory of the self that was at once individualistic and materialistic faced the challenge of providing an account of free and voluntary action – an indispensable component of a theory of the self as an autonomous agent – in a vocabulary which on the surface appears unsuited to it: one of mechanisms, motions, and causes. The notions of deliberation, volition, and rational choice, would have to accord with the language of mechanics. This Hobbes provided, first, with an analysis of deliberation as calculation. Deliberation is the act of calculating the probabilities that a particular course of action will satisfy a desire. It involves the repeated succession of competing appetites, aversions, and their associated trains of thought, a simple oscillation of passions culminating in the formation of an intention or will. Deliberate or wilful behaviour is that prompted by an impulse that represents merely the last in a series of succeeding impulses experienced by the subject in the course of deliberation. Unless interrupted by other concerns, the act of deliberating lasts for as long as the possibility of performing an action is open to the self, or within its power to act or forbear. 'Of necessities,' Hobbes writes, '… there is no deliberation'[12] since it is only acts that are within one's capacity to perform or forbear that are subject to calculations of utility.

Where there is no hope of carrying out a course of action, there is no deliberation.

A second necessary condition of deliberation is that any act subject to the utility calculus must belong to the future. One may have no expectation of changing past or even present action. In addition, appetites as Hobbes speaks of them 'are expectations of the future.'[13] One experiences desires only for future goods – either to gain something that one currently lacks or to maintain possession of what one currently holds. Similarly, aversions and fears take exclusively futural things as their objects. Deliberation for Hobbes can in no sense be said to be guided by moral judgments since the categories of good and evil are mere epiphenomena of the internal motions of the organism. What passes for the good is that for which one experiences a desire, and is thus derivative.

> But whatsoever is the object of any man's appetite or desire that is it which he for his part calleth *good*; and the object of his hate and aversion, *evil*; and of his Contempt, *vile* and *inconsiderable*. For these words of good, evil, and contemptible are ever used with relation to the person that useth them, there being nothing simply and absolutely so, nor any common rule of good and evil to be taken from the nature of the objects themselves.[14]

The Hobbesian individual is no less a rational being than it is a creature of passion. Taking up the classical notion of the human being as a rational animal, Hobbes provides a decidedly modern and materialist reading of the concept of rationality. The rational self is the prudent maximizer of utility. Through an understanding of the causal processes at work in its environment, the individual is able to devise strategies for its own advantage and to determine the most effective means of realizing its ends. While reason in the epistemological sense is defined in *Leviathan* as 'nothing but *reckoning* (that is, adding and subtracting) of the consequences of general names agreed upon for the *marking* and *signifying* of our thoughts,'[15] moral rationality takes on a specifically prudential connotation. It is the faculty that reckons the consequences of proposed courses of action, identifying ways and means of possible gratification. Rationality is essentially a problem-solving capacity which never loses sight of its own advantage.

The notion of volition also receives a mechanistic treatment consistent with his accounts of deliberation and rational choice. Voluntary human behaviour in the language of materialism and mechanics is understood as behaviour that has its genesis in the individual's own will, where will is taken to represent the last in a series of appetites or aversions experienced in the course of deliberation. While the passions themselves are said by Hobbes to be involuntary – for the reason that they are not prompted by, or do not proceed from, the will since the will is itself a passion – any behaviour that proceeds from the will is voluntary. Voluntariness remains strictly within the ambit of causal processes, and is in no sense a free will that is genuinely self-determining, spontaneous, or *sui generis*. It represents neither a break with necessity nor an interruption in the play of causal forces. There being nothing in the world that takes its beginning from itself, no *sui generis* motion of any sort, the human will is not free in the sense of representing a rupture in the chain of causality. It is a perfectly necessary response to a given set of conditions as these are represented to the self in deliberation. Human behaviour necessarily proceeds in accordance with one's utility calculations and may not be knowingly evil or imprudent (it being a contradiction in terms, in Hobbes's account, to be attracted by what one determines to be evil).

Behaviour that is not voluntary may be either involuntary or a combination of the two. The former includes all motions of the individual that proceed not from the will but from the direct necessity of natural forces, such as the acts of falling or being pushed. In such instances, the motions of objects in the external environment directly (that is, without the mediation of the will) produce the motions of the organism. This type of behaviour is not preceded by deliberation and the reckoning of utility nor does it proceed from the will. Mixed actions represent a combination of voluntary and involuntary elements, 'as when a man is carried to prison he is pulled on against his will, and yet goeth upright voluntary, for fear of being trailed along the ground.'[16]

Although Hobbes speaks of the individual as being a free agent both in the state of nature and in civil society, the meaning of freedom as well is translated by him into the vocabulary of physical causality. Human liberty is conceived in a manner that is consistent with the necessity of causal processes and, as in his analysis of volition, conspicuously lacks any element of the nonmechanical, the nonphysical, or the nontangible. There is nothing spontaneous in human conduct, including that which is called free. Hobbes defines freedom in negative terms as a mere absence of constraint on voluntary behaviour. It denotes the lack of impediments or opposition from objects (including persons) in the external world to those motions that are within the individual's power to perform and that one has a will to carry out. A free agent, accordingly, 'is *he that in those things which by his strength and wit he is able to do is not hin-*

dered to do what he has a will to.'[17] Free actions are simply voluntary motions that are unimpeded by outward things.

In sum, the self of Hobbesian materialism is an appetitive machine ever mindful of its own advantage and all of whose endeavours are readily comprehended in the vocabulary of mechanics. Human action and interaction are only so many motions belonging to what are essentially physiological beings. The categories of motion, mechanism, cause, and so on are all that are needed to provide a thorough account of human existence, from the physiological to the psychological to the political. These latter realms of human existence, far from being separate domains each calling for its own distinct set of categories and methods of analysis, form a single domain of inquiry and may properly be viewed within a single vocabulary – that of matter in motion.

While an extended critique of the Hobbesian conception of the self (as well as of the accounts that follow, all of which are associated with early liberal thought and most of which characterize the self in similarly ahistorical and asocial terms) is reserved for Chapter 3, a specific comment about the language of materialism is called for at this point. Hobbes's proposed reduction of all things human – from physical movements to actions, interactions, practices, emotions, mental states, reasonings, and so on – to simple matter in motion represents a plain oversimplification and misunderstanding of the majority of human experience. What in particular it excludes from its account is precisely what gives our experience its characteristically human import: the quality of significance or meaning. Any experience that is worthy of the name has a meaningful character which a mechanistic explanation utterly fails to represent. It fails to understand the intangible, spontaneous, and extra-physiological character of humanly significant experience and action. In seeking to translate these into the language of mechanics – in particular the notion of free, deliberate, and voluntary action – it forces them into categories in which they do not belong. Too much is lost in the reduction of complex human phenomena to the terms of such a vocabulary. While it is the case that explanations of physiological and causal processes may be of relevance to descriptions of certain courses of action, this is far from implying that there is nothing more to human action than such processes. To suppose otherwise, as two of Hobbes's critics point out, 'is rather like saying that kissing is simply a mutual movement of the lips or that work is moving lumps of matter about.'[18] As (partially) accurate as such statements may be, they are singularly unilluminating on account of what is lost in the translation from humanly significant experience and action to mere motions of the organism. They provide no understanding of the meaning-ful – perhaps even existential – character of much of human life.

Modern materialism offers only a gross and impoverished vocabulary for understanding the constitution of the self. This is nowhere more evident than in Hobbes's account of deliberation and volition. What is missing in the account of deliberation is its most important feature: the element of decision or choice. Deliberation, in addition to involving an oscillation of passions, involves decision. With decision and choice comes the possibility that one could have chosen otherwise. As mercurial as the notions of deliberation, volition, and freedom are, and as difficult as it may be to provide such notions proper philosophical expression, it is imperative that their difficulty and complexity be preserved rather than effaced in the interests of simplicity or scientific elegance, as Hobbes is inclined to do. The categories of materialism and mechanics seem plainly unable to comprehend the self-determining character of so much of human action and experience. That there is something more to action than reaction – a hard-wired response falling strictly within the play of causal forces – is not negated by the difficulty we experience in identifying the something more. Phenomenologically, we experience voluntary action as the interruption of chains of causality and the initiation of new ones, even while we experience difficulty in providing a theoretical account of how this is so. That it is so is a commitment that could only be given up for the sake of a greater and competing commitment to a metaphysical theory, and at the price of overlooking much of human experience and renouncing almost completely our prephilosophical modes of self-understanding.

Locke: The Rational Proprietor

Perhaps the most central thinker in classical liberal thought, John Locke appropriated key premises of Hobbesian individualism while renouncing others and rejecting his more illiberal conclusions (most notably his commitment to absolute power). The political philosophy of Locke, unlike that of some other classical liberal (or proto- or near-liberal) theorists including Hobbes and Rousseau, presents no difficulty of classification, resting squarely within the category of liberal thought. Both Locke's premises, including those that concern the constitution of the self, and conclusions are paradigmatic of early liberalism. It is here that we find the philosophy not only of moral individualism present in Hobbes's thought (a thinker on whom Locke relies heavily), but also that of political individualism, a doctrine that is sacrificed in Hobbes on the altar of absolute sovereignty.

Following Hobbes, Locke's political philosophy begins with the individual self in its original moral condition, the state of nature. In this natural and presocial environment, the conduct of the self is governed solely by considerations of prudence, a notion that Locke construes primarily in economic and quasi-economic terms. For Locke, it is the vocabulary of economics as well as mechanics that reveals the true nature of the self both in the state of nature and in modern society. The Lockean self is not only an egoist by nature but a proprietor as well. It is an owner of both the land and other goods upon which it happens in the state of nature, and with which it mixes its labour, as well as of itself and its capacities. The individual is in the first instance the proprietor of its own person. The first rule of its nature is to seek its own happiness primarily through the accumulation of resources essential to its preservation and well-being. The Lockean individual is required by nature to subdue and appropriate some portion of its environment with a view to its own advantage. Reason enjoins the individual to take private possession of land, to improve it through labour, and to enjoy the benefits that it yields. The rational individual is thus the industrious labourer and the shrewd calculator of utility. Civil society is conceived in similarly economic terms as a set of free and voluntary relations between rational proprietors, and the state as a contractual device for their mutual advantage. Locke speaks ahistorically of the fundamental constitution of the self as underlying equally the conduct of individuals in the state of nature and in modern times. It is the same self that performs its cost/benefit analyses in the economy of seventeenth-century England as that which originally enters into the social contract.

If Locke took up Hobbes's view of the self as a rational egoist ever-concerned with satisfying its appetites, potentially at the expense of other persons, and devising strategies and calculations to this end, the two thinkers parted company in an important respect. Whereas Hobbes had viewed individuals as natural competitors or even adversaries, in addition to being antisocial, Locke held the view that there is at least an element of sociability in human nature. This nature is perhaps most accurately described as semi-social. While governed by prudence, Lockean individuals are not without a capacity both to comprehend rationally and to abide by natural law, making it unnecessary for an absolute sovereign to compel individuals to respect the rights of others. They are capable of understanding the law of nature through reason and of conducting themselves according to its dictates, including those that incline them toward other human beings. As Locke writes:

> God, having made Man such a Creature, that, in His own Judgment, it was not good for him to be alone, put him under strong Obligations of Necessity, Convenience, and Inclination, to drive him into *Society*, as well as fitted him with Understanding and Language to continue and enjoy it.[19]

Prompted by inclinations toward their fellows, Lockean individuals are capable of setting rules for themselves and following them on the grounds of utility. While incapable perhaps of showing direct concern for others, they are at least capable of indirect concern, since without the company of other persons, individuals would fail to appease certain natural inclinations or exercise their cognitive faculties.

The human being's natural condition, then, is one of semi-sociality. It is naturally disposed toward the company of others while remaining the sole proprietor of itself and its capacities. Its inclination toward, and relations with, other individuals are of the highest importance to it and form the basis of many of its evaluations and opinions. Much of the Lockean individual's conduct is informed by a view of the good life that is learned within its associations with other persons and is influenced by their judgments. Notwithstanding this, however, the individual is sole owner of itself in the sense that it is obligated to no one for its capacities or talents and is subject to no moral obligation to which it has not freely consented. Its faculties and its labour are strictly its own and may not properly be placed at another's disposal against its will. All persons being free and equal by nature, none may be subjected to the will of another or forced to part with their property for the sake of another. For Locke, one cannot be said to be indebted either to the society in general or to any person in particular for one's abilities, faculties, or property. These are the private possessions of the self, and may only be exploited by others by securing the individual's consent, primarily through the voluntary exchange of goods and services. Human relations may to a large extent be conceived on the model of trading: individual contractors enter into agreements with others with an eye to maximizing utility. This holds true as much in ethical as in economic relations. It is also perfectly permissible from a moral point of view, on condition that such actions do not violate the rights of other persons.

At the heart of Locke's doctrine of moral individualism is his view of the person as a fundamentally self-directed and autonomous agent. A premise central to any individualistic moral or political theory, the individual is constituted as a free agent capable of self-determination in its actions. While a creature of appetite, it possesses the capacity to decide freely which of its desires it will act upon and in what manner. The individual, in Locke's account, determines which of its appetites it will pursue and calculates ways and means by which it will pursue them. The individual deliberates, as Hobbes also maintained, but not merely in the sense of experiencing an oscillation of passions. Rather, it decides – freely chooses – which course of action it will follow. It does so, moreover, not merely with the aim of achieving maximum gratification for the appetites, but in accordance with an overriding plan of life and conception of the good.

Herein lies perhaps the most crucial difference between the Hobbesian and Lockean formulations of moral individualism, a difference that would have far-reaching implications for their respective theories of political obligation. For Locke, the act of deliberation is spoken of not in crude mechanistic terms, but in a vocabulary of choice, self-determination, and free will. In deliberation, the self examines its appetites both in Hobbes's sense of reckoning utilities as well as in the further sense of deciding on or judging their worthiness in light of a set of ethical commitments. It aims at, and is fully capable of, achieving critical distance from the passions, and is accordingly not passion's slave. While always motivated by its own happiness, the individual, in deliberating on a possible course of action holds a perceived good, as it were, in suspense while deciding whether it accords with its plan of life and view of the good. The appetites are thus guided by reasoned judgment, as Locke describes in *An Essay Concerning Human Understanding*:

> For all that we desire is only to be Happy. But though this general *Desire* of Happiness operates constantly and invariably, yet the satisfaction of any particular *desire* can be suspended from determining the *will* to any subservient action, till we have maturely examin'd whether the particular apparent good, which we then desire, makes a part of our real Happiness, or be consistent or inconsistent with it. The result of our judgment upon that Examination is what ultimately determines the Man, who could not be *free* if his *will* were determin'd by any thing, but his own *desire*, guided by his own *Judgment*.[20]

The individual exercises choice in a considerably more robust and genuine sense than in Hobbes's account, one that interrupts the supposed necessity of causal forces. As a free agent, it holds in suspension and weighs the merits of an object of desire before deciding how it will act.

The Lockean individual is capable of self-determination both in conduct and in understanding. It possesses the freedom and rationality to choose its actions as well as its beliefs about the world without resorting to the authority of others. As an empiricist, Locke holds that individuals are so constituted as to be capable of gaining knowledge independently (of authority, revelation, and so on) through the senses. The understanding that they acquire about natural law and morality properly governs conduct, while the failure to exercise their faculties freely and intelligently represents a betrayal of their rational nature. As a choice-making being, the individual who fails to determine its own manner of conduct according to self-chosen ethical values or its own understanding according to the evidence of the senses is in either case acting in contravention to the law of nature. Individuals betray their nature in subordinating themselves to the judgments of others.

Another central notion in Locke's theory of moral selfhood is the concept of 'concerned consciousness,' a notion closely associated with his theory of personal identity (which I shall only touch upon briefly). The problem that the latter theory sets out to resolve concerns the principle of unity in human experience, or the manner in which all of the scattered experiences undergone by a person over time may be integrated to constitute the self. How are discrete perceptions related to a self, such that they could properly be characterized as belonging to that self? Locke's view is that personal identity is understood in relation to consciousness, and in particular memory. Reflexive consciousness of thought and action is the unifying principle on which the individual identity of the self is constituted and distinguished. The identity of the self persists over time by virtue of the spatio-temporal continuity of consciousness, and its identity at any given moment in time is its consciousness at that time. If personal identity consists of reflexive consciousness, it is known by virtue of memory. The latter, according to Locke, serves an epistemic function in making the self known to itself, although it is not memory but consciousness that is constitutive of its identity. Personal identity is reflexive consciousness and becomes known in memory since it is memory that re-presents past perceptions.

If it is reflexive consciousness that serves as the principle of unity that identifies the self as the unique being that it is, it is concerned consciousness that makes up its moral identity. Taken as a moral category, the self is that which shows concern for its happiness and for everything that tends to produce it. It is constituted as the self that it is through appropriation of the actions that it performs, or by claiming title to them. The self, Locke writes:

> is a Forensick Term appropriating Actions and their Merit; and so belongs only to intelligent Agents capable of a Law, and Happiness and Misery. This personality extends it *self* beyond present Existence to what is past, only by consciousness, whereby it becomes concerned and accountable, owns and imputes to it *self* past Actions, just upon the same ground, and for the same reason, that it does the present. All which is founded in a concern for Happiness, the unavoidable concomitant of consciousness, that which is conscious of Pleasure and Pain, desiring that that *self*, that is conscious, should be happy. And therefore whatever past Actions it cannot reconcile or appropriate to that present *self* by consciousness, it can be no more concerned in, than if they had never been done: And to receive Pleasure or Pain, *i.e.* Reward or Punishment, on the account of any such Action, is all one, as to be made happy or miserable in its first being, without any demerit at all.[21]

Once again it is the vocabulary of economics, as well as legality, that Locke employs in his account of moral selfhood. It is an account of a being that is constituted as the self that it is by 'appropriating,' 'owning,' and 'imputing to itself' actions undertaken in its past, and in so doing becomes accountable for them. The moral self is the proprietor of its own acts. It becomes itself by taking possession of, and as a consequence assuming responsibility for, its own moral property – its conduct.

It is through concerned consciousness that such appropriation occurs. As a being that is by nature concerned with its happiness, the moral agent claims ownership over actions designed to bring about this aim. In claiming actions as its own, they become a part of the self and define its moral constitution. Concerned consciousness thus extends beyond mere awareness or recollection of past actions to include an identification of the self with these. The moral self is not merely cognizant of past actions but actively concerned about them since it is through conduct that one either attains or fails to attain happiness. The notion of consciousness central to Locke's theory of personal identity takes on both an ethical and a legal connotation in his account of the person as a moral agent. The self as a moral and legal notion is the owner of its acts, and accordingly is accountable for them.

Locke's view of the self surely represents an advance over Hobbesian individualism, primarily because it integrates the actions of the self into its moral being. By supplementing mechanistic with economic language, Locke is more successful than Hobbes both in recognizing the centrality of, and in giving philosophical expression to, the notions of self-determination and freedom in the constitution of the individual. The Lockean self is a choice-making agent in a way that Hobbes's individual is not. It is a being with a will capable through its exercise of breaking the bonds of causal necessity and becoming an autonomous agent.

Notwithstanding this advance over Hobbes's account of the individual, Locke's view also shares some of its shortcomings, beginning with the fact that it is in ahistorical terms that both philosophers speak of the self. Locke had as little historical consciousness as Hobbes. (This criticism will be taken up in Chapter 3.) Moreover, he attained only the briefest of glimpses into the essentially social character of the self, speaking of it only as a semi-social being in its original condition. While this again represents something of an advance over Hobbes, it is a minor one indeed in comparison with accounts of human subjectivity that would later come on the scene. It would be with Jean-Jacques Rousseau that classical liberalism would encounter its first critic of note to insist that moral and political philosophy speak in a thoroughgoing manner of the historicity and sociality of the self.

Rousseau: The Historicized Self

Whether the political thought of Rousseau is properly characterized as liberal or illiberal is eminently contestable. As with Hobbes, Rousseau's defence of unlimited state power unquestionably places his liberal credentials in some doubt, even while many of his other premises and principles clearly fall within the liberal tradition. Whether one regards Rousseau as a liberal, near-liberal, or illiberal, he undoubtedly represents one of classical liberalism's most notable – if not always friendly – critics.[22] Among his more suggestive criticisms is that if we wish to understand the moral constitution of the self we must cease viewing it in ahistorical terms and instead offer a developmental account of both the individual and its relations with the social whole. The individual, in the political thought of Rousseau, becomes a social and historical construct. It is no longer the possessor of an immutable nature as it had been for Hobbes and Locke, but is a product of social involvements, conventions, and institutions.

Rousseau's basic premise is that human beings become what they are in the course of history and within a network of social involvements.

Their constitution represents the outcome of a long process of development extending from the original condition of individuals in the state of nature to the present. It is in terms of this developmental process that the moral constitution of the self must be understood. If we wish to understand its present constitution – and explain in the process how human beings became corrupted, as Rousseau insisted they had – then we must provide an account of the evolutionary process that created it, beginning with an account of the individual in the state of nature.

Liberalism's quest for origins continues in the political thought of Rousseau and takes a distinctive turn. The original condition of human beings is described by Rousseau as one of perfect natural freedom and complete asociality. At this zero point of human development, the state of nature is populated with atomistic individuals who display no social traits whatsoever and who, from the perspective of the present, appear barely human. Existing prior to all human artifice – before the bonds of friendship and family, language, morality, customs, and institutions – the individual was an entirely solitary being living a life of splendid isolation. Here was the mythical noble savage whose actions, while prompted by natural inclinations, were autonomously self-chosen by agents who were by no means passion's slaves. The Rousseauan individual was free not only in Hobbes's sense of being unconstrained by obstacles in its environment to satisfy its desires, but also in the metaphysical sense of possessing freedom of the will. It was both inwardly and outwardly free, and it was this capacity for free will and autonomy that was at the heart of its nature. The will possessed the capacity to cause or initiate self-chosen courses of action, and in a manner that is not merely determined by impulse but guided by judgment. While in the state of nature impulsive action tended to be the rule, the capacity for judgment was also present, if only in latent form.

The Rousseauan noble savage represented the epitome of the myth of the rugged individualist, the asocial atom who was a perfectly complete and independent moral whole. Its independence extended beyond the material to the moral realm in the sense that its moral identity was entirely self-contained and its conduct was governed exclusively by self-love. The realm of the moral was constituted entirely of questions concerning the individual's relationship with itself. Other individuals, from the perspective of the self, did not exist as centres of consciousness of the same kind as oneself, but were (as with Hobbes) obstacles in one's path or means to an end. At most (and going beyond Hobbes), others were potential objects of pity. The sentiment of pity, directed toward the suffering of other individuals, represented the first glimmer of social consciousness in the state of nature. It was this sentiment as well that prevented the state of nature from deteriorating into a state of war by producing a universal reluctance to inflict injury upon other individuals.

If self-love and pity governed human nature in its original condition – if it is these two traits that remain when all the qualities of socialized humanity are stripped away to reveal its original constitution – the gradual transition from the state of nature to social life was accompanied by profound changes in not only forms of human association but also the makeup of the self. The initial stage of this transition, the period of nascent society, marked a permanent break from natural harmony. Alienation from the natural order, previously unknown in human experience, came about as individuals entered into lasting relationships and began to subordinate instinct to the requirements of civility. The institution of fixed dwellings, family, and other forms of social life occasioned profound changes in the individual, including the development of language and reason. These in turn made possible the maturation of the intellectual capacities as well as the higher sentiments. The eventual formation of social norms, institutions, and enduring forms of community life at once edified and alienated human beings from their natural roots. It was a transition fraught with difficulty and danger as individuals chanced cooperation and mutuality, eventually leading to the formation of government. Self-love itself became socialized as the judgments of other individuals took on a new importance. Formerly complete and independent persons became increasingly dependent on others as well as institutions, conventions, and shared beliefs for their well-being and identity. The moral realm, no longer limited to the individual's relationship with itself, expanded to include all forms of interaction between persons. One's view of the good became intertwined with and dependent on the opinions of others, a crucial element in Rousseau's account of the steady corruption of human nature made possible by the entry of individuals into lasting forms of social life. Its former independence was replaced by multiple forms of dependence and interdependence which went contrary to the self's original nature, producing a permanent conflict between nature and society. Resolving this conflict became the overriding goal of social life, precarious and doomed an undertaking though it was. Being antisocial by nature, any manner of social existence would inevitably corrupt the self. At best, the tension could be minimized by creating institutions patterned on human nature itself, which would leave individuals as free as they had been before their entry into civil society.

The fundamental aim of the social contract was to replace the natural freedom that had prevailed in the state of nature with civil freedom. Only under this condition would it be prudent for contracting parties to submit themselves to the rule of law, as a means of better protecting themselves and ensuring the freedom that is essential to their nature. Natural freedom Rousseau understood as the independence of the individual in realizing its aims. This type of freedom or independence is not governed by rules of any kind and imposes no obligations on others. By contrast, the kind of freedom or liberty sought in civil society is governed by rights and obligations enshrined in law. Civil freedom extends well beyond personal independence to include rules protective of all individuals alike, rules that are intended by their generality and impersonality to replace the generality and impersonality of the law of nature. Civil liberty exists only where there is the rule of law since that alone guarantees the protection of individual freedom.

At a certain stage in its development, then, the individual realizes that it is no longer self-sufficient, that its wants exceed its capacities, and that cooperation (including the commitment to respect the civil freedoms of others) is a vital part of its happiness. Atomistic individuality gives way to a socialized individuality, one that intimately links the moral identity of the self with the social whole. Entering civil society, the individual renounces both its material and moral independence in becoming a part of community life. The moral identity of the self is now understandable only with reference to a shared way of life. It adopts a social mode of comportment and becomes a member and inheritor of a variety of customs, norms, and attitudes. In becoming a citizen, its individuality finds expression only in the various forms of mutuality and belonging.

Politically, this takes the form of an interpenetration of individual and general wills. A key postulate of Rousseau's theory of the state argues that the individual will by means of the social contract becomes identified ever more perfectly with the general will. One's view of the good is largely shaped by the body of sentiments, conventions, shared expectations, and norms of behaviour that together constitute what Rousseau terms the general will. This important, if vague, notion is understood by Rousseau to signify not a mere aggregate or majority of individual wills, each whole and complete unto itself, but the will of the polity itself. Each individual comes to identify with and feel at home within the collective political body. The self-sufficiency and completeness that the individual experienced in the state of nature is permanently lost in civil society, and is replaced by a sense of belonging and identification with the social whole. To preclude the alienation that threatens to dissociate the individual from both its natural roots and other persons, it is the general will that provides the self with a sense of its own identity as a moral agent. In taking on the traits of a moral being, the polity itself possesses a will which tends to the well-being of each of its members alike. By its nature, the general will could not conceivably run counter to the will of any individual, nor especially could it ever will that any citizen be harmed. Employing an organic metaphor, Rousseau writes:

> It cannot be believed that the arm can be injured or cut off without the head feeling pain; and it is no more believable that the general will can consent to any member of the state being injured or destroyed by any other, whoever he may be, than that the eyes of a man having the use of reason can be put out by his hands.[23]

It bears emphasis that the general will, as Rousseau conceives of it, is not reducible to the sum of individual preferences, nor a majority of these, but represents the collective will of the body politic itself. This is a will that is neither discoverable nor representable democratically.[24]

This interpenetration of self and other after the formation of civil society finds its highest expression in the virtue of patriotism. This highest of civic virtues (according to Rousseau) represents the marriage of public and private interest, and is a central feature of a just state. The patriotic individual's highest concern is the good of all, subordinating all other ends to this no matter what personal sacrifice this may entail. For this individual, the nation is as much a part of oneself as one is a part of it. Patriotism involves a feeling of participation in something larger than the self, even while knowing that one's homeland is not identical with oneself. While self-interest remains as much a part of the constitution of the individual after the formation of civil society, self-interest itself develops from an essentially private to a public sentiment. Self-love is cultivated into a form of civic virtue that places public over private, collective over individual, interests.

It is with respect to the will, then, that Rousseau analyses the self both prior to and after the institution of civil society. In the state of nature, the will was free – if only in latent form – and its objects were limited to the domain of personal interest. Even in this original condition, the individual was capable of reasoned choice, although it is less its rational than its *sui generis* character that distinguishes both Rousseau's conception of the will from the Hobbesian view and human action (as Rousseau views it) from the mechanistic behaviour of animals.

> Nature lays her commands on every animal, and the brute obeys her voice. Man receives the same impulsion, but at the same time knows himself at liberty to acquiesce or resist: and it is particularly in his consciousness of this liberty that the spirituality of his soul is displayed. For physics can explain, in some measure, the mechanism of the senses and the formation of ideas; but in the power of willing or rather of choosing, and in the feeling of this power, nothing is to be found but acts which are purely spiritual and wholly inexplicable by the laws of mechanism.[25]

The capacity for conscious choice, informed by reason and judgment, is primarily what separates the human from the subhuman order. As the constitution of human beings develops from nascent to civil society, the freedom of the will becomes increasingly manifest and provides the basis of moral accountability. Willing comes to signify a conscious act of deciding on or freely choosing a course of action on the basis of reasons one understands as one's own, and is contrasted with subordination to the demands of another or to one's own passions. Human action, properly speaking, is never unwitting or performed under any kind of unreasoning compulsion.

According to Rousseau, in the course of human development the will becomes progressively impartial – that is, increasingly oriented toward the common good – as well as more manifestly free and autonomous. The will becomes truly autonomous in legislating for itself principles of conduct that accord with the general will. What Rousseau terms 'moral freedom' (as distinguished from both natural and civic freedom) is obedience to generalizable and voluntarily self-imposed rules. While freedom of this kind is defined in terms of obedience, it is decidedly not a mere compliance with just laws, but includes a strong and necessary element of volition. The principles that the morally free individual imposes on itself and which govern its actions must be authentically self-chosen. It is the synthesis of will and principle, and not any form of servility, in which moral freedom consists. In addition to the requirement of voluntariness, true moral autonomy must accord with the general will. Both the manner and content of human willing matter from the standpoint of whether conduct that proceeds from the will is morally free. The laws one imposes on oneself must be generalizable standards of mutuality. Moral freedom presupposes the existence of civil society since it is only where there is the rule of law, and a law that is representative of the general will, that the self can practise civic virtue. The individual in civil society, then, is permanently confronted with the paradox that its moral freedom and identity are bound up with the very thing that threatens to corrupt it – the network of social involvements that characterize it as the kind of self that it is.

Rousseau's socialized conception of individuality is closely related to not only the doctrine of the general will but also his organic theory of society. Following Hobbes, Rousseau speaks of the totality of persons inhabiting a nation under the rule of law as a social body of which each citizen is a member. It is conceived as possessing all the features of a unified self rather than merely a collection of self-contained individuals. As Rousseau writes in *Discourse on Political Economy*:

> The body politic, considered as a single entity, may be regarded as a living body organized similarly to that of a man. The sovereign power corresponds to the head; laws and custom are the brain, which controls the nerves, and is the seat of the understanding, the will, and the senses, while the organs of sense are the judges and public officers; commerce, industry, and agriculture are the mouth and stomach, making nourishment available to all; public finance is the blood which economic wisdom, perfecting the function of the heart, guides throughout the body, distributing life and subsistence; the citizens are the limbs and body that make the whole machine move, live, and work, and which cannot be injured in any part without a sensation of pain being transmitted to the brain, provided that the animal is in a healthy state.[26]

Organic metaphors pervade Rousseau's political writings and suggest a view of society as a fundamental unity possessing a single will. While strictly a conceptual creation, such an 'organism' has an identifiable moral character together with a will not analysable as the sum of individual wills. As an organic being, it is characterized as having a far greater degree of solidarity than early liberal doctrine was accustomed to accept, with its typically atomistic view of persons in civil society.

While it is one of Rousseau's lasting contributions to political philosophy to have recognized that the constitution of the self (at least, the self of modern civil society) is a social artefact, and to attempt to work out the implications of this observation in the theory of the social contract, it is clear that his contribution is not without difficulties. Placing a new emphasis on the essentially social and historical character of the self, Rousseau prompted liberal thought to reexamine its typically ahistorical and atomistic understanding of the individual. Herein lies perhaps the main import of his critique of early liberalism. The shortcomings of his view are most visible in his attempt to get beyond liberal thought in arguing, most notably, that the individual must, to be truly free, place itself entirely at the disposal of the general will and surrender to a body politic that claims absolute power over all citizens. Rousseau appears to have had no misgivings about the notion that moral freedom is only to be found in a condition of complete surrender to the state, and is curiously sanguine about the corruptive influence of absolute power. A familiar criticism of Rousseau's thought is that his commitment to the principles of individual autonomy and moral freedom is oddly coupled with paternalism and collectivist egalitarianism. It is at the very least paradoxical that the self should become morally free and autonomous in the measure that it surrenders its rights to an all-powerful sovereign, even when this represents a voluntary decision on the part of the individual. It is all the more paradoxical when such a complete surrender is accompanied with no legal guarantee that the individual will under no circumstances be harmed by the state. Rousseau's assurances that the body politic, by its nature as an organic entity, could not possibly cause harm to any of its members, and that 'the sovereign is always what it should be,'[27] surely ring hollow to contemporary ears. The problems and injustices from the standpoint of individual rights to which such sentiments potentially give rise are self-evident to witnesses of modern political practice and require little comment.

What modern political observers have long realized is that the demands of individual liberty and collective unity cannot be philosophically reconciled in so facile a manner as Rousseau proposes in his theories of the general will and the organic society. The tension that exists between these two demands is very real and not capable of any simple or straightforward reconciliation of the sort that his account offers – if, that is, they are capable of reconciliation at all. On the face of it (at the very least), seeking to bring about both political solidarity and individual freedom within the terms of a social contract is an exercise of harmonizing what are essentially conflicting objectives, the difficulty of which should not be underestimated. The conditions of possibility of individuality and community are by no means mutually exclusive, however the manner and difficulty of their reconciliation – should it prove possible at all – is inadequately conceived by Rousseau. While seeking to harmonize these two kinds of considerations, he manages only to subordinate the individual self to the collective will in a thoroughgoing and ominous manner. As moral identity becomes ever more nationalized, the individual is a thoroughly moulded construction devoid of significant differentiation from others. Its individuality (about which Rousseau is rightly concerned) is overwhelmed by the requirements of collective membership.

Benjamin Constant expressed a similar view in his critique of Rousseau. The arguments of *The Social Contract*, Constant objected, which insist that both individual wills and individual rights be subordinated to the general will place liberty on perilous ground and ironically in its own name. As well, placing no limits on the power of the state to interpret and to put into practice the content of the general will exposes citizens – especially nonconformists – to the threat of tyranny. If, as Rousseau maintains, the conditions themselves of social life threaten to corrupt our individual natures then surely unlimited state power poses a threat that is greater still. Rousseau's assertion that the general will is always right and could never demand the sacrifice of any individual clearly invites a sceptical response. A necessary condition of writing the content of the collective will into law and putting it into practice, Constant observes, is the delegation of power. The sovereign, which (it is asserted) is always what it should be, must delegate its powers to deputies and various bodies which, it is certain, are not always what they should be.

> When no limits are imposed upon the representative authority, the people's representatives are no longer the defenders of liberty, but rather candidates for tyranny: and once tyranny is constituted, it is likely to prove all the more terrible when tyrants are more numerous. Under a constitution which includes national representation, the nation is free only when its deputies are subject to restraint.[28]

Whatever it may mean in political practice to reconcile the requirements of individuality and community, it cannot mean the complete surrender of private interests and individual rights to the collective will. Political philosophy must at once identify and secure the conditions of individual selfhood while concerning itself with the requirements of a civil society. It must describe a legal order that in some manner harmonizes sociability with individual freedom, and in a manner more successful than in the thought of Rousseau.

Kant: The Rational Will

From the inception of the tradition, liberalism has consistently placed one or another conception of the will at the heart of its accounts of the self, from Hobbes's deterministic 'last appetite' through Locke's anti-deterministic notion of self-determination to Rousseau's conception of the will as a *sui generis* sentiment of autonomy. Liberal principles of justice and human rights, understood largely as necessary conditions of autonomous action, seem necessarily to presuppose a notion of the individual as an agent with a strong capacity for self-direction. The liberal self must be capable of interrupting and initiating causal processes, of choosing its own values, and governing its conduct in accordance with self-chosen reasons. In short, it must possess a will – an ability to author freely its own beliefs, values, and actions.

The importance of the will in an account of the self as a moral agent was not lost on Immanuel Kant. Both the German idealist's moral and political philosophies make the notion of the will a central theme. As with his ethics, Kant's approach to liberalism is founded on a view of the will as the most human of faculties. The only unqualifiably good thing on earth, Kant's ethics maintained, was a good will. It is this faculty that raises human beings above the order of nature by liberating them from the causal necessity that governs animal behaviour. Human action is no mere effect of naturally given appetites or instincts, but is a product of self-conscious design. It is affected, but not determined, by inclination. Like Locke and Rousseau, Kant categorically rejected Hobbes's deterministic conception of the will, viewing it instead as a faculty of uncaused causality. The will, for Kant, is the cause of human action in the sense that it represents the wholly undetermined power to initiate courses of action on the basis of self-chosen principles of reason. Human freedom, both metaphysical and political, depends on the individual's capacity to determine its own conduct in accordance with its evaluative judgments. As Kant writes:

> The will is a kind of causality belonging to living beings in so far as they are rational. Freedom would then be the property this causality has of being able to work independently of determination by alien causes; just as natural necessity is a property characterizing the causality of all non-rational beings – the property of being determined to activity by the influence of alien causes.[29]

Volition is an essential property of a being understood to be both a free and a morally accountable agent. The will of such an agent, according to Kant, is the cause of itself and is in no sense an effect or product of the 'external' (including the social) environment. It possesses the power of absolute origination.

Following Locke and Rousseau, then, Kant conceives of the moral self as a choice-making being whose will is both free and essential to its constitution. The influence of Rousseau is particularly evident in Kant's notion of autonomy. The Kantian self is its own law-giver, as Rousseau also held, and its moral autonomy consists in the fusion of the will with principles generated by the categorical imperative. An essential part of the individual's freedom is its capacity to govern its own actions in accordance with principles of reason. These principles are in no sense imposed on the will from without – by laws or norms that the individual had no part in fashioning or authorizing – but represent self-chosen standards of conduct. The autonomy of the self as a moral agent consists in its self-legislative capacity, or in its freedom to act according to the determinations of its conscience.

The moral autonomy of the individual, Kant holds, is possible only in civil society and only under the rule of law. The state of nature is devoid of true moral autonomy for the reason that it is without constitutional and civil laws in which persons may see their will reflected and by which they may voluntarily order their conduct. Moral autonomy includes both metaphysical and political conditions of possibility. Metaphysically, it is made possible by the faculties of reason and the will, while politically the autonomy of the self is dependent on the establishment of just laws. Political liberty in particular is an essential empirical precondition of moral autonomy. Only in a society that creates and guarantees for each individual a sphere in which it is free to determine its own values and follow its conscience is it possible for the self to achieve autonomy. Political liberty, while far from guaranteeing that individuals shall voluntarily prescribe for themselves impartial principles of practical reason, is a necessary precondition for this to occur. Liberal principles of right create a set of empirical conditions suited to, or that help to foster, the development of morally autonomous selves. They create conditions in which persons are able to make up their own minds about how they wish to – or determine they ought to – conduct themselves. Since it belongs to the nature of moral autonomy to be an affair of inwardness, it cannot in any manner be imposed on persons by constitutional or civil laws, or indeed by anything but the will of the individual. When it occurs, it represents a personal achievement which is at the very most fostered or rendered possible by just laws. These are laws, moreover, in which the individual must see itself reflected. If it cannot – as is evident – institute its own laws, it must have an equal right of participation in the process by which they are created, laws which must govern the actions of all alike. Moral autonomy is only possible when persons, either alone or collectively, prescribe their own laws. Only under this condition is the moral personality of the self compatible with the rule of law.

At the heart of Kant's conception of the individual as a moral agent is a major distinction central to his transcendental idealism between the self as a phenomenal and a noumenal being. This fundamental distinction in Kantian metaphysics separates the order of phenomena, or things as they appear to consciousness, from noumena, the realm of things in themselves. As Kant argues in the *Critique of Pure Reason*, it is only phenomena that are knowable by human beings since their form is derived from the structure of the mind while the noumenal realm, being antecedent to experience, remains unknowable. Kant's metaphysical account of the self incorporates this distinction, generating a view of the individual as both a phenomenal and a noumenal being. Human beings have a dual nature, belonging at once to the orders of sense and intelligibility. As phenomenal, the self is an empirical being subject to causal and other natural laws, and inclined to act on the basis of desire. As a noumenal being, it is free in that it possesses a rational will which elevates it above the order of causal necessity, makes it capable of self-legislation or moral autonomy, and observes the laws of practical reason.

It is, of course, the latter that, in Kant's estimation, represents the true essence of moral selfhood (the self in itself, as it were). The true nature of moral agency is located not in the sensible world – in the order of causality and appetite as it had been for Hobbes – but in the intelligible world of freedom and reason. The noumenal self is possessed of a free and rational will which is capable of governing action in accordance with self-prescribed maxims. The intelligible subject is morally autonomous and fully capable of acting not only in accordance with, but also from a sense of, ethical duty. As part of his metaphysical doctrine, Kant maintains that there must be a principle of unity in human experience which holds together diverse perceptions within a unified consciousness. There must be something standing behind the phenomena – behind one's perceptions, choices, desires, and so on – that makes them one's own, an intelligible self by virtue of which the phenomena of everyday experience are unified and related to the subject. This noumenal substratum is prior to the subject's choice of ends, prior to its various experiences and courses of action, and is their metaphysical ground. While empirically unknowable, it is what makes moral experience possible. It is that by virtue of which persons are morally responsible agents and the necessary presupposition of human freedom.

There is a second sense in which the self is an autonomous being according to Kant's conception. In addition to the capacity for self-legislation, there is in the fundamental constitution of moral agents an inherent unsociability, or a tendency on the part of the individual to isolate itself from the social whole and to pursue its personal endeavours in an egoistic fashion. Kant speaks of 'the *unsocial sociability* of men, that is, their tendency to come together in society, coupled, however, with a continual resistance which constantly threatens to break this society up.'[30] The self continually vacillates between its social and antisocial tendencies, and resolves this tension only imperfectly. On the one hand, the individual is fully aware of its need for social involvements, cooperation, recognition, and human mutuality. The innumerable requirements of human life, including in particular the development and expression of the higher faculties and sentiments, are properly met only when human beings come together to form a stable society. On the other hand, individuals possess an unmistakable tendency to separate themselves from others as a condition of personal autonomy. We desire to be individuals – not merely members of a social whole but individuated and independent selves committed to what are essentially private and personal ends. The individual is permanently torn between its need for social involvements and its desire to direct everything according to its own wishes. It desires at once to belong and to dominate. This inherent tension within the moral constitution of the individual, Kant maintains, is largely responsible for the developments of higher culture. The arts, sciences, and even the social order itself represent the 'fruits of his unsociability,'[31] since it is through the development and training of our private capacities that these are brought into existence. Competition and conflict with others tend toward the discipline of the faculties and the general edification of social life.

Civil society represents both the proper resolution and the highest achievement of our unsocial sociability. This unceasing vacillation of social and antisocial inclinations is resolved – albeit imperfectly – within a liberal republic in which individual freedom is universally guaranteed. The antagonism that results from human unsociability is resolved not in a lawless condition but in a political order that creates the greatest possible freedom for the individual compatible with the freedom of all. Under this condition, the natural antagonism between individuals is prevented from escalating into a Hobbesian war of all against all, and instead is harnessed for the betterment of all. Human capacities are progressively developed through competition and conflict with others, just as 'trees in a forest, by seeking to deprive each other of air and sunlight, compel each other to find these by upward growth, so that they grow beautiful and straight – whereas those which put out branches at will, in freedom and in isolation from others, grow stunted, bent and twisted.[32] A liberal order which guarantees for the individual a sphere in which to pursue its affairs – within the limits of respecting the same autonomy of others – harnesses individual unsociability in a way that allows persons to excel while generating other beneficial consequences for the social whole.

It is on account of the Kantian self's capacity for practical reason and its possession of a free and rational will that it is accorded absolute value. The free will is potentially a good will, the highest good for Kant. This metaphysical core of selfhood justifies conferring upon the human individual a dignity which transcends all merely contingent value and which obliges us to treat persons as ends in themselves rather than as mere means to our own ends. For Kant individual dignity is unconditional and absolute for the reason that its possessor is a being equipped with rational capacities not the least of which is a free will. Treating persons in a manner befitting their rational nature – as autonomous ends in themselves – entails showing respect for human choices, with all the political implications that this involves.

The main implication of Kant's view that the individual must be the 'intelligible cause' of its actions and seek happiness in its own way is that individual freedom constitutes the first principle of a just political order. The liberty of the individual, in both its civil and political aspects, is of the highest significance for Kantian liberalism. Civil freedom accords persons the right to pursue self-chosen ends under the protection of general laws while political freedom pertains more specifically to the right of participation in fashioning the laws themselves. Both political and civil liberty are essential to our rational natures – they are political conditions of moral agency itself – as well as being ultimately traceable to the categorical imperative, the cardinal principle of Kantian ethics. The principal feature of a just constitution is that it respects and maximizes the freedom that is essential to the true nature of the self, and it does so by placing identical constraints on the conduct of all persons.

Justice itself is defined by Kant as a harmony between one's own freedom and that of all others under the rule of law. 'A constitution allowing *the greatest possible human freedom* in accordance with laws by which *the freedom of each is made to be consistent with that of all others* – I do not speak of the greatest happiness, for this will follow of itself – is at any rate a necessary idea, which must be taken as fundamental not only in first projecting a constitution but in all its laws.'[33] Political and legal institutions serve as guarantors that human dignity will be properly respected and that the freedom and rationality essential to the moral being of the self will be permitted to flourish.

At the heart of classical liberal doctrine is the postulate, formulated in various metaphysical vocabularies, that it is the moral constitution of the self that is the foundation of all political legitimacy. A just order is one that creates conditions suited to individual autonomy in accordance with its metaphysical nature. Whether this nature is comprehended in the categories of transcendental idealism, scientific materialism, social construction, or utilitarian economics, it is that most celebrated invention of early liberalism – the individual – in whose service politics and laws are to be placed. It is above all to safeguard the individual's moral being, its metaphysical essence, that a liberal order is founded. While liberalism, being a politics of individuality, requires a theory of the self as part of its philosophical underpinning, it is unfortunate that the metaphysical vocabularies taken up by the founders of the liberal tradition seem unsuited to describe its moral constitution. Whether it is necessary to assert that the self, in order to be viewed as a being of absolute worth, must carry somewhere in its innermost recesses a deep core of being – some metaphysical substance which entitles it to be treated with dignity – is, at the very least, open to question. Contemporary liberalism would be well served by finding a different answer to this question than that provided by its classical founders.

2

Utilitarian and New Liberals

If the self of classical liberalism was conceived primarily within the vocabulary of atomistic individualism – of materialist and idealist metaphysics, and of utilitarian economics – the notion of moral selfhood in liberal thought from the late eighteenth century to the dawn of the twentieth underwent profound transformation. Nineteenth-century liberalism contained both important elements of continuity with earlier liberal thought as well as significant modifications with respect to political principles and assumptions concerning the individual and society. That century witnessed both the appropriation of atomistic individualism in utilitarian strains of liberal doctrine as well as its wholehearted rejection in the 'new liberalism' of late-nineteenth- and early-twentieth-century British thought. Utilitarian liberals – principally Jeremy Bentham, James Mill, and John Stuart Mill – carried forward in differing ways the materialistic, hedonistic, and egoistic individualism of Hobbes and Locke. They were succeeded by the so-called new liberals – Thomas Hill Green, Leonard Trelawny Hobhouse, and John Atkinson Hobson, among others – whose discontent with the classical doctrine was more pronounced, and who turned toward developmental, evolutionary, and organic notions to articulate the self and its relations with the social whole. Before turning to discuss these notions in some detail, I shall first describe the manner and extent to which the classical doctrine fell out of favour among liberal theorists of the nineteenth century.

First and most obviously, both utilitarian and new liberals rejected contractarian methodology together with the myth of the state of nature. Both as a historical hypothesis and a moral fiction the fable of the solitary individual in the state of nature was summarily dismissed by the majority of nineteenth-century liberals. The best anthropological and historical evidence available indicated that there had most likely never been a time during which human beings existed in a presocial condition, no 'original' state of rugged individuality for philosophers to speculate about. It was becoming increasingly apparent that forms of interpersonal association were as original to the condition of human beings as reason itself, and that accordingly the project of identifying the hypothetical terms of an original social contract was an exercise in futility. The contractarian method, according to some, ignored the intimate bond that had always existed between persons in the form of family, tribal, and neighbourhood associations. Human conduct had always been regulated by beliefs, customs, and laws and had never experienced the kind of 'perfect freedom' spoken of by the founders of the liberal tradition. Political theorizing could no longer turn on the question of what atomistic contracting parties would agree upon in a presocial condition – which of their 'natural rights' they would give over to the state on prudential grounds – not only because such a state had never existed in history but also on account of a growing scepticism concerning natural rights. Metaphysical notions of natural rights and duties as transcendental deliverances somehow inherent to the constitution of the individual began to lose favour among liberal theorists. Human rights were coming to be conceived on a less metaphysical, and more utilitarian, basis – as contingent upon not only social recognition and the rule of law but also the principle of utility.

Society, for utilitarian and new liberals, was no longer to be viewed on the contractarian model as an artefact, an entirely contingent and wilful union of individual right-holders entered into for purposes of mutual security and felicity. Human relations, laws, and institutions were not contractual items created by morally independent individuals. What, in short, was found wanting in classical liberalism was a proper appreciation of the socially interdependent character of human existence. Society was neither an artefact nor a merely contingent fact of human existence. The rule of law, the presence of institutions, shared practices, customs, and various forms of social relations all constituted 'original' features of human life. The state of nature no longer represented the truth of the human condition, and accordingly was not a fitting point of departure for political reasoning. Such reasoning instead became explicitly oriented toward the common welfare, with 'welfare' being construed primarily in terms of the seemingly impartial greatest happiness principle. The transformation of liberal thought that occurred during the nineteenth century took place both at the level of practical political reasoning and at the philosophical and metaphysical level, comprehending the individual and its relations to the social world. Changing conceptions of the self and society provided new foundations for the increasingly reform-oriented and interventionist character of liberal thought, culminating in the new or left liberalism that paved the way for twentieth-century welfare politics. Describing this process of transformation of the classical doctrine is the task of the present chapter. Following the structure of Chapter 1, I begin with a general overview of the liberalism of this period and follow with more detailed descriptions of some of its principal figures.

The Transformation of Liberal Doctrine

Toward the end of the eighteenth century, what had seemed to be essential ingredients of liberal philosophy had proved to be dispensable indeed. The myth of the state of nature, the social contract, and natural rights were seen to be unnecessary and highly implausible foundations for liberal morality. Contractarian methodology was being replaced with the new and seemingly scientific doctrine of utilitarianism, which promised to ground political theorizing on a new scientific account of human nature. The content of political obligation would be grounded in a materialistic, hedonistic, and egoistic theory of moral selfhood, carrying forward in modified form premises derived from Hobbes. Jeremy Bentham, following Hobbes rather explicitly in certain respects, formulated a theory of the state based on the ends that all persons pursued by nature, in particular pleasure and the absence of pain. Utilitarian liberalism was erected by Bentham on the twin pillars of moral hedonism and psychological egoism, both continuations of Hobbesian doctrine. Bentham's *Introduction to the Principles of Morals and Legislation* opened with the famous passage:

> Nature has placed mankind under the governance of two sovereign masters, *pain* and *pleasure*. It is for them alone to point out what we ought to do, as well as to determine what we shall do. On the one hand the standard of right and wrong, on the other the chain of causes and effects, are fastened to their throne. They govern us in all we do, in all we say, in all we think: every effort we can make to throw off our subjection, will serve but to demonstrate and confirm it. In words a man may pretend to abjure their empire: but in reality he will remain subject to it all the while. The *principle of utility* recognizes this subjection, and assumes it for the foundation of that system, the object of which is to rear the fabric of felicity by the hands of reason and of law.[1]

Bentham held not only that the individual is morally obligated to pursue pleasure but that it is bound to do so by nature. Human conduct necessarily proceeds from a motive either toward satisfaction or away from dissatisfaction, as Hobbes had maintained. All such conduct is ultimately traceable to simple pleasures – fourteen in number – and pains – twelve in number – which Bentham painstakingly described in a catalogue of human motives. Above all, human life, according to Bentham, is governed by a desire not for power but security, understood as the freedom from fear and want. The Benthamite individual is motivated solely by calculations of personal utility, a view shared by James Mill. The elder Mill maintained similarly that action is invariably caused by egoistic and hedonistic motives, where motive is understood as the idea of a pleasure brought about through voluntary action. The younger Mill would prove to be of two minds on this issue. While appearing to take up the hedonistic view of human nature espoused by Bentham and the elder Mill – writing in *Utilitarianism* that 'happiness is desirable, and the only thing desirable, as an end; all other things being only desirable as means to that end'[2] – John Stuart Mill appropriated only a modified version of moral hedonism and rejected psychological egoism outright.

Liberalism's Hobbesian heritage was more thoroughly overcome by Thomas Hill Green and the new liberals of the late nineteenth century. Much of Green's critical commentary on the condition of the liberalism of his time was directed at the metaphysical foundations of utilitarianism, principally the hedonist thesis. The egoistic hedonism of the utilitarians not only failed to account adequately for the psychology of the moral life, ignoring motives of altruism or even self-perfection, but failed on ethical grounds to provide a worthy ideal for human conduct. The utilitarian philosophy had only carried further, and not replaced or even improved upon, Hobbesian premises. Human conduct involves not merely the maximization of personal or collective gratification, Green argued, but a constant striving for excellence or virtue, a process oriented toward personal and social development over the satisfaction of the appetites.

The new liberalism promised to rethink the metaphysical foundations of the tradition, and drive it away from its original atomistic premises. This it accomplished by rejecting both psychological egoism and moral hedonism, the twin pillars of the utilitarian creed, and incorporating in their place new theories of human sociability and development. As Green announced in the *Prolegomena to Ethics*:

We will suppose then that a theory has been formed which professes to explain, on the method of a natural history conducted according to the principle of evolution, the process by which the human animal has come, according to the terminology in vogue, to exhibit the phenomena of a moral life – to have a conscience, to feel remorse, to pursue ideals, to be capable of education through appeals to the sense of honour and of shame, to be conscious of antagonism between the common and private good, and even sometimes to prefer the former.[3]

A new emphasis on the social embeddedness of the self, and associated motives of altruism, cooperation, and social harmony were asserted by the new liberalism to be both psychologically possible and morally laudable. Moral and social evolution were moving in the direction of an altruistic collectivism, the virtual antithesis of the classical doctrine.

The most fundamental transformation in the liberal view of the self concerned this new emphasis on human sociability. Atomistic individualism, while by no means universally accepted among classical liberals, began to lose favour during the latter half of the nineteenth century with new liberals and, to a lesser extent, John Stuart Mill. Mill, while sometimes criticized for viewing the individual in overly atomistic terms, also viewed it as a social being by nature. 'The desire to be in unity with our fellow creatures,'[4] the sentiments of friendship, communication, the various moral feelings, and so on attest to the profound embeddedness of the individual within a network of social relations. The fact of human sociability extends, Mill pointed out, to the individual's self-understanding. Social involvements are so habitual and necessary to human life that, Mill writes, the individual 'never conceives himself otherwise than as a member of a body.'[5]

Social relations and institutions were increasingly viewed at this time as natural and essential to the life of the individual rather than as mere contingencies or artefacts as they had been for earlier liberalism. Individual ends are shaped and attained in association with other persons both in the sense that we enlist the cooperation of others to realize our ends and that such ends are not articulated in a social vacuum. They are informed by the judgments, values, and traditions of the culture to which one belongs. The individual is always embedded in an indefinite number of social relations from the private and personal to professional, economic, political, and other forms of association. Whether these relations are private or public, cooperative or antagonistic, human beings, as

Hobhouse writes, are 'drawn together by hate, by the passions of pride, by the love of competition – by a thousand motives which are far from being purely sympathetic or wholly good.'[6]

This new appreciation of sociability was used as a key premise in the justification of the gradual turn taken by nineteenth-century liberals away from the largely 'negative' conception of liberty that had prevailed among the tradition's founders and toward a strongly interventionist state with a correspondingly 'positive' conception of freedom. A gradual shift was taking place in liberal thought from the earlier preoccupation with individual inviolability and the limits of state power to a view of the state as an active promoter of human happiness. Utilitarian liberals were advocating programs of social reform that advanced the greatest happiness of the greatest number while new liberals were calling for degrees of government intervention that altogether blurred the ideological boundaries between liberal and socialist politics. Among both utilitarian and new liberals, a new confidence was being placed in the capacity of public institutions to create social harmony in a manner that they believed coincided with the personal freedom and well-being of the individual. The older scepticism concerning the state's capacity both to know and to promote the good was gradually receding. What replaced it, beginning with Bentham, was a creed that called for the rights of the individual to be placed alongside the collective welfare as twin goals of public policy, a view that justified large-scale additions to the powers and responsibilities of the state.

Utilitarian liberals continued to presuppose a Hobbesian, or 'negative,' conception of liberty. Persons were free to the degree that they were left alone by the state to pursue self-chosen action. This created a prima facie case against any legal restriction of choice: because such restrictions necessarily constituted violations of liberty, the utility promoted by any given law must outweigh the utility of leaving persons free to act as they choose. This conception of liberty, equally present in the thought of Bentham and Mill, would be called into question toward the end of the century by Green, Hobhouse, and other reform-minded liberals. Green in particular undertook a fundamental transformation of the notion of freedom. His concept of 'positive freedom' was intended to replace the overly formal and negative character of the traditional notion with a view of liberty as the personal capacity to realize the end of self-development. Freedom for Green was 'a positive power or capacity of doing or enjoying something worth doing or enjoying, and that, too, something that we do or enjoy in common with others.'[7]

Green's reinterpretation of freedom was not without political consequences. Since liberty was coming to be viewed under Green's influence
as an active power of self-development rather than the absence of coercion, legislators who wished to promote freedom no longer needed to
concern themselves in the old liberal manner with carefully defining the
limits of state intervention in human affairs. Indeed, Green's main worry
with respect to the issue of government intervention was not that there
was too much of this (as had been Mill's complaint), but that there was
too little. The state's responsibilities, according to Green and his follow-
ers, included radical (and previously quite illiberal) reform measures in
the form of planned remedies of social ills. Radical reform in political
policy – including the introduction of formidable restrictions and regulations governing factories, housing, education, the ownership of land,
and the production and consumption of alcohol – was called for by
Green in the name not only of the common welfare but liberty itself.
Such reforms were specifically designed to further the cause of individual
self-realization, given a new appreciation of the social character of the
self. Remedying various social ills was an indispensable condition of the
development of individual character.

The new liberals who followed Green carried his notion of positive
freedom still further in their calls for social reform. Advocating a greater
use of state power to remove obstacles to the collective happiness, reformers such as Hobhouse and Hobson called for a variety of legislative
measures designed to promote the well-being of the social 'organism.'
These figures envisaged a government of rational planners whose function was to subject human affairs to ever-increasing degrees of legislative control, and in the name of freedom. Social (including economic)
relations were to be managed according to rational design. Public policy
consisted exclusively of ways and means of realizing the ends of collective happiness, economic security, harmony, and other socially approved
ends. Hobhouse advocated reforms ranging from unemployment insurance to old-age pensions, health insurance, and education, all to be managed by government and all requiring a nearly socialist concentration of
power in the hands of legislators. With Hobhouse, Hobson, and other
new liberals, the tradition's sceptical stance regarding the state and the
good would be virtually overturned in a wave of rationalist optimism.
The rhetoric of progress, evolution, and scientific rationality dissolved
the older scepticism, effectively blurred the distinction between liberal
and socialist principles, and paved the way for welfare politics.

The dissolution of the classical antagonism between individuality and the requirements of civil association coincided with new trends in the scientific thought of the nineteenth century, principally within the field of biology. That science's most celebrated thesis – Darwinian evolution – would have a radical effect on liberal thought toward the end of the nineteenth century, as some social reformers fastened on this notion as an apparent scientific confirmation of their political ends. In keeping with the positivist spirit of the age, the new liberalism sought to ground its proposed measures of reform on a scientific foundation. Liberal thinkers like Hobhouse and Hobson believed that the new methods and principles developed in the scientific disciplines required total allegiance from all serious areas of thought and were readily transferable to the humanistic disciplines of ethics and politics.

It was above all Darwin's theory of evolution that new liberals appropriated to lend support to their reform programs. While Social Darwinism claimed the allegiance of relatively few, the theories of social, political, and moral evolution derived from Darwinian science carried considerable weight among liberal thinkers of the time. Civilization was believed to be progressing toward a condition of greater equality, cooperation, and altruism, and away from the individualism of the earlier liberal tradition. At once a biological, sociological, ethical, and political doctrine, evolutionary theory asserted that in human affairs the general direction toward which the social organism was moving was one that involved a deeper appreciation of the profoundly social, and indeed collectivist, nature of human existence. The 'progressive' self was a thoroughly socialized self.

There was nothing new in the new liberalism's endeavour to make political morality scientific or reconcile it with the scientific trends of the age. The mantle of scientific respectability had long been sought by liberal theorists from Hobbes to the utilitarian liberals of the nineteenth century. Both Bentham and Mill hoped to replace outmoded metaphysical and theological conceptions of human beings with one that reflected the scientific thought of their day. Bentham in particular wished to fashion a political and moral 'arithmetic' which would, by totting up various quantities of pleasure and pain, generate principles that were in keeping with a scientifically respectable conception of the individual and society. Morality and politics both belonged to the province of scientific knowledge with all of the authority which that title bestows. By reducing our moral and political lives to the quest for maximum gratification, utilitarian discourse sought a degree of simplicity, clarity, and exactitude which rivalled that attained by the other sciences. What was wrong with the moral and political thought of his day, Bentham believed, was that it had failed to implement the scientific method in the service of the collective happiness. It had failed to purge normative discourse of qualitative and nonutilitarian notions, producing a confusing mixture of incompatible categories. A scientific politics would permit only a single criterion of evaluation – the standard of pleasure and pain – and it would tolerate only quantitative distinctions between them. While Mill, taking a less extreme view than Bentham, recognized qualitative distinctions between the pleasures and acknowledged that morality was an art rather than a science, his liberalism as well was believed to be founded on a scientific understanding of human beings.

Coinciding, then, with the scientific trends of the times, liberalism came by degrees to gain an appreciation of sorts of sociability, and with this came radical reformulations of liberal principles. Nineteenth-century liberalism's gradual (and limited) recognition of the social character of the individual coincided – and not accidentally – with an equally gradual turn to the left. A socialized self seemed to require a socialized politics. It required a socialized conception of liberty itself, which it received in the distinction between positive and negative freedom, the former being given increasing priority over the latter. Freedom came to be viewed not merely as the absence of constraint on individual action, but as the personal capacity or power to realize one's ends in accordance with the common good, a conception of freedom that logically entailed wholesale additions to powers of state intervention.

As well, liberty was placed by both utilitarian and new liberals on a new and decidedly contingent basis. It would now depend for its moral justification on the more foundational principles of utility, self-development, and the common welfare. Beginning with Bentham, liberty would be placed alongside collective expediency as twin goals of public policy, thereby losing its former primacy within liberal doctrine. In itself, Bentham argued, freedom is not intrinsically pleasurable and is only a means of achieving that which is, specifically security. But for its connection with security – a value of the highest importance to Bentham – liberty would have little value indeed. According to the logic of utilitarianism, it was only on account of their consequences for collective happiness that human rights in general were granted moral legitimacy. Bentham expressed the utilitarian view of human rights in the following terms:

That in proportion as it is right and proper, i.e. advantageous to the society

in question, that this or that right, a right to this or that effect, should be established and maintained, in that same proportion it is wrong that it should
be abrogated; but as there is no right which ought not to be maintained so
long as it is upon the whole advantageous to the society that it should be
maintained, so there is no right which, when the abolition of it is advantageous to society, should not be abolished.[8]

Even John Stuart Mill, the most celebrated and eloquent defender of individual liberty of the nineteenth century, claimed to defend this principle solely on the grounds of utility. Eschewing 'abstract right,' or any
conception of justice that was independent of the principle of utility, Mill
set about, in *On Liberty*, to provide a moral justification of freedom that
derived directly from his utilitarianism. While it is debatable whether all
of the arguments he presented in that text in support of liberty were in
fact utilitarian arguments, Mill professed to believe that all public policy
and moral conduct ultimately depended for their justification not upon
principles of human rights but the greatest happiness of the greatest
number.

If happiness, and not liberty, was the proper end of government for
the utilitarians, much the same held true for the new liberalism. The
well-being of the social 'organism' was to be deliberately pursued
through a variety of public policy measures and became the highest
standard of appeal for political reasoning. In keeping with their new appreciation of sociability, Hobhouse, Hobson, and other reform liberals
came to adopt (in differing ways) an organic model of society reminiscent of Rousseau's. The social utility for these thinkers was an organic
notion that, quite unlike the Benthamite view, regarded social utility as
more than the mere sum of individual utilities. Organic conceptions of
society typically maintained both that interdependence was an inescapable characteristic of human life and that a society is never without
a unified collective life and character which is something apart from the
lives and characters of individual citizens. While important disagreements existed among new liberals concerning the exact nature and implications of the organic model of society,[9] there was considerable
agreement that earlier liberal thought had failed to comprehend the
potential for social harmony as well as its inherent value.

If Green, Hobhouse, and Hobson shared a fuller appreciation of
human sociability and interdependence than their liberal predecessors,
these thinkers also carried liberal thought further toward socialism than
their predecessors. For 'progressive' thought, collective expediency, not

individual rights, served as the ultimate standard of judgment for public policy. In what amounts to a virtual reversal of the classical doctrine, Hobhouse stated that society 'may do with the individual what it pleases provided that it has the good of the whole in view ... It contemplates, at least as a possibility, the complete subordination of individual to social claims.'[10] Hobson similarly held that 'the rights and interests of society are paramount: they override all claims of individuals to liberties that contravene them.'[11]

Whether a collectivist politics is logically entailed by the failure of atomistic individualism is a question that will be examined in detail in subsequent chapters. For now, it suffices to point out that for the new liberals of the late nineteenth and early twentieth centuries, this question was answered largely in the affirmative. It was no accident that a liberalism that was by degrees coming to realize the socially embedded character of the self was also taking a gradual turn toward the left; a socialized conception of individuality seemed to call for a socialized conception of justice and liberty. The failure of the metaphysics of individualism entailed the failure of the politics of individualism, or so it was thought. I shall now turn to a more detailed discussion of the theories of moral selfhood adopted by four of the leading figures of liberal thought from the late eighteenth century to the beginning of the twentieth century.

Bentham: Homo Economicus

Jeremy Bentham's philosophy of the self is best understood in relation to Hobbes. From Hobbes, Bentham inherited both a materialistic and deterministic view of human beings as well as an egoistic and hedonistic conception of moral agency. While rejecting Hobbes's contractarian methodology, Bentham appropriated a theory of the self that very closely resembled the earlier contractarian view. The individual is inclined by nature to maximize personal utilities in all areas of practice, specifically to pursue pleasure and avoid pain. An orthodox empiricist and materialist, Bentham is as inclined as Hobbes to explain human action solely in terms of the physical motions of the organism. Much as our knowledge of the world is produced by sense impressions impacting on the mind, human behaviour is a programmed response to causal forces, a necessary effect of the forces – both external and internal – acting upon it. The individual is governed by a constitution that permanently inclines it to preserve itself and its motion as well as to achieve a maximum of hedonistic gratification.

Bentham's discussion of the 'springs of human action' in his somewhat tedious catalogue of the various causes of behaviour distinguishes between simple and complex pleasures. The simple pleasures are those that are not divisible into constituent parts while the complex are those that are. Complex pleasures are constituted by a combination of two or more of the fourteen simple pleasures, the fourteen being the pleasures of sense, wealth, skill, amity, a good name, power, piety, benevolence, malevolence, memory, imagination, expectation, relief, and the pleasures dependent on association.[12] Pains as well are distinguished by Bentham into the simple and complex, the simple pains being those of the senses, privation, awkwardness, enmity, an ill name, piety, benevolence, malevolence, memory, imagination, expectation, and the pains dependent on association.[13] All pains and pleasures, both simple and complex, Bentham terms 'interesting perceptions.' Complex interesting perceptions may be composed of either two or more pleasures, two or more pains, or a combination thereof. He also distinguishes pleasures and pains into four classes – physical, moral, political, and religious – and asserts that the value of each is contingent on its intensity, duration, certainty, proximity, productiveness (i.e., the probability of its being followed by another pleasure or pain of the same kind), purity (i.e., the improbability of a pleasure producing a pain, or vice versa), and extent (i.e., the number of individuals likely to be affected by it). Bentham's notion of a 'felicific calculus' or moral arithmetic involves a tallying up of the values enumerated above with an eye to determining which course of action or legislative measure is most likely to produce the maximum pleasure and the minimum pain among the available alternatives.

The utilitarian self is thus a quasi-economic agent – *homo economicus* – which is constantly on the lookout for means of securing maximum advantage for itself. The inclination to maximize utilities is not only the single ultimate source of human motivation, but the foundation of all morally good action as well. A proponent of both psychological egoism and moral hedonism, Bentham maintains that the self-interested pursuit of pleasure is not only morally virtuous but psychologically necessary. One cannot but act in the manner that one believes will maximize personal satisfaction. Virtuous conduct satisfies the further condition that such action proceeds on the basis of a correct calculation of utility. Following Hobbes, Bentham conceives of the self and its actions in decidedly mechanistic and quasi-economic terms. The human condition, although not a perpetual war of all against all, is one in which all actions and interpersonal relationships are of strictly instrumental value to the individual. Other persons are never more than means to one's own ends, there being no bonds of fellowship among human beings that transcend the single-minded pursuit of gratification. For Bentham, 'there are but two persons in the world (1) Self, (2) Mr. All-besides,'[14] the latter of whom is either a useful means of achieving pleasure or an obstacle in one's path. Altruistic action (i.e., that which aims at securing another's good as an end rather than a means) represents on Bentham's account a psychological and moral impossibility for human beings.

Bentham also follows Hobbes in adopting a deterministic view of the will. All intentional acts, Bentham holds, are caused by motives which may be either the desire for pleasure or aversion to pain. If the motive is pleasure, an action is undertaken on the expectation that it will produce that consequence. The will, like the understanding, operates according to a certain logic or set of fixed rules which Bentham attempts to explain within a psychologically egoistic vocabulary. While compelled by its nature to pursue and maximize pleasure, the utilitarian individual is also confronted with a 'choice' of sorts between alternative pleasures as well as means of pursuing these. The calculation of utility, although a rational procedure, remains wedded to a deterministic view of the will: one not only acts in accordance with one's utility calculations, but does so by necessity. Reason remains passion's slave.

Although Bentham could not have been more dismissive of the free-will thesis in his philosophy of the self, viewing the debate concerning freedom and necessity largely as an irrelevance on account of the plainly determined character of the will, he did nonetheless attribute considerable importance in his political thought to the notion of self-determination or autonomy. Human conduct, while not free in the metaphysical sense, ought to be free in the political sense to the extent that this is conducive to the greatest happiness. Since motion (ever-increasing motion) constitutes the defining characteristic of human beings, conduct (conceived in materialistic terms as the physical motions of the organism) must be self-actuated in order to be properly human. Only the agent can decide upon the principles of motion that are most conducive to its interest, as Bentham expresses it:

No man can allow another to decide for him as to what is pleasure, or what is the balance, or the amount of pleasure: and hence a necessary consequence is that every man of ripe age and sound mind ought on this subject to be left to judge and act for himself, and that attempts to give direction to conduct inconsistent with his views of his own interest is no better than folly and impertinence.[15]

Although, as with Hobbes, the notion of self-determined or self-chosen action is philosophically problematic for Bentham given his materialistic and deterministic premises, as a liberal Bentham remains committed in his political writings to individual liberty and self-interest. To be happy, individuals must in large part determine for themselves wherein their happiness lies rather than have this determined for them by others or the state. The proper role of government, accordingly, does not extend to dictating a detailed plan of life to individual citizens. Determining what constitutes one's interests ought largely to be left up to the individual.

His liberal credentials thus established, Bentham nonetheless parts company with classical liberalism's tendency to elevate individual rights and freedoms over all other kinds of political considerations. Parallel to, and in fact more fundamental than, his commitment to liberal freedoms is a commitment to the general welfare, the political corollary to the moral principle of utility. In particular, it was the supreme value of security that ranks above freedom in Bentham's hierarchy of political values. Individual liberty, while a principle of considerable importance in his view, depends for its value and justification on its being a necessary condition of achieving political security. Freedom, for Bentham, is very far from being an end in itself. It is not a source of pleasure on its own and is accordingly of only instrumental value. All of the liberal freedoms, from rights to personal protection to property rights, are conceived by Bentham as so many measures designed to bring about stability in human life above all other ends.

The assertion that Bentham, by subordinating individual freedom to collective security, abandoned liberal doctrine is most likely mistaken. His utilitarian methodology provided a new ground for liberal principles in general, yet in so doing it placed such principles, and perhaps liberty above all, on a decidedly contingent basis. It placed freedom alongside the collective welfare as twin goals of public policy, displacing the former's erstwhile status as the first principle of a liberal order. According to the new utilitarian creed, a just political order is defined as that which secures happiness as an end, and liberty and individuality as means only. The latter principles, however, are considered by Bentham to be rationally grounded and of no small importance in calculations of utility. Illiberal measures designed to compel persons to be happy or to fashion a utopia would no doubt have met with Bentham's disapproval. Utilitarian legislation is to furnish individuals with an environment in which to pursue happiness by their own standards rather than to determine for them the manner in which they are to live.

Bentham maintains that public policy formulated along utilitarian lines is better suited to the new set of social conditions that, he believed, were taking shape in late-eighteenth-century England. The displacement of traditional religious practices and moral customs, together with the loosening of communal ties and the increasingly impersonal character of social relations, made necessary a radically new approach to both ethical and political reflection. Such reasoning, Bentham holds, must reflect the fundamentally impersonal character of the relations it is meant to govern. It is to assume considerably less about the ethical obligations and ties of affection that had habitually governed human relations and replace these with a thoroughly impersonal, rational, and impartial mode of reflection. Individuals are to be viewed merely as isolated units in the quantitative calculus of utility, as atomistic centres of pleasure and pain, each of whom is to count for no more and no less than one from the vantage point of morality and the law. What is most fundamental about moral agents is what all hold in common: the unending quest for personal advantage. From both an ethical and political standpoint the personal characteristics, identity, and self-understanding of the individual are completely irrelevant in estimating utility. As an arithmetical mode of reasoning, the utilitarian calculus could cope only with a highly abstracted conception of the self, one stripped down to what it considers the bare essentials of human agency. All unquantifiable considerations are accidental and morally uninteresting. Legislators are to overlook such accidental features and confine their attention to majorities and minorities, larger and smaller collectivities whose interests and preferences are to be impartially tallied. The principle of impartiality is to regulate not only government policy but, to the extent to which individuals are enlightened, moral relations as well. Rational persons, in Bentham's view, are naturally inclined to pursue their personal interest in a way that coincides with the common good, so much so that were all individuals perfectly enlightened a general condition of benevolence and social harmony would inevitably result.

Bentham's utilitarianism logically lends itself to a form of liberalism that places a new emphasis on democracy and representative government. The tallying of votes is, as political practices go, in keeping with both the spirit and methodology of utilitarianism. Moreover, elected representatives are more likely to demonstrate a concern for the overall social utility and less inclined to abuse the power of political office. While Bentham was never inclined to place any great faith in the wisdom of the people, he believed that they are more apt to secure the general happiness than a government of the 'enlightened.' Representative government is the most rational form of government that could exist, not only in the England of Bentham's day but, in view of the universal uniformity of human nature, in any part of the world.

In no significant way does Bentham's utilitarian philosophy of the self represent an advance over Hobbes, on whom the founder of utilitarianism so heavily relies. Bentham's political conclusions are clearly less objectionable than Hobbes's, but the conception of the individual that underlies both of these figures' political views is so strikingly similar that Bentham cannot be said to have overcome liberalism's Hobbesian heritage or even adequately grasped the need to do so. It is Hobbes's contractarian methodology and political principles that Bentham rejects. He continues to presuppose a highly abstracted and atomistic view of the self and succeeds only in introducing a different method by which to inquire how a self thus constituted might get what it wants. If the contractarian method does not allow us properly to determine what moral and political conditions a materialistic, determined, egoistic, and hedonistic subject will find satisfactory, then perhaps the utilitarian method will. Bentham's critique of Hobbes fails to extend below the surface of political philosophy to address questions concerning the fundamental make-up of the self, the nature of moral action, and the relation between the two.

As a student of the Enlightenment, Bentham inherited its passion for rational order. Utilitarian social reform represents a series of measures designed to remedy society's ills after the fashion of the engineer and to facilitate the individual's all-consuming quest for order and security. The values of the utilitarian self are largely restricted to the conservative and security-oriented dimension of human character, resulting in an abstract, truncated, and thoroughly one-dimensional characterization of the self. In the rage to reduce the complexity of both the individual personality and social reality to the simplicity of utility maximization – to the order of the quantifiable and the scientifically manageable – Bentham leaves out of his account not only any understanding of the social, historical, and cultural embeddedness of the self but any sense of the self-creative, dynamic, and imaginative aspects of the human personality. The life of the Benthamite individual is pleasurable but soulless, rational but alienated, comfortable but unfree, purposive but meaningless. It pursues only the ends that are programmed into its nature and is only in the most superficial sense autonomous. It is no accident that Bentham, given his view of the self, was unconcerned in his political writings with the problems that would later preoccupy the younger Mill. The dangers of social conformity and the stifling of individuality, the threat of a tyranny of the majority and the prospect of a government of authoritarian social planners did not trouble Bentham at all. There were to be no limits to the greatest happiness principle, no constraints on the power of legislators and social engineers to manufacture human happiness as they saw fit. Bentham's utilitarian liberalism contains the seeds of authoritarianism made possible in part by his failure to overcome the Hobbesian legacy.

Mill: Utilitarian Individuality

If the utilitarian liberalism of the nineteenth century endeavoured to overcome and transform key aspects of the classical doctrine, from its moral foundations and methodology to its new emphasis on the minutia of social reform, it was with John Stuart Mill that the attempt achieved partial success. Mill's utilitarian predecessors managed to renounce only some of the more obvious shortcomings of the earlier doctrine, including its myths of the state of nature and the social contract, but failed to question the constitution of its most basic unit of analysis and philosophical starting point, the individual. The Benthamite individual is merely the Hobbesian appetitive machine with minor variations, with all (or some) of the authoritarian consequences for political practice that this implies. The moral self that comports itself toward social reality in the machine-like and mercenary fashion of the hedonistic egoist is one that must be strictly enjoined by the state in order for a semblance of justice and social harmony to prevail. The Hobbesian/Benthamite self logically lends itself to an authoritarian, or at least a strongly activist and paternalistic, state – one, moreover, that threatens to undermine the very individuality that liberalism professes to value. This observation was certainly not lost on Mill. Starting out from many of the same philosophical assumptions as Bentham and James Mill, the younger Mill clearly comprehended the need to overturn more of the Hobbesian heritage than his utilitarian predecessors had attempted or thought necessary. It was not only contractarian methodology and authoritarianism that needed to be jettisoned in Mill's view, but key premises in Hobbes's conceptions of individuality and moral action.

Like so many of his liberal forebears, Mill is an orthodox empiricist in epistemology, viewing both knowledge and human character as products of experience. The source of all knowledge, morality, and personality lies in the order not of the transcendental, the theological, or the a priori, but of the empirical. Human knowledge consists solely of generalizations from sense experience and is in no case a priori or dependent on an extra-empirical order. Moral reasoning and character are likewise to be explained on a decidedly nontranscendental basis. Individual character or identity, from which all voluntary action proceeds, is a result of its experience. Similarly, ethical and political standards are to be recovered from the phenomenal world of human practices and judgments rather than any transcendental or theological standpoint. These standards, moreover, are to be oriented solely toward the attainment of human happiness, and are not to appeal to any a priori or abstract conception of right apart from this end.

As mentioned above, Mill is largely sympathetic with the utilitarian theory of motivation even while proposing modifications intended to protect the Benthamite theory from its critics. Bentham's catalogue of the springs of action, while essentially correct as far as it goes, seems to Mill to be incomplete insofar as it excludes from its account some of the more important sources of human motivation. It overlooks the moral sensibilities of conscience, virtue, honour, self-respect, and so on, in insisting that it is exclusively the consequential aspect of human action that has motivational force. Moral agents, Mill observes, are indeed motivated in some of their actions by ethical considerations which are not properly construed merely as means of attaining pleasure. Virtue, for Mill, is capable of being an end in itself for moral agents, as are the ends of 'spiritual perfection' and self-respect, none of which appear as sources of pleasure in Bentham's account. Mill denies, however, that this recognition entails the failure of the hedonist thesis, that happiness is the only thing desirable as an end. These other values, while ends in themselves, constitute a 'part' of the individual's happiness and are therefore not distinct from it. Hedonism may be defended if ends other than pleasure (narrowly conceived) are understood to represent an ingredient of our happiness. As Mill writes in *Utilitarianism*:

> The ingredients of happiness are very various, and each of them is desirable in itself, and not merely when considered as swelling an aggregate. The principle of utility does not mean that any given pleasure, as music, for instance, or any given exemption from pain, as for example health, is to be

looked upon as means to a collective something termed happiness, and to be desired on that account. They are desired and desirable in and for themselves; besides being means, they are a part of the end. Virtue, according to the utilitarian doctrine, is not naturally and originally part of the end, but it is capable of becoming so; and in those who live it disinterestedly it has become so, and is desired and cherished, not as a means to happiness, but as a part of their happiness.[16]

Originally only a means of experiencing pleasure (or happiness conceived as pleasure), an end may come to function simultaneously as a means and as a part of the end of happiness. This may obtain for any number of values from money, fame, and reputation to virtue, honour, and self-respect. In being desired for their own sake, they come to represent constituents of happiness itself. The moral sentiments, accordingly, are fully capable of motivating conduct in a hedonistic account, but only if such sentiments are construed as parts of our pleasure.

Mill parts company more significantly with Bentham where he distinguishes between the higher and lower pleasures and insists that true happiness is identified with the former. Pleasure, Mill believes, is indeed the only end that persons desire for its own sake. Here Mill follows Bentham explicitly. They begin to differ where Mill feels obliged to respond to critics of utilitarian psychology, in order to defend it from its critics and accommodate objections with which he himself is sympathetic. In particular, the objection that the hedonistic thesis presupposes a rather crude and undignified view of human beings which appears to undermine our conception of persons as moral beings prompts Mill to draw his famous distinction between the pleasures. His reformulated hedonism asserts that while happiness or pleasure is the only thing desirable as an end, it is only the pleasures approved by rational reflection that constitute our true happiness. There are, moreover, qualitative differences among the pleasures which are properly ranked in terms of higher and lower, superior and inferior. The higher pleasures (ones involving the exercise of the higher faculties of taste, judgment, and discrimination) yield not only a greater quantity of satisfaction than the lower but a superior quality as well. Their greater worth is determinable not by all persons alike but by those 'most competent judges' who have experienced both the higher and the lower pleasures. The only proof of something's desirability is the fact that it is desired, and the only proof of the superior desirability of the higher pleasures is that experienced judges have determined this to be the case. What these judges decide to be higher among the pleasures is the true source of human happiness, thus responding adequately, Mill supposes, to the objection posed above. Hedonism, thus qualified, incorporates a higher view of the self, one that finds its greatest happiness among the nobler pursuits as ends in themselves.

Mill accepts a modified version of the hedonistic conception of the self handed down from Bentham but categorically rejects the latter's psychological egoism. Mill refuses the thesis that voluntary action is always motivated by the desire for pleasure on the grounds that habit, in addition to pleasure, is a powerful source of the individual's motivation. Quite apart from the pleasurable effects that it may produce, an action may be performed for the simple reason that it is habitual. The motivation for continuing to perform a certain action may be quite different from what originally inspired an individual to undertake it. Originally motivated by pleasure, one may continue in the performance of an act unconsciously or even when one would prefer not to for the simple reason that in becoming habitual an act may become a purpose in itself.

Mill is of two minds concerning both the Benthamite theory of motivation and the metaphysical determinism to which it is conjoined. While dissatisfied with the full-blown determinism of Hobbes and Bentham, Mill accepts in his scientific writings what he calls the doctrine of philosophical necessity, which states that 'given the motives which are present to an individual's mind, and given likewise the character and disposition of the individual, the manner in which he will act might be unerringly inferred; that if we knew the person thoroughly, and knew all the inducements which are acting upon him, we could foretell his conduct with as much certainty as we can predict any physical event.'[17] In keeping with the fashion of the day toward developing a scientific sociology, Mill follows his utilitarian predecessors and views human action as subject to the same strict law of causality as that which governs the material order. Given an understanding of a person's character and motives, that person's conduct and volition are no less predictable than events in the physical world and are equally subject to causal necessity. Conduct and volition are jointly determined by the circumstances in which an individual acts together with their character and motives. Yet Mill also maintains that all these supposedly causal factors are themselves within the control of the agent, at least to a degree. Mill oddly combines a commitment to the doctrine of philosophical necessity with a decidedly antideterministic conception of personal agency. Motives cause one's actions, yet one is not compelled to obey any particular motive but may choose this freely. Character is the necessary effect of circumstances which dispose the self toward certain appetites and motivations which in turn cause behaviour, yet one also has the capacity to alter one's character. This is achieved by altering the circumstances in which appetites and habits are formed, in effect becoming both the cause and the effect of one's circumstances. One is said to have a character in the degree that one modifies through free acts of volition one's desires and actions rather than passively accepting what one's culture enjoins.

The circularity that results is brought about by two incompatible philosophical commitments between which Mill would never choose. The metaphysical determinism which holds centre stage in Mill's scientific writings is pushed to the side in the ethical and political works by a strong conception of personal agency. *On Liberty* in particular gives expression to an antideterministic and libertarian view of moral agents. The self is both a rational (i.e., utility maximizing) and free agent nearly to the point of eccentricity. Making choices for Mill is the most human of acts and the foundation of liberal politics. 'He who exercises deliberate decision,' as one commentator writes, 'employs all those faculties which are specifically human: observation; reasoning and judgment; purposive choice; and, once the choice is made, the firmness of will and self-control to hold fast to the decision.'[18] Mill the moral individualist regards the individual as a 'self-acting unit' capable of exercising autonomous choice in its actions. It is neither a merely conditioned social product nor passion's slave but a free and self-determining agent. Its choices are to reflect its own personality rather than conform to a 'one size fits all' plan of life.

The doctrine of philosophical necessity important to Mill the scientist is overshadowed in his political philosophy. Liberalism, as Mill knows, must incorporate a robust conception of individuality, something not possible for a deterministic view of human beings. The liberal self is an agent in a rather strong sense, and the very antithesis of what metaphysical determinism asserts. Whether Mill would have conceded this point or not, he nonetheless speaks in his political philosophy of a self that is either fully autonomous or capable of becoming so in its moral life. *On Liberty* presents a sustained critique of the conditions that threaten human autonomy – not including, unfortunately, the doctrine of necessity itself. Mill's critique is directed at the social and political conditions that conspire to negate individuality and to replace it with the drab conformity that Mill observed in his day. Custom and tradition are primary culprits as it is largely in their name that individual expression and creativity are thwarted. Uniformity of thought and action, conformity to the fashions of the day, and the unthinking submission to convention are the nemeses of individuality. 'Society has now fairly got the better of individuality,' Mill writes, 'and the danger which threatens human nature is not the excess, but the deficiency, of personal impulses and preferences.'[19] A thousand pressures to conform to prevailing attitudes and habits are experienced by persons in the course of everyday life, narrowing our choices to those approved by others or by the authority of custom. The choices that we make are not properly our own when the options from which we may choose have been unduly circumscribed.

Mill asserts in *On Liberty* that 'if a person possesses any tolerable amount of common sense and experience, his own mode of laying out his existence is the best, not because it is the best in itself, but because it is his own mode.'[20] The fact that they are self-chosen renders a person's actions and values their own moral property. Herein lies perhaps the most significant point of difference between Mill and the earlier utilitarians: whereas Bentham's theory of the state is largely based on a conservative, security-loving view of the self, Mill's more libertarian principles presuppose a spontaneous and self-creative agent. The latter prefers experiment over stability, difference over uniformity, plurality over homogeneity, and freedom over security. Freedom is valued by Mill as not merely a means of attaining security but an indispensable presupposition of individuality. Individuality is defined in large part as the power to make choices and the principle of individual liberty (the principle that guarantees to each citizen the right to exercise such choice) becomes, for Mill, a necessary political condition of its realization.

'The principal question in human affairs'[21] accordingly concerns the limits that are to be imposed on the power of the state. How are public institutions to create a just fit between the requirements of personal autonomy and social control? Mill's view, in short, is that the liberty of the individual ought to be maximized to the extent that it is compatible with a respect for the liberty of all. The sphere in which personal choice may be exercised is to be constrained only by the identical domain of choice of other persons. The sole justification for state interference in individual conduct is to prevent such conduct from harming, or violating the rights of, other persons. As long as persons observe this condition, they may pursue self-chosen goals in whatever manner they prefer without interference from the state.

Mill, of course, claims to defend the principle of individual liberty on utilitarian grounds alone and without appeal to any notion of 'abstract right' by offering a series of arguments to demonstrate its compatibility with the overall social utility (arguments that I shall not rehearse here). Mill believes that liberal principles, and in particular individual freedom, could be more rigorously defended on (arguably) utilitarian grounds than had been done by previous utilitarians, and that as a result liberty would properly be viewed as not only a means to the end of security, as it had been for Bentham, but an essential dimension of individuality itself. Without appealing to natural rights or to a transcendental notion of justice, as had many previous liberal theorists, Mill holds that liberty is an indispensable principle of political organization. Without it, the numerous social benefits that this principle makes possible would not be achievable. Justice, while conceived solely in terms of utility, is the most imperative and binding element of morality, and liberty is the most imperative principle of justice. Liberal principles govern only what Mill terms 'other-regarding,' and not 'self-regarding,' conduct. The distinction between self- and other-regarding action is vague, as his detractors have been quick to emphasize, but may be described as the distinction between actions that primarily (not exclusively) and directly affect the interests of the agent performing them – the self-regarding – and actions that primarily and directly affect the interests of others. Although Mill sometimes speaks of self-regarding actions as producing no effects whatever on other persons (a class of actions that, one would think, is exceedingly small and limited mainly to trivial acts), the most adequate rendering of this phrase is the class of actions that chiefly, and not solely, affect the agent's interests, even while they may affect or otherwise interest others (usually indirectly). However one interprets this distinction, it is only other-regarding action that is to be governed by law in a liberal order while the self-regarding is to remain under the exclusive jurisdiction of the individual agent. Within this sphere, the individual is sovereign.

Mill's liberalism awards highest importance to the notion of individuality even while, as a utilitarian, he maintains an appreciation (albeit a modest one) of the social character of the self. So much of the life of the individual, Mill remarks, is taken up with social involvements of one sort or another that one never conceives of oneself in truly atomistic fashion as an isolated agent, but only as a member of one or more collectivities. Human life has a thoroughly intersubjective and interdependent character which the earlier liberalism had not properly conceived. Recognizing this fact politically entails that a strict principle of impartiality must govern all state institutions. Legislators, Mill maintains, must not play favourites among citizens but fashion laws that impartially apply to all alike. Impartiality and disinterestedness, for Mill, are principles of no small importance in both moral and political philosophy. What is of ultimate moral importance for utilitarianism is not the promotion of one's personal happiness but the general welfare. A utilitarian liberalism must therefore counsel legislators to cultivate a disinterested attitude toward individuals and confine their attention to abstract notions of collectivities, majority and minority preferences, and so on. Impartial and equal concern for all persons better captures the recognition of sociability while satisfying the utilitarian maxim.

Whatever final verdict one pronounces on the utilitarian liberalism of John Stuart Mill, it is undoubtedly more successful than the liberalism of Bentham and James Mill in overcoming the Hobbesian legacy, even if it does not carry this as far as one might hope. The atomistic individualism of Hobbes and Bentham is most definitely present in Mill's liberalism, albeit to a lesser extent. He remains very much committed to the hedonistic theory of motivation implicit in utilitarian morality, albeit in a modified form, as well as to a rationalistic and at times mechanistic view of individual conduct. His political philosophy is most successful, and perhaps most liberal, where his affiliation with Bentham is least apparent. His rejection of psychological egoism together with his partial dissatisfaction with moral hedonism and determinism (in their Benthamite formulations) help him to renounce the authoritarian implications of Bentham's liberalism, although Mill's utilitarian commitments compel him to subordinate liberty and other principles of human rights to the greatest happiness principle. As a liberal, Mill wished to raise the priority of individual freedom higher than earlier utilitarians had placed it, by construing it as more than a means toward the higher end of security. He attempts to lend a superior binding force to this principle even while continuing to toe the utilitarian line according to which all principles other than the greatest happiness are at best means toward its realization. This logically entails, as Bentham was willing and Mill was unwilling to recognize, that legislative measures that promote the collective happiness while violating individual liberty are perfectly acceptable and in fact morally required. Mill's attempt to rebut this implication is valiant but ultimately unsuccessful. A liberalism grounded in utilitarianism necessarily places human rights and freedoms on a decidedly contingent basis as long as conflict between the general happiness and individual rights remains a practical possibility.

Green: Individuality Socialized

The transformation of classical liberal doctrine that began with the utilitarian thinkers of the nineteenth century took a more radical turn in the so-called new liberalism initiated by Thomas Hill Green. With Green, Hobhouse, and other reform liberals, the legacy of Hobbes was more thoroughly overcome than it had been by either Bentham or Mill. Sociability took on an importance that it had only begun to receive among utilitarian liberals, while the atomistic individualism still present in Mill's thought was replaced by an organic view of the relation between the individual and the social whole. The new liberalism would renounce both atomistic notions of the self and the negative conception of freedom with which they had traditionally been associated, replacing these with an understanding of liberty as a 'positive' power or capacity to attain ends that promote self-development and coincide with the common good. Green and those who followed in his wake sought to socialize both liberal morality and its philosophy of the self.

The foundation of Green's moral and political theories is a philosophical idealism reminiscent of Kant's. The human mind plays an active role in the construction of knowledge, lending structure to sense experience by means of a priori concepts and laws of the understanding. Knowledge is not what it had been for the empiricists, a simple product of sense experience, but the joint product of sensations and the active faculties of the subject. Green's idealism extends beyond the theory of knowledge to the metaphysics of the self. According to this view, there is a divine or spiritual principle at the core of human nature, and the moral life essentially is an attempt to realize this principle in human affairs. The individual self is an instantiation or 'reproduction' of the one supreme and 'eternal self-conscious subject of the world.'[22] The human being, Green believes, is a particular manifestation of this singular and timeless self. This somewhat mysterious spiritual principle is universally present in human nature and constitutes the metaphysical essence of the self as well as the universal ground of moral obligation. It is in light of this principle – 'the ground of human will and reason'[23] – that the individual in Kantian fashion is accorded absolute value as an end in itself. Green describes the self as the metaphysical basis and unifying principle of human experience. The self stands behind and imposes unity upon scattered experience. It is, as he writes in the *Prolegomena to Ethics*, 'not something apart from feelings, desires and thoughts, but that which unites them, or which they become as united, in the character of an agent who is an object to himself.'[24]

As a moral agent, the self must be conceived very differently than either the contractarian (with the partial exception of Kant) or utilitarian liberals had understood it. Indeed, much of Green's critical commentary is directed specifically against the egoistic and hedonistic conceptions of individuality prevalent among liberal theorists. The Hobbesian/Benthamite individual, Green maintains, represents a complete misunderstanding of moral agency. The self, while interested to be sure in its own happiness, is motivated primarily by a principle of self-development or self-perfection which is not properly comprehended in a vocabulary of egoistic hedonism. Its ultimate end as a moral agent is not the maximization of pleasure but the betterment of the self through the development of the higher faculties and devotion to the common good. Essential to Green's moral idealism is the view that persons aspire to better themselves in a manner that neither the contractarians nor utilitarians could properly understand. The motivation to better, or to make the most of, oneself is not a hedonistic desire for gratification – or even the 'higher' pleasures spoken of by Mill – but a properly moral aspiration, independent of desire, to become something better than one is. It is an aspiration to be more, not to have more, and to exercise one's faculties not for the sake of the happiness one expects to attain thereby but as an end in itself. Nor is self-perfection, as Mill had argued, a 'part' of the ultimate end, but the whole of it.

The moral vocation of the self consists in 'the growth of a personal interest in the realization of an idea of what should be, in doing what is believed to contribute to the absolutely desirable, or to human perfection, because it is believed to do so.'[25] The individual is capable of being motivated by moral aspirations, including the cultivation of the self and the improvement of human life in general. Abstract conceptions of what a person might become motivate much of human conduct, including that which is distinctively human. This moral idealism, according to Green, offers a better account of our experience of the moral life than hedonistic and egoistic views, both of which fail to do justice to the notions of obligation, virtue, self-sacrifice, and the common good. Such notions had been forced by both contractarian and utilitarian theorists into vocabularies in which they did not belong, resulting in an impoverished, one-dimensional understanding of moral experience.

The moral vocation of the self is something that can be achieved only within society. The 'natural' condition of individuals is social for the reason that the capacity for self-development at the heart of human nature could realize itself only within social relationships. Only there could the higher faculties be developed, including the moral capacities of virtue, self-sacrifice, and concern for the common good. The old liberal idea that in order to comprehend the human condition one must abstract from all merely 'accidental' social involvements and characteristics could not have been more mistaken, Green believes, since it is precisely such involvements that make possible the development of the self. The human spirit can only realize itself in a social condition.

The individual is at once autonomous, self-governing, and mindful of its rights while capable of showing equal concern for others' well-being. Egoism and altruism being equally prevalent in the human heart, the mark of the virtuous character is the inclination to pursue self-perfection in a manner that also promotes the common good. As a social being, the individual's personal good could no more be separated from the common good than the individual itself could be understood in abstraction from social relationships. A moral being by nature, there is no need to inquire in the classical liberal manner into the 'origin' of moral obligation since this is as much a part of the human being's constitution as the desire for social intercourse.

What is not original or inherent to human nature, again in contrast with the classical view, are human rights. These Green understands as social conventions only, and while their importance as conventions is considerable indeed, they remain subordinate to the common good. Political and civil rights are not derived from natural rights but arise within civil society as institutions likewise protective of the individual and collective goods. The rights of the individual are properly conceived not as rights against the state or the general community but as powers secured to the agent to act for its own ends in accordance with a self-chosen conception of the good. The classical antagonism bound up with the notion of individual rights (as 'against' other persons or the state) is dissolved by Green and replaced with a quasi-organic view reminiscent of Rousseau's. The common good, a notion central to Green's liberalism, can be secured only if all individuals are granted the same rights or powers to pursue their own moral vocations as these are conceived by the agents themselves. These rights in turn are granted on the supposition that they will enable individuals to contribute to the general welfare. This entails, as Green expresses it, that

A right against society, in distinction from a right to be treated as a member of society, is a contradiction in terms. No one, therefore, has a right to resist a law or ordinance of government, on the ground that it requires him to do what he does not like ... If the common interest requires it, no right can be alleged against it.[26]

Seeking to correct the excessive individualism of the earlier liberalism, Green places considerable emphasis on the right of the community to govern the individual in the interests of the common good. Individuality takes second place to the public interest as does the prudential to the altruistic virtues. Although understood in organic or complementary terms, the common good takes priority in Green's writings over the private good. The individual will is merely a 'partial expression'[27] of the general will. The moral imperative to perfect the self finds expression only in socially approved ways and with the well-being of others uppermost in mind. The principle of the common good is to be the highest standard to which individuals and public institutions alike are responsible. It alone is the final authority on all matters of public policy, even if this involves considerable individual sacrifice.

Green distinguishes his account of the self from both the Hobbesian and utilitarian views by insisting on not only the essentially social character of human beings but the freedom of the will. The capacity for choice so essential to liberal morality had been inadequately conceived, Green holds, by philosophies of the self that are deterministic. Liberal politics, he realizes, must incorporate a robust and antideterministic conception of agency, one that regards individual action as something more than a programmed and predictable effect of causal forces without or within the agent. Voluntary actions, although determined or caused by motives, are not for that reason unfree in any meaningful sense but are products of a free will. A motive is improperly construed as a kind of force alien to and acting on either the agent, the will, or the act itself. Rather, a motive 'is the act on its inner side;'[28] it is the 'idea of an end, which a self-conscious subject presents to itself, and which it strives and tends to realize.'[29] A motive, moreover, is always an expression of one's view of the good, and is never merely a brute instinct or animal want unmediated by an idea of one's personal good. In voluntary action the agent chooses or fashions its own motive by freely deciding on the end it will and ought to pursue, and is not in any sense compelled by causal forces to choose a particular end. Neither is it accurate to describe conduct, as Mill had, as a joint effect of character, motives, and circumstances, even with the qualifications that Mill introduced (that each of these causes is to a degree subject to the agent's modification). Green writes:

> It would be better to say that moral action is the expression of a man's character, as it reacts upon and responds to given circumstances. We might thus prevent the impression which the ordinary statement, in default of due consideration, is apt to convey, the impression that a man's character is something other than himself; that it is an alien force, which, together with the other force called circumstances, converges upon him, moving him in a direction which is the resultant of the two forces combined, and in which accordingly he cannot help being carried.[30]

Mill's ambivalence with respect to the free-will thesis is not present in Green's account. For the latter, the moral agent is a being of free will and is the author of both its motives and the actions that follow them.

If freedom belongs to the metaphysical and moral constitution of the self, its value to the individual is wholly dependent on the manner in which it is exercised. Liberty, according to Green, is the right not to act however one wishes but to pursue self-perfection in accordance with the common good. Its value is neither ultimate nor intrinsic but instrumental. Nor is freedom a part of the ultimate good, as Mill had argued. It is valued as a means to an end only and is of less moral importance than the virtues of self-sacrifice and benevolence. Personal conduct and public policy alike are to serve the collective good, while freedom and human rights generally are mere expedients to this end.

Green's rejection of atomistic individualism carries significant implications for his interpretation of liberal principles, and especially for freedom itself. A moral agent thoroughly socialized in its nature could not be free, as the older liberalism had supposed, simply by being left alone. Freedom would have to be understood not as a negation, an absence of constraint on voluntary action, but in new 'positive' terms as a power to attain self-chosen ends. Green distinguishes positive from negative freedom and equates true liberty only with the former. Construing freedom in Hobbesian fashion as a simple lack of constraint had lent moral legitimacy to a variety of social, political, and economic inequalities, including formidable economic disparities between rich and poor. True liberty could not signify the right to do as one pleases if this involves causing suffering for others, but could only be the right or power to pursue one's moral vocation in accordance with the common good. Freedom is thus limited in meaning to the freedom to pursue 'worthy' ends. Thus, as Green expresses it:

> When we measure the progress of a society by its growth in freedom, we measure it by the increasing development and exercise on the whole of those powers of contributing to social good with which we believe the members of the society to be endowed; in short, by the greater power on the part of the citizens as a body to make the most and best of themselves. Thus, though of course there can be no freedom among men who act not willingly but under compulsion, yet on the other hand the mere removal of compulsion, the mere enabling a man to do as he likes, is in itself no contribution to true freedom.[31]

Green's theory of positive freedom requires that legislators interested in promoting individual liberty must turn their attention toward enhancing the social and economic conditions of the people. Liberal causes could only be pursued through a greater involvement of government in the life of the individual. Legislative measures from education to public health, land, factory, and temperance reform are necessary means of ensuring that all persons are able to contribute to the collective good. Financial security, material comfort, leisure time, and sobriety are only a few of the conditions necessary to self-development, and each requires degrees of state activity that had previously been viewed as illiberal. Such reforms, Green asserts, are to be advanced not under the socialist banner but in the name of liberal freedom itself. The wholesale expansion of state power advocated by these reformers was urged not against, or in competition with, individual liberty, but in its own name. For Green, it is not the case that this period in liberal history was witnessing a decline or 'balancing' of individual freedom with the collective welfare, as this period is sometimes described, but that one conception of freedom was replaced with another. It was replaced with an idea of liberty that incorporates a transformed, socialized view of human beings. The gradual turn to the left that liberal thought was to take in the latter part of the nineteenth century and into the twentieth, in part as a favourable response to Green, was understood as removing barriers to not only human happiness and well-being but freedom as well.

Hobhouse: The New Liberal Self

The transformation of liberal thought from its original Hobbesian premises hit full stride during this period in the political philosophy of Leonard Trelawny Hobhouse, perhaps the most significant philosophical exponent of the new liberalism. With Hobhouse, the legacy of Hobbes was almost completely overcome as this concerns both principles of political morality and the philosophy of the self. Building on aspects of Green's thought, Hobhouse articulated a view of the individual moral agent as organically related to the social whole, and as a social being in a strong quasi-Rousseauan sense. The social organism as a whole is asserted to be progressing toward a condition of increasing harmony, cooperation, and equality between its members, lending credence to a strongly interventionist and egalitarian political order. With Hobhouse and other like-minded reformers, the theoretical boundaries that had separated liberal from socialist thought would all but disappear. The socialized self, it was asserted, requires a socialized politics.

Hobhouse's account of the self as a moral agent begins with a defence of the freedom of the will. His view, largely similar to Green's, is that the individual is a metaphysically free agent whose actions, while prompted by motives, are not governed or determined by any causal factors aside from autonomously chosen reasons. Motives, Hobhouse writes, are not causal forces acting on the agent 'but external objects in one shape or form – things or persons as they are or as they may be.'[32] In voluntary action, 'the will decides, and there is the beginning and the end.'[33] The will is cause and not effect, determined by neither internal nor external factors in fashioning choices for conduct. An act of will involves the adoption of an end as a reason and purpose for action. The subsequent action is performed for the sake of this autonomously chosen end and is thus freely decided upon and performed.

From Green, Hobhouse also appropriates a nonatomistic and socialized view of the self in contrast with both the Hobbesian and utilitarian accounts. Society is conceived as a much more intimate union than traditionally viewed by liberals, the members of which are each organically related to the whole. On the organic model of society, individuals are thoroughly interdependent and, as Green held, the good of one is ultimately inseparable from the good of all. The well-being of the self is not achievable in isolation nor are its ends fashioned or pursued apart from others. Both the public and private lives of the individual are thoroughly taken up with an indefinite number of relationships and concerns generically described as social. These relations, whether harmonious or antagonistic, envisaged or tacit, form the fabric within which individuals live out their lives. Hobhouse cautions, however, against carrying the organic model too far and conceiving of the social body as an organism with a life or identity apart from that of the persons who compose it. There is a danger, Hobhouse realizes, implicit in organic metaphors (of which Rousseau was unaware) that the individual, understood as a mere cell within the greater social body, could become disconcertingly subordinate to the general society. The danger is present, he asserts, only if the latter is taken to represent a mysterious entity of some sort existing apart from or above concrete individuals rather than as consisting entirely of individuals. Hobhouse writes:

> Society consists wholly of persons. It has no distinct personality separate from and superior to those of its members. It has, indeed, a certain collective life and character. The British nation is a unity with a life of its own. But the unity is constituted by certain ties that bind together all British subjects, which ties are in the last resort feelings and ideas, sentiments of patriotism, of kinship, a common pride, and a thousand more subtle sentiments that bind together men who speak a common language, have behind them a common history, and understand one another as they can understand no one else. The British nation is not a mysterious entity over and above the forty odd millions of living souls who dwell together under a common law. Its life is their life, its well-being or ill-fortune their well-being or ill-fortune. Thus, the common good to which each man's rights are subordinate is a good in which each man has a share. This share consists in realizing his capacities of feeling, of loving, of mental and physical energy, and in realizing these he plays his part in the social life, or, in Green's phrase, he finds his own good in the common good.[34]

The social body, while having 'a certain collective life and character' and being 'a unity with a life of its own,' is nonetheless nothing over and above the individual citizens who compose it. 'The nation' is constituted entirely of the concrete phenomena of social life: persons and the practices, institutions, and sentiments that tie them together. Unlike cells, individuals possess powers of self-determination and autonomy, capacities that ought not to be placed entirely at the disposal of the collective whole. The organic model, as Hobhouse (following Green) views it, is intended primarily to underscore the interdependence of human beings rather than to elevate society or the state to a position superior to that of individuals.

The social body, thus understood, is asserted by Hobhouse to be involved in a process of evolution. Social and ethical development both characterize the present condition of society and coincide to fashion by degrees a state of cooperation and collective responsibility among all persons. Although human history does not unfold in a necessary sequence of stages or progress according to iron-clad laws, there is evolution within both the individual and the general society. Developments depend not on any kind of social determinism but on the wills of individual persons, these being the true causes of evolution. Such evolution is therefore subject in a high degree to human control and is the very antithesis of an automatic process. Nor is this process properly construed in Social Darwinian terms as a struggle for survival. Rather, human development leads toward ever-increasing degrees of harmony and concern for the common good. For Hobhouse, it is collectivism and altruism rather than the survival of the fittest that are the true marks of social and moral evolution. The development of individuals and the social body as a whole is characterized by an increasing complexity of interdependence and an organic unity of the will. The individual becomes an increasingly socialized, interdependent, and altruistic moral agent as the process of evolution continues.

Organicism and evolution converge in Hobhouse's view to indicate jointly the direction toward which political reform properly aims. 'Progressive' reform measures aim to maximize social harmony, cooperation, and equality through utilitarian planned social improvements or state engineering projects. Government, the principal agent of the communal body, is given the responsibility of furthering the evolutionary process through legislative measures designed to promote the development of individual minds and the nation as a whole. The development of both depends on not only choices fashioned by individual wills but the collective will operating through democratically governed public institutions. For such institutions to further rather than forestall the cause of social progress, they must hold the notion of collective harmony as their highest moral standard and work to eradicate inequalities and other 'disharmonies' in the social body. Public policy is to serve the collective ends of cooperation, unity, and harmony, and in so doing displace the individual ends (including negative liberty) that had prevailed in the earlier liberalism. Collective or organic unity is to prevail over individuality, solidarity over difference, and homogeneity over plurality. Only in this way will the recognition of sociability and of the nature of moral selfhood accurately translate into political practice.

As rational beings, individuals are capable of and inclined toward putting into practice what Hobhouse terms the principle of harmony.

'The essence of the rational impulse in the world of practice,'[35] the desire to harmonize one's personal good with the collective welfare is the mark of not only an evolved self but a rational one as well. Practical reason, in a socialized view of the self, operates not according to the utilitarian maxim but on the basis of the principle of harmony. This principle seeks as complete a reconciliation of the communal and the individual goods as is practically possible and the removal of all elements of recalcitrant individuality.

> According to the Principle of Harmony the object of moral endeavour is to establish and extend harmony and remove disharmony. Any person may have within him elements and capacities of harmony with others and also disharmony. What is inharmonious if it cannot be modified must be destroyed, but to repress or even to fail to stimulate and promote any element capable of harmonization is contrary to the moral purpose ... [E]very man has a duty to and a claim upon every other, with whom he is in actual relation, in respect of the elements of potential harmony in his nature. The common good is the realized harmony of these elements in all members of the community.[36]

Persons who live in keeping with their rational and social natures also live in accord with others, to the point that no significant conflict exists between the good of one and the good of all. Hobhouse, again following Green and roughly in keeping with the utilitarian view as well, denies the final authority of individual rights, subordinating these in principle to the common welfare. Private ends that are 'disharmonious' with collective ends are morally improper and do not warrant state protection on grounds of civil liberty. As liberty is understood as the freedom to contribute to the collective well-being in a manner that befits one's unique talents, or the right to pursue self-realization in any manner that contributes to socially beneficial ends, there can be no liberty for the individual to pursue an entirely egoistic existence. For Hobhouse, as for Green and the utilitarian liberals, individual freedom is a means to an end and is morally justifiable only on the condition that its enjoyment promotes the collective good. Human rights in general, while deserving recognition by the state, are neither the sole ends nor even the main ones to be served by public policy. Instead, the state is to respect the public will and to promote the general utility whatever the implications may be for individual rights. Hobhouse's liberalism, founded on the principle of harmony, carries to an extreme the logic of Benthamite utilitarianism; in a liberal order,

Hobhouse writes, the community 'may do with the individual what it pleases provided that it has the good of the whole in view … It contemplates, at least as a possibility, the complete subordination of individual to social claims.'[37]

Far from being an end in itself (as it had been for Mill), individuality for Hobhouse is a potential breach of social unity. Beliefs, attitudes, lifestyles, and so on, that are not in keeping with collective sentiments are to be carefully overseen by the state. Evolution, Hobhouse asserts, is leading in the direction of an organic collectivism which respects human rights and freedoms while construing these as majoritarian notions. Freedom ultimately is the freedom not of the individual to pursue self-chosen ends without threat of coercion but of majorities to impose their will on minorities. It is the right of a majority to remind minorities and individuals that they are social beings and accordingly must abandon all 'alien sentiments' which threaten to disrupt the collective harmony. A self-described liberal collectivist, Hobhouse does not hold the value of individuality in the highest regard since doing so harkened back to the atomistic individualism of old.

Properly recognizing in our political practices the sociable, interdependent, and evolving nature of the self is possible only for a collectivized liberalism, Hobhouse maintains, since other variants of liberal doctrine only perpetuate the Hobbesian legacy in one form or another. The turn toward collectivism is the political corollary to the philosophical recognition of human sociability. It is the principle that fits best with the recognition of the individual as a member of a social body. As a socially embedded being, the individual is an inheritor of obligations and rights that belong to one as such a member, and rights which at no time are more than instruments of the collective welfare. A morality of altruism and a politics of collectivism are the only alternatives to the asocial atomism of Hobbes.

As might be expected from the above, Hobhouse's liberalism calls for a more activist and paternalistic state than had been advocated by earlier liberal theorists. The state is to intervene actively in the lives of its citizens in paternalistic fashion and always with a view to the common good. It is to trouble itself less with the matter of 'negative' individual rights than liberals such as Locke, Kant, and Mill had preferred, and to elevate in their stead the values of community and family life, social unity, and other collective ends. The sphere of permissible coercion is to be enlarged in order that both the common welfare, 'efficiency,' and freedom itself may better be realized. 'The conditions of life' in general are to be controlled by a democratic government to the maximum degree compatible with respect for human rights, among which are to be counted basic welfare rights or entitlements as we would now speak of them. Welfare measures such as old-age pensions, unemployment and health insurance, and so on, are recommended by Hobhouse along with an egalitarian policy of income redistribution. Such measures serve to rationalize social life generally and in the process quicken the pace of evolution, the latter representing an advance to the extent to which conditions of human life are subject to rational (i.e., state) control.

Calling for a more activist, egalitarian, and paternalistic state than was commonly advocated in the tradition, Hobhouse's liberalism barely distinguishes itself from socialism. It lays the foundation for welfare politics and calls on public institutions to regulate and control conditions deemed important to the common welfare while shying away from more immoderate socialist policies such as instituting state ownership of the means of production. Hobhouse's aim is to defend the activist state from within the liberal tradition, as had Green, and to do so in a fashion that would reformulate central aspects of the classical doctrine. Liberty, a principle central to any variant of liberalism, is not to be opposed in Hobbesian and Benthamite fashion to restraint, nor self-determination to determination by others, so long as the self is conceived as organically related to the social whole and a participant in the evolutionary process. Rational control, rather than a threat to freedom, is an essential means of expanding it and indispensable to the cause of social development.

I shall postpone for later chapters the question of whether a proper recognition of human sociability logically entails not only an abandonment of the Hobbesian legacy but the prioritizing of welfare politics over an individual rights-based conception of justice. Whether the politics of welfare – utilitarian, organic, or collectivist – is what is needed in order for a proper appreciation of the social embeddedness of the self to be possible is a question that utilitarian and new liberals were content to answer in the affirmative, and one which I shall table for the time being.

3

Neoclassical Liberals and Communitarian Critics

If it is an accurate observation that the liberal tradition from Hobbes to Hobhouse is characterized by considerable diversity, at the levels of political ideology, methodology, and the view of the self, the observation still more adequately describes liberal theorists of the twentieth century. The assortment of twentieth-century writers working in this tradition ranges broadly at the level of ideology from egalitarian social democrats, barely distinguishable from moderate socialists, to libertarians at the opposite end of the spectrum; while at the methodological level liberal doctrine has been defended on a variety of grounds from nineteenth-century utilitarianism to contractarianism to new variants of Hegelianism and postmodernism. Liberalism has established itself as the dominant political tradition of the Western world and the central debates of the times occur primarily between liberalism's rival factions rather than between liberal and nonliberal modes of thought. As liberalism has come increasingly to constitute the mainstream of political discourse in the West, it has simultaneously undergone the same fate as befalls any sizable tradition of thought; it has divided into an increasing number of sects whose resemblances are not always readily apparent. Whether all philosophers, politicians, and legislative measures characterizable as liberal share among them a core doctrine of any sort is highly unlikely. More plausible is the suggestion that liberalism should be viewed in terms of a Wittgensteinian family resemblance, linking in a nonobvious manner such thinkers as those discussed in the first two chapters together with twentieth-century writers John Dewey, Friedrich A. Hayek, Isaiah Berlin, John Rawls, Robert Nozick, Ronald Dworkin, Joseph Raz, Charles Larmore, David Gauthier, and Richard Rorty, along with such legislative policies as the New Deal, the welfare state, free trade, and the market economy. Currently, the political principles cited as liberal are the primacy of individual rights and state neutrality between competing conceptions of the good life, although clearly not all thinkers we would wish to characterize as liberal defend both or either of these principles.

If liberalism is a creed without a core doctrine, both ideologically and methodologically, it is no less divided over the philosophy of the self. Recent liberal conceptions of moral agency have incorporated premises from not only the tradition's founders – principally Hobbes, Locke, and Kant – but also Hegelian, socialist, and postmodern schools of thought. The diversity that prevailed among liberal conceptions of the self during the eighteenth and nineteenth centuries became heightened in the twentieth century. As a consequence there is not, nor has there ever been, a unified liberal philosophy of the self. It has largely been liberalism's critics, especially those on the political left, who have thought that it presupposed such a unified conception, while the more careful observer would assert that the liberal tradition incorporates a variety of moral, psychological, and metaphysical assumptions which again constitute a family resemblance but not a unified account. Terms such as 'atomistic individualism' and the 'unencumbered self' that are often applied to liberal thought represent at best partial descriptions which cast more shadow than light in many instances, as I shall argue in the present chapter.

Liberal philosophy has witnessed a renaissance since the 1970s beginning with the publication of John Rawls's *A Theory of Justice*, an influential work in which the contractarian methodology of the seventeenth and eighteenth centuries was pronounced anew. The revival of contractarianism which continued through such figures as Robert Nozick and David Gauthier has introduced some modifications to the original methodology and generated ideological positions nearly as diverse as those of the tradition's founders. What has received less attention among contractarian liberals, however, is the view of the self which in all important particulars is directly appropriated from Hobbes, Locke, and to a lesser extent Kant. Like the return of the repressed, the Hobbesian legacy which the new liberalism attempted to move beyond has been fully restored in contemporary liberal thought by neoclassical contractarians, but no less so by utilitarians who have also loomed large in twentieth-century liberalism. If any general statement is possible concerning liberal thought on the self in the twentieth century, it is that the metaphysical accounts put forward by the tradition's founders have largely become a source of embarrassment to be overcome either through the introduction of a new and nonmetaphysical theory of the self or, more recently, by bracketing entirely the matter of the moral and metaphysical constitution of human beings. The latter view, seemingly the more radical of the two, succeeds only in evading an inescapable series of questions concerning liberalism's fundamental unit of analysis and source of political legitimacy. In proposing to bracket the matter of the fundamental constitution of the individual, this view renders entirely mysterious the issue of who or what liberal politics is expressly designed to safeguard and why the values of individuality, liberty, and so on, should warrant the priority that liberals attach to them. Moral and political philosophies invariably contain assumptions about the self – none more so than liberalism – which require express formulation for the purposes of both philosophical articulation and political argumentation. If liberalism is indeed a politics of individuality, it behooves its philosophical proponents to explain how individuals are constituted and why the rights that we attribute to them are asserted to be of the highest moral and political importance.

One source of twentieth-century liberalism's metaphysical embarrassment is the hypothesis, familiar to socialists, Hegelians, postmodernists, and even liberals themselves, that human beings are far from being the asocial atoms invoked by Hobbes: beings unaffected in their choices or their moral being by the network of social conditions – the lifeworld, traditions, ways of life, shared beliefs, practices, language, etc. – in which they find themselves always already situated. Individuals are social beings in a manner that classical liberalism failed to realize. Liberal theorists have differed over the full meaning and implications of this truistic belief; some (new liberals and egalitarian social democrats) believing it to entail an abandonment of limited government and calling for an actively interventionist and paternalistic welfare state, while others draw more conservative or even no conclusions concerning public policy. Since the time of J.S. Mill and T.H. Green, liberals have been unable to deny the fact and import of human sociability. The source of disagreement has turned to the implications of this recognition for public policy and for political philosophy itself. While some authors have denied that the recognition of sociability carries any interesting consequences for liberal politics whatsoever, the majority have believed this recognition to entail (directly or indirectly) a move to the left of the ideological spectrum. Whether couched in terms of 'positive freedom,' 'social democracy,' or egalitarianism, liberal thought in the twentieth century took a historic turn to the left which coincided with the recognition of the socially embedded character of human existence.

This move was prompted in part by liberalism's critics on the left, many of whom have urged that liberal principles should be abandoned entirely for a version of socialist politics. Most recently, a group of critics working within the Aristotelian and Hegelian traditions has put in question numerous liberal premises, including several pertaining to the self. Communitarians have asserted that the philosophical underpinnings of liberal politics can no longer be taken seriously and that their rejection entails the replacement of the values of individuality with those associated with community life and the common good. The contemporary debate between liberals and communitarians, the heart of which concerns the philosophy of the self, represents the most philosophically interesting debate in which liberals are currently engaged and it is this debate which the present chapter takes up and to which it offers a contribution.

Employing the structure of the first two chapters, I shall begin by surveying the scene of twentieth-century liberalism, focusing on the conceptions of the self that it has most often presupposed. I single out John Rawls and Robert Nozick for extended discussion on account of the attention that their political writings have received and also their representativeness of the current state of liberal thought concerning moral selfhood.[1] These sections are followed by a detailed description of the communitarian critique of liberalism advanced by writers such as Charles Taylor, Alasdair MacIntyre, and Michael Sandel. Following this, I offer a reply on behalf of liberalism to the communitarian challenge. Briefly, I argue that liberals do indeed have an important lesson to learn from the neoaristotelian and neohegelian critique, but that this does not require the abandonment of liberal principles, including the neutrality thesis and the primacy of justice. What it demonstrates is the need for a radical overhaul of liberal thought concerning moral agency, a project that I undertake in Part II of this study.

The Philosophy of the Self in Contemporary Liberal Theory

Neoclassical liberalism is a rights-based theory of justice formulated in express opposition to the utilitarian and organicist liberalisms discussed in Chapter 2. The latter schools of thought, which succeeded the tradition's original contractarianism and predominated throughout much of the nineteenth and twentieth centuries, had placed individual rights on an inadequate moral basis by subordinating these to the principle of the general welfare. Respect for human rights for both utilitarian and new liberals was strictly a contingent matter while the possibility of their subordination to the general utility remained in principle a possibility of state action. That some may be sacrificed for the good of others, neo-contractarians maintain, is an intolerable implication of these two strains of liberal thought, and one that must be offset by removing human rights from the vicissitudes of the utilitarian calculus and assigning them priority over all other types of ethical and political considerations, including the common welfare. The fundamental mistake of utilitarian and new liberals was to overlook the fact that human beings are indi-viduated agents as well as members of collectivities, and the significant fact of their separateness renders the romantic idea of a 'social organism' or 'body politic' unsuitable and dangerous as a description of actual human societies. Its danger lies in the possibility of states treating indi-vidual citizens as mere units or appendages of the social body, hence mere means to the end of the collective welfare (or more accurately, the satisfaction of the majority or ruling interest). There is, neoclassical lib-erals hold, no such entity as a society conceived as a kind of quasi-agent possessing a good distinct from that of its constituent members and to which the latter could potentially be sacrificed for the greater good of all. 'There are,' as Nozick writes, 'only individual people, different individ-ual people, with their own individual lives. Using one of these people for the benefit of others, uses him and benefits the others. Nothing more.'[2] This seeming truism is all too often obscured in organicist and utilitarian discourse.

Taking the fact of human separateness seriously entails the rejection of the existence of both a social entity distinct from the persons who com-prise it and a social good distinct from individual goods or any common element uniting them. It further entails taking up Kant's injunction that we treat persons always as ends in themselves and not mere means to others's ends, even if the others in question constitute a majority of per-sons. All persons are to be treated as ends not only on account of their separateness but also their rational natures, as Kant held. Moral agents are not merely pleasure-seeking but rational beings, and rationality con-veys a dignity and inviolability on persons which properly constrains the calculus of social utility. Since straightforward maximization poten-tially reduces some persons to the status of sacrificial offerings for the benefit of others, these liberals conclude that the utility calculus must it-self be constrained by human rights rather than the reverse. A rights-based morality secures human liberty more completely than either the utilitarian or new liberalisms had managed.

If the experience of twentieth-century politics teaches any lessons surely one is that the Hobbesian/Rousseauan idea, optimistically re-vived by Green and Hobhouse, of a social organism (distinct or not from the persons comprising it) renders individual rights and freedoms con-tingent, derivative, and ultimately unstable. The values of individuality invariably become subordinated to those of community life, with con-sistently disastrous consequences for human rights. Responding to this, many contemporary liberals have reinstated the classical doctrine that liberty and justice are the principal values of a liberal order. The primacy of rights thesis is variably expressed as the view that 'justice is the first virtue of social institutions'[3] (Rawls), that human rights are 'side con-straints'[4] (Nozick) on individual and state action or 'political trumps held by individuals'[5] (Dworkin). However it is formulated, the primacy of justice thesis states that no ethical or political value may justify the sacrifice of individual rights. Rawls aptly states the thesis as follows:

> Each person possesses an inviolability founded on justice that even the wel-fare of society as a whole cannot override. For this reason justice denies that the loss of freedom for some is made right by a greater good shared by others. It does not allow that the sacrifices imposed on a few are outweighed by the larger sum of advantages enjoyed by many. Therefore in a just society the liberties of equal citizenship are taken as settled; the rights secured by justice are not subject to political bargaining or to the calculus of social interests.[6]

Considerations of justice delimit the scope within which persons may formulate their ends and pursue their conceptions of the good life.

In a manner antithetical to utilitarianism, contemporary liberalism conceives the right as prior to the good. Accordingly, principles of justice must not incorporate or depend for their justification on any particular conception of the good, but must remain neutral between those concep-tions that are contested within the society. As far as possible, the laws that govern a just state should take a neutral stand in debates that con-cern controversial ethical and philosophical doctrines, and apply the principle of tolerance rather widely. There being a variety of ethical doc-trines and personal ideals, and no uncontroversial method of adjudicat-ing between them, persons must be at liberty to decide for themselves how they will live, what ends they will pursue, and what beliefs they will hold. That reasonable persons disagree about such matters entails giving individuals a wide latitude for personal choice, if not out of re-spect for the particular beliefs or ends being chosen, then out of respect for the agents themselves. State neutrality has been defended on several

grounds, including scepticism concerning the possibility of rational ad-
judication between competing views of the good, and the value of personal experiment with different ideals – a necessary means, on some
accounts, to the end of individual autonomy. While the argumentation
varies, a degree of consensus currently prevails among liberal theorists
concerning the related doctrines of the primacy of justice (the priority of
the right over the good), state neutrality, toleration, and pluralism. In addition to the set of rights and freedoms traditionally defended by liberal
theorists, it is this constellation of values that most readily identifies contemporary liberals as such.

Where these theorists part company is less over the worthiness of liberal principles than over their interpretation and relative priority. The
practical significance of principles of equal respect and concern, neutrality, and freedom are matters of considerable dispute. The matter of their
consequences for public policy has produced a range of ideological
stances from the social democratic egalitarianism of Rawls and Dworkin
to the libertarianism of Nozick. Liberalism currently comprises a wide
spectrum of ideological positions each representing a particular conception of how this constellation of political values is properly applied and
given priority. While the Lockean ideal of the minimal state continues to
have its defenders, the dominant view among contemporary liberals is
largely sympathetic with the moderately leftward turn taken by liberal
politics during the early and middle twentieth century.

As mentioned, the latter decades of the twentieth century witnessed a
broad return from utilitarian to classical contractarian methodology. No
longer a historical hypothesis, of course, the theory of the social contract
has been rehabilitated as a useful moral fiction, the basic idea of which
remains the same as that formulated by the tradition's founders with
some methodological refinements carried over from contemporary economic theory. The introduction of decision-theoretic models into contractarian discourse is believed by many to raise the original Hobbesian
method to a higher order of abstraction and rigour agreeable to the analytical temperament of Anglo-American philosophy. The vaunted clarity
and systematicity of the utilitarian doctrine would have to be matched
by a new contractarianism with greater analytical rigour. The mode of
argumentation produced by this incorporation into liberal discourse of
models of rational choice is a novel phenomenon. While the employment
of economic and quasi-economic vocabularies to describe moral agents
is itself nothing new in liberal theory, the recent turn toward decision-
theoretic models is undeniably unique, indeed an innovation in moral/

political argument. A tribute to methodological rigour, this new rational-ist – one might say positivist – mode of argument, complete with technical jargon, is sure to bedazzle the most exacting economist, mathematician, or logician.

Notwithstanding these new methodological contributions, contractar-ian liberalism remains committed to the basic Hobbesian idea of gener-ating principles of justice from the (now decidedly hypothetical) terms of a social contract struck not between asocial appetitive machines but mutually indifferent utility maximizers bound by no prior moral ties. For purposes of analysis, we are to bracket all contingent and morally ir-relevant considerations about ourselves and inquire which principles of association would meet with the approval of rational choosers. An es-sential feature of the method is that all choosers occupy a hypothetical condition of perfect equality and freedom, whether this is conceived as the state of nature or the somewhat less fanciful initial choice situation of decision theory or Rawls's original position. In either case, rational agents are to select those principles that allow them to maximize utility in the most efficient manner possible while unrestricted by prior moral beliefs or bonds of affection of any sort. The legitimacy of principles selected in this way rests squarely on their agreeableness to rational per-sons, and observing these principles in the course of our moral lives is the mark of our rationality. While different writers take their inspiration from different classical thinkers – for instance, Rawls from Kant, Nozick from Locke, and Gauthier from Hobbes – the essential contractarian idea that principles of political organization are to be products of an express (if counterfactual) agreement between rational agents and in no case imposed on persons by a higher authority remains in place. The domain of morality is comprised exclusively of rules, principles, and procedures agreed upon by hypothetical deliberators in a hypothetical choice situa-tion. It is the fact of agreement – explicit and voluntary, albeit hypothet-ical – that conveys moral legitimacy, and decidedly not the authority of settled practice or tradition. Herein lies contractarianism's liberating potential: in liberating us from all unchosen obligations, we are free to carry on our lives observing only those constraints to which we as ratio-nal beings would freely consent. We remain morally autonomous, self-legislating agents in the sense dear to Rousseau and Kant.

If the basic contractarian conception of morality remains largely what it had been for the founders of liberal thought, so too do its conceptions of reason and the self. The legacy of Hobbes and his progeny persists un-abated in much of current liberal philosophy. The self continues to be understood in classical fashion as a rational being, and in the sense unique to modernity. Reason, both theoretical and practical, is a mono-logical and formal affair of rule-governed inference from premises taken as given. Theoretical reason begins with a set of basic premises from which it produces deductions *more geometrico*, and occupies an authori-tative ahistorical vantage point on the world of practice. The paradigm of deduction, although frequently neglected in argumentation, remains the regulative ideal of contractarian theorists – the eternally sought, if never fully realized, model of rational discourse. Practical reason as well remains understood in formal Hobbesian fashion as a strictly instru-mental procedure of securing maximum advantage for oneself. Moral agents are rational in the specifically modern sense that they are gov-erned by prudence alone, and continually occupy themselves with dis-covering the most efficient means of attaining that which they desire. Borrowing the language and assumptions of much contemporary eco-nomic and social theory, individual agents are each assumed to possess a set of ends or preferences, coherently and hierarchically arranged, which they endeavour to maximize in the most efficient manner possi-ble. In estimating how one is to act, one ascertains one's desire, surveys the available possibilities of action, estimates which of these is most likely to bring about the greatest net balance of satisfaction over dissatisfac-tion, and chooses.

Practical reason, for contractarian liberals, is once again the slave of the passions. The preferences held by moral agents are entirely subjec-tive both in the trivial sense of belonging to the subject and in the non-trivial sense of being without objective measure. Moral subjectivism denies that human ends admit of either rationality or irrationality, or that they may be morally praiseworthy or blameworthy. From a moral point of view they are to be regarded as given (indeed arbitrary), beyond both justification and critique. Moreover, such values are relative in the sense that they vary to an extent from person to person. Lacking both universal and objective worth, human values, they conclude, must be both relative and subjective. The work of practical reason is purely quan-titative and instrumental; it is to reckon the consequences of possible ac-tions, estimate relative probabilities of their satisfying our preferences, tallying costs, and so forth.

Neoclassical liberals share with their contractarian and utilitarian forebears the view of the self as in essence an individualistic utility max-imizer, or in Nozick's phrase a 'value-seeking I.'[7] This represents the essence of moral agency no less for contemporary writers than for Hobbes or Bentham. Most obviously in the case of authors employing decision-theoretic models such as Nozick and Gauthier, persons are assumed to maximize utilities no less in their ethical and political than in their economic relations; the difference between these realms turns not upon the self's mode of comportment – this remains fixed – but the ends to be attained therein. The principles of rational self-interest, ethical hedonism, and psychological egoism remain common, if frequently unarticulated, assumptions of contractarian thought. These logically distinct yet related premises typically pass among neoclassical liberals as settled assumptions requiring neither thematic articulation nor philosophical justification. They make up our ordinary prereflective understanding of ourselves as rational beings and accordingly do not call for extended comment. For this reason they seldom receive it, despite the criticism to which these assumptions have been subjected from a number of sources, including (as we have seen) some liberals themselves.

A possible exception to this within the contractarian camp is Rawls himself. While his parties in the original position are straightforward maximizers of utility, Rawls denies that rational choosers are altogether egoistic. Because the parties stand behind a veil of ignorance concealing all personal interests and attributes from view, the choices they make necessarily reflect only generalized interests. A condition of impartiality is imposed on rational choosers by the context of choice itself, effectively eliminating any difference between egoistic and altruistic behavior. On closer inspection, however, it would appear that Rawls is not the exception on this matter that he asserts himself to be. He writes:

> Every interest is an interest of a self (agent), but not every interest is in benefits to the self that has it. Indeed, rational agents may have all kinds of affections for persons and attachments to communities and places, including love of country and of nature; and they may select and order their ends in various ways.[8]

Were we to grant this, it would still appear that Rawls is committed to a view of rational choosers as primarily egoistic maximizers and not maximizers *simpliciter*. The veil of ignorance as a device is introduced precisely to impose impartiality on choosers who presumably are not already impartial. It is precisely because rational choosers are partial to their personal good, 'by nature' as it were, that there is a need to impose an impartiality condition on them by means of the veil. Were the principal motivations of rational agents not egoistic, it is difficult to conceive why impartiality would need to be imposed from without. Is not what the parties are to be ignorant about – their egoistic desires primarily – the source of the problem that principles of justice are to remedy? It appears that Rawls is not an exception after all to the usual view among contractarians of moral agents as (at least primarily) self-interested maximizers of utility.

The assumption of rational self-interest is perhaps the strongest assumption concerning the self commonly, if not uniformly, made by neoclassical liberals. A common feature of contemporary liberal thought is a certain trepidation about incorporating strong or controversial assumptions into political philosophy, particularly assumptions about the good but also the constitution of the self. The idea is to avoid relying on a conception of the self that is controversial, thus leading those who dispute that conception to reject liberal politics as well. The aim is to set out from a minimal set of assumptions in order to avoid exposing liberal principles to attack on the grounds of false premises and also to avoid biasing the issue of justice by a presupposition about the good. If liberal justice is to be neutral between competing views of the good, it must avoid any preconceptions in its mode of argument. Regarding the constitution of the self, a distinct note of scepticism is audible in much of the contemporary literature owing in part to widespread scepticism about metaphysics in general. Although contractarianism appears to show more than a historical affinity to the doctrines of materialism and empiricism, most of its current proponents would deny that the former depends for its justification upon the latter. Frequently liberals insist on the complete separation of the political from the metaphysical, the epistemological, the psychological, and the ethical. On the matter of the self some writers, including Dworkin and Larmore, expressly deny that liberalism presupposes any special set of assumptions regarding this while others, such as Rawls and Rorty, deny that it relies on a specifically metaphysical account. Still others, who may or may not wish to deny either of these hypotheses, prefer to avoid discussing the matter altogether, leaving the assumptions about the self that may be implicit to their own views unthematized. Perhaps the most common view of the self upheld by contemporary liberals is something we may call metaphysical agnosticism. It prefers to assume either nothing or, failing that, as little as possible about the constitution of moral agents.

Despite such avowals, however, liberal politics invariably draws on assumptions about the self, and typically they are stronger and more controversial than liberals claim to realize. The contractarian method itself contains presuppositions about moral agents which not all of its proponents would wish to defend. Philosophers who would not defend the Hobbesian account of the self, in its moral or metaphysical aspect, frequently employ the method of political reasoning that these very premises made intelligible. It is a method that presupposes not only that moral agents are in essence rational egoists but that they are bound by no moral obligations or ties not of their express choice. The self 'initially' (and here again it is assumed that it is intelligible to speak of the self as in an 'initial' or premoral condition able to choose rationally the terms of its entry into society) possesses no moral categories, is encumbered with no obligations or claims upon itself, and draws no distinction between what actions it may perform and what it may not. It is conceived as unconcerned about the interests of other individuals. Its motivations are asocial, its choices amoral and strategic.

All relations between persons – ethical, political, economic, etc. – conform to the model of the contract, rendering society a contingent affair of mutual accommodation in accordance with terms explicitly chosen and voluntary. In the contractarian view, it is not only reason but society as well that is construed in strictly instrumental fashion. Persons enter into social – including cooperative – relations for prudential reasons, and begin to take an interest in others's interests for the same reasons. The classical model of the self, reason, and society remains firmly in place.

Yet what does not remain a part of current liberal doctrine, indeed what could no longer be taken seriously, is the premise that human beings are not deeply embedded in a variety of social circumstances. That moral agents in point of fact are always situated within particular life-worlds and traditions, that they are always participants in practices and a way of life which precede them, that they are speakers of a particular language and view the world through a particular categorial framework are familiar theses difficult to deny by even the most convinced individualist. For the most part contemporary liberals are inclined, perhaps with trepidation, to grant this set of theses in one form or another and allow that their new liberal predecessors were at least partially correct to take the fact of human sociability seriously, even if they would refuse the organicist interpretation of sociability that new liberals offered along with the collectivist political implications that stem from it. The noted trepidation is largely explained by the historical, and seemingly logical, connection between the socially embedded conception of the self and socialist politics. It remains a common assumption among liberals and nonliberals alike that a strongly social conception of the self logically entails an antiindividualistic and socialist politics. Not wishing to grant this conclusion, liberal theorists frequently assert that the fact of human sociability is a mere truism from which no interesting political consequences follow. Assuming a defensive posture, liberals often reply to the various schools of thought which emphasize social embeddedness both that their position is truistic and politically irrelevant and that liberalism's classical tale of an original state of nature and social contract is only a moral, not a metaphysical or historical, hypothesis. It is a mere thought experiment which assumes little about actual moral agents; it assumes remarkably little and yet generates many far-reaching conclusions about the nature of justice. So goes the standard liberal reply.

This chapter and those that follow reject both the assumption noted above – that the social embeddedness thesis entails socialist or other illiberal politics – and the usual reply by which liberals counter it. Liberalism cannot deny that individuals are social beings in a strong constitutive sense, moreover it never needed to deny this. The recognition of social embeddedness undermines no part of the liberal conception of justice, but not because it is merely truistic or politically irrelevant. Indeed it is neither, as I hope to demonstrate in later chapters.

Before doing so, I take up, in the next two sections, conceptions of the self at work in the political liberalism of John Rawls and the libertarianism of Robert Nozick, two representative and important figures in neoclassical liberal thought.

Rawls: The Original Chooser

That Kantian politics can be had without Kantian metaphysics is a premise central to Rawls's rehabilitated contractarian liberalism. Dissatisfied with the implications for justice and individual rights of the utilitarian and new liberalisms, Rawls initiated an important methodological turn in recent decades back to the tradition's original preutilitarian roots and the political methodology of Hobbes, Locke, Rousseau, and Kant. It is the contractarian method that will place liberal principles of justice and human rights on a secure moral foundation, Rawls believes, and particularly in its Kantian formulation. Liberal justice requires that all persons be treated as ends in themselves, as dignified and rational agents in the manner that Kant proposed. This entails that their rights must not be subject to the vicissitudes of the utilitarian calculus or subordinated to any alleged higher good such as the general welfare.

As we saw in Chapter 1, Kant defended liberal principles (in particular, the primacy of individual freedom) on both moral and metaphysical grounds. The doctrines of transcendental idealism and the noumenal self were as important for his conception of justice as the categorical imperative itself. Political philosophy, Kant believed along with other classical liberals, requires a comprehensive moral and metaphysical grounding. This foundational conception of politics, characteristic of Enlightenment thought, Rawls rejects, in part if not completely. In particular, he replies that Kantian metaphysics is entirely detachable from liberal politics. The domain of the political is independent of the metaphysical. Consequently, a theory of justice need not, indeed ought not, allow itself to be drawn into metaphysical debate about the fundamental constitution of the subject. Political liberalism must assume as little as possible and, where it can, remain neutral on issues of metaphysics, epistemology, and moral psychology no less than on the question of the good. A theory of justice that incorporates strong assumptions from any of these eminently contestable domains does not provide the theory with philosophical support but adds to its vulnerability.

Though inclined toward empiricism, Rawls asserts that the version of liberal politics that he defends assumes an appropriately neutral or agnostic position on the matter of the metaphysics of the self. He adamantly rejects the assertion proposed by Michael Sandel[9] that 'justice as fairness' carries specific metaphysical implications about the self, implications specifically Kantian in form. Sandel's charge is that liberal politics cannot avoid these implications, a charge that Rawls dismisses in rather cursory fashion.[10] What liberalism presupposes, according to Rawls, is not a comprehensive metaphysical account of human beings but a narrower, and properly political, conception of citizens. It incorporates premises about the self to be sure, but these assumptions are of a normative, not metaphysical, nature.

Remarking that the category of the person lends itself to investigation from a variety of perspectives both philosophical and scientific, Rawls asserts that from the point of view of justice the only relevant premises concerning the self are those comprising a notion of political citizenship. All accounts of the person that are not of a directly political nature are to be bracketed from consideration. More specifically, Rawls distinguishes three normative conceptions of the self, of which only the first is of major interest to the theory of justice: 'that of the parties in the original position, that of citizens in a well-ordered society, and finally, that of ourselves – of you and me.'[11] Contractarianism is an essentially hypothetical enterprise, a normative thought experiment rather than a historical hypothesis that is interested less in actual moral agents than the artificial rational choosers inhabiting the original position, Rawls's counterpart to the state of nature. These hypothetical creatures provide theoretical expression to a conception of citizenship appropriate to liberal democracies, representing as they do actual moral agents stripped of all attributes of a personal and morally irrelevant nature.

That actual persons are in fact socially and culturally situated, Rawls is not concerned to deny. Indeed, he expressly recognizes that sociability is neither a trivial nor a contingent fact of human existence.

> [S]ocial life is a condition for our developing the ability to speak and think, and to take part in the common activities of society and culture. No doubt even the concepts that we use to describe our plans and situation, and even to give voice to our personal wants and purposes, often presuppose a social setting as well as a system of belief and thought that are the outcome of the collective efforts of a long tradition.[12]

These considerations, however, together with all the traits of the person that produce inequalities or substantial differences are bracketed by Rawls as morally irrelevant.

The parties in the original position are constituted only by those traits that Rawls considers to be of moral interest. As these are few in number, he introduces the veil of ignorance as a methodological device designed for the purpose of abstracting from those facts about persons that do not warrant consideration in fashioning principles of justice. Understanding that the original position is a counterfactual 'device of representation' populated with similarly counterfactual rational parties, the basic idea is to imagine what terms of association such parties would agree on if their deliberations took into consideration only morally relevant facts. What principles of justice would rational maximizers agree on if deprived of knowledge concerning their personal ends, characteristics, identity and other 'idiosyncrasies,' along with those of others? They are to be ignorant of their particular time and place, their position in the socio-economic order, their individual talents, beliefs, and propensities, and more significantly their personal conception of the good life. Their knowledge about themselves and others is to be of an entirely general nature: 'the general facts about human society, ... political affairs and the principles of economic theory, ... the basis of social organization and the laws of human psychology'[14] are all available to the parties. Particularities must be eliminated from view. By abstracting from these and transposing ourselves into the original position, it becomes possible to view the social world and our place in it *sub specie aeternitatus*. The original position, Rawls believes, represents the moral point of view which, as he expresses it in *A Theory of Justice*, regards human circumstance from 'the perspective of eternity.'[15] 'The' (singular) moral point of view is an ahistorical and asocial vantage point on human affairs from which authoritative pronouncements concerning the nature of justice are issued.

The method of abstracting from particularities, all of which are assumed to be morally irrelevant and unworthy of inclusion in the discourse of justice, imposes a strong impartiality condition on the reflecting parties. It introduces as well a large measure of distance to aid reflection – distance from our habitual attitudes and practices, from ends both personal and shared, and from the traditions of thought in which we participate. In short, the contractarian method involves an almost Cartesian level of abstraction in order to make possible a distanced perspective on human affairs – a perspective of this world, but a world highly abstract, circumscribed, and virtually metaphysical.

Accordingly, the parties in the original position are identified not with ourselves but with persons stripped down to their moral essentials. So stripped, the individual occupying the original position is a kind of Kantian 'noumenal self,'[16] as Rawls himself describes it in a metaphysical moment. In choosing principles of justice we are to imagine ourselves as noumenal beings looking out on the social world from an ahistorical vantage point. As such, we are perfectly free to decide what terms of political association are most advantageous to ourselves, understanding again the lack of distinction between egoistic and benevolent motivation once the veil is imposed. As there is no knowledge of personal characteristics to distinguish oneself from another, what is conducive to one's own interest must be equally agreeable to others identically situated. The parties are law-givers to themselves, or in Kantian language they are morally autonomous, self-legislating agents whose choices are autonomous, unconditioned, and generalizable. Rawls's noumenal self is morally and rationally autonomous, and able to formulate and act upon rational decisions. In implementing such decisions, or acting in accordance with principles chosen impartially, one gives expression to one's nature as a rational being while treating others as ends in themselves. One is not merely maximizing utilities in the crudely utilitarian sense of pursuing optimal pleasure, but realizing one's rational nature. Herein lies the key distinguishing feature between the utilitarian's and Rawls's conceptions of rational agency – that whereas the former considers the self's most fundamental characteristic to be the capacity for pleasure and pain, for the latter it is the capacity for self-legislation that is fundamental. What does not distinguish the two views is the particular interpretation of rationality attributed to human beings. The same prudential and instrumentalist conception of rationality presupposed in classical contractarian and utilitarian doctrines continues in unaltered form in Rawls's work.

Rawls's rational agents possess two moral capacities. The first is the capacity to articulate and act from impartial principles of social cooperation, or to possess a sense of justice, while the second is the capacity to fashion and pursue a particular conception of the good life. The former takes us beyond utilitarian doctrine, for which justice is a contingently useful strategy in the pursuit of one's ends rather than an unconditional sense of right constraining the selection of ends. The sense of justice leads one to act on impartial principles out of respect for persons, an idea difficult to translate into the vocabulary of utilitarianism. The second moral power, on the other hand, the capacity to hold a particular view of the good, is easily translatable into utilitarian language. It is the capacity 'to form, to revise, and rationally to pursue a conception of one's rational advantage, or good.'[17] Acting sometimes in egoistic fashion and sometimes with benevolent intent, individuals pursue self-chosen ends which are fashioned (or capable of being fashioned) into a coherent and long-term plan of life. Individuals are capable of estimating what is of value in human life, of devising plans and satisfying their rational desires in a manner consistent with a sense of justice. The common possession among individuals of these capacities, along with their rationality, makes it possible to conceive of persons as free and equal by nature. The fact of their possession constitutes persons as free agents, while the fact of their equal possession – in some requisite minimum degree – renders us equal as well.

Rawls remains firmly within the liberal tradition in conceiving of moral agents as rational utility maximizers, primarily if not solely motivated by self-interest. The parties in the original position are as committed to optimizing utility as are Hobbesian individuals, although they are constrained from doing so by both a sense of justice and the veil. Their interest is in attaining their rationally chosen ends, and securing the liberty and other conditions necessary for doing so. While their particular, or extra-veil, interests are presumed to vary widely, among these are certain 'primary social goods' which all parties have a fundamental interest in maximizing. These primary goods are values of both a basic and general nature in that they underlie whatever particular view of the good persons may select once the veil is lifted. Regardless of one's final ends or personal plan of life, one is presumed to take a more basic interest in maximizing the primary goods of self-respect, individual rights and freedoms, opportunities, and wealth. Parties in the original position share a general interest in securing their particular interests. They are aware that all persons desire these general ends whatever other, or particular, values they hold, and accordingly select principles of association that accord with this knowledge. Since primary social goods are necessary conditions of the realization of final ends, whatever these may be, the account of primary goods defended by Rawls represents an objective yet 'thin theory of the good.' A thicker theory is ruled out on grounds of the legitimate plurality of final ends.

It bears emphasis that the most fundamental interest of Rawls's original choosers lies in the capacity for rational choice itself. Primary goods, notably self-respect, liberty and other basic rights, the possession of opportunities and a degree of wealth, are indispensable to not only the attainment of one's personal utilities but more fundamentally the capacity for autonomous choice, the *sine qua non* of moral/political agency. Rawls's identification of primary goods clearly reflects an individualistic conception of agency, one for which closed opportunities, the absence of freedom, and the presence of formidable socio-economic hierarchies are inimical both to happiness and to rational agency itself.

It is, according to Rawls, both the capacity for autonomous choice and the principles of justice that we would select in a condition of perfect freedom and equality that 'reveal our nature' as moral agents.[18] Significantly, it is our view not of the good but of the right that reveals our fundamental moral constitution, not our chosen ends but the procedural rules that govern our pursuit of ends, whatever these ends may be. The reason Rawls holds this view has become a matter of some controversy. As he writes in *A Theory of Justice*, this is so 'for the self is prior to the ends which are affirmed by it.'[19] The self, according to Rawls, is to be identified with its conception of justice rather than the good on account of the contingency and revisability of the latter. An important element of distance exists between the agent and its chosen ends, rendering the latter permanently subject to revision by the individual. To identify the self with its ends, even with an overriding or dominant end, would suggest that its view of the good is beyond choice. It entails that persons are inevitably bound to certain value configurations which they may not alter.

Yet since these are alterable by the self, the self must be in a sense prior to its chosen values. The exact nature of this priority – whether moral, ontological, or a combination – is a matter of some dispute, as I shall discuss later in this chapter.

Rawls's view, then, represents no major departure from the conception of the self presupposed in earlier contractarian and utilitarian liberalisms. The legacy of Hobbes, Locke, Kant, Bentham, and Mill is visible in his work, minus some of their more troubling metaphysical premises. This is not surprising in view of the fact that Rawls's primary interest with respect to the self is not to present an overhauled conception but more modestly to incorporate fewer traditional assumptions than has been customary. It is less to refute such assumptions than to bracket as many of them as is possible. As a consequence, Rawls's moral agents continue to fit the description of instrumentally rational maximizers of utility, acting primarily in accordance with self-interest and encumbered by no moral ties or obligations not of their express choice. Persons possess coherent preference-orderings, all of which are ranked in terms of relative importance and maximized in an optimally efficient manner. Rawls does add one special assumption of note, namely that rational choosers are not subject to envy of other persons. They aim at a simple maximization of primary goods for themselves without regard to their relative possession by others.

Rawls cannot be faulted for attempting to rid liberalism of much of its metaphysical baggage, particularly the theories of the self present in Hobbesian materialism and Kantian transcendental idealism. For attempting to defend liberal politics without these classical assumptions, Rawls may well be commended. Yet the particular gesture by which he seeks to accomplish this is open to dispute. Rawls's metaphysical agnosticism comes closer, in the language of psychoanalysis, to a simple repression of liberalism's troubling and, by most contemporary accounts, unacceptable metaphysical impulse than a more productive 'working through' toward some more satisfactory condition. Political philosophy cannot, as Rawls wishes, be separated altogether from all other philosophical disciplines, including in particular ethics and the philosophy of the self. Political philosophy is not the 'free-standing'[20] field of investigation Rawls wishes it to be, but inevitably incorporates premises from these other fields. Although Rawls expresses the intention to incorporate no controversial assumptions about persons, the contractarian method which he employs is itself already committed to a particular conception of moral agency, one hardly beyond dispute even among liberals.

Even when modified along Kantian lines, the contractarian self remains at heart a rational egoist indifferent to the interests of other persons and whose essential mode of comportment is decidedly strategic. The rationality that governs it is a purely instrumental and strategic sort. Moral relations are engaged on the contract model and always with an eye to personal advantage. More fundamentally, the moral constitution of the self, the contractarian model assumes, is describable in all essentials in ahistorical fashion. All traits of the person deemed a matter of cultural or historical contingency, or of a personal and particular nature, are accidental to moral agency and accordingly are of no moral or political relevance. None of these premises is beyond controversy or even especially weak. Moreover, they most certainly extend beyond political philosophy proper.

If the contractarian method is to carry any persuasive force, the concept of moral agency that it presupposes must be defensible. It must bear more than a passing resemblance to actual persons or our ordinary prereflective understanding of ourselves as moral/political agents. Part of the persuasive force that classical contractarian and utilitarian liberalisms attained among their adherents rested on the perceived adequacy of the Hobbesian/Benthamite view of the person. That view appeared to possess moral, economic, philosophical, and scientific legitimacy as well as to hold out a certain liberating potential for politics. It was not merely the conception of the self that assumed less than rival doctrines. It was the one that expressed a comprehensive and, it seemed, true account of human beings as they actually are. Yet with the turn that contemporary contractarianism has taken toward conceiving of itself as a wholly hypothetical enterprise, much of its persuasive force has evaporated. Principles of justice now represent the products of an agreement that never was among persons who never were. The terms of the consensus, the individuals who arrived at it, and the condition of freedom and equality that made it possible, are each highly counterfactual theoretical constructions, raising an obvious question as to the persuasive force of political principles thus generated for actual human beings. Why ought beings like us take an interest in agreements reached by beings like those occupying Rawls's original position? If the answer cannot be that they are us, it must be that they resemble us in important respects. Their rationality and fundamental mode of comportment must model our own for the contractarian method to possess any persuasive force. The parties in the original position must possess all morally relevant and 'essential' characteristics of actual persons, yet whether this is true of Rawls's deliberators is doubtful on several grounds.

First, it is doubtful whether instrumental rationality is an adequate conception of human reason. Since the time of the Greeks, philosophers have argued in one fashion or another that there is something fundamental to the constitution of human beings about reason. To this, liberals have added that the dignity and inviolability of the person squarely rests on its being a rational agent, yet when rationality is construed in quasi-economic fashion as the power to get what one wants, such conclusions do not readily follow. Whatever truth these beliefs reveal about human beings and justice is not captured in the contractarian interpretation of reason as the capacity merely to pursue utility with optimal efficiency. There is more to moral/political reason than is dreamt of in contractarian philosophy. (I shall return to this topic in Chapter 5.)

Second, the analogy between moral agents and instrumentally rational egoists whose moral relations are entirely strategic and constrained only by expressly chosen principles is highly dubious. Modelling ethical and political relations on economic relations accomplishes the very opposite of what contractarianism promises; far from asking us to assume less about the self and its various relations, it requires us to assume the highly controversial and, in my view, untenable assertion that economic relations provide an appropriate model of moral relations. Both ethical and political relations are badly misunderstood on such terms. Indeed, whether even economic practice is properly conceived along Hobbesian lines is highly contestable. In each of these relations, the assumptions of contractarianism are at best incomplete and at worst false.

Third, that all attributes of the self that are in any sense nongeneral – be they particular, personal, culturally or historically contingent, etc. – are for that reason morally irrelevant is at best a strong assumption and at worst a dubious one. The argument that who we are or conceive ourselves to be in our capacity as moral agents should be irrelevant to our choice of political arrangements seems a strange proposition. We may wish to bracket a good many attributes of this kind when determining public policy – indeed it is very often wise to do so – yet to bracket them all in a priori fashion is to dismiss much of what constitutes us as moral agents and human beings. Too few attributes of the self qualify on Rawls's account as morally relevant, resulting in an overly abstracted and ahistorical view of moral agents.

Whether it serves any useful purpose to ruminate on the hypothetical deliberations of hypothetical creatures in a hypothetical condition of perfect freedom, equality, and impartiality is a question best answered in the negative. In short, Rawls's deliberators are not us; they are only rational in a narrow and quasi-economic sense of the term, they deliberate in a vacuum, are only marginally characterizable as moral agents, and are barely human. For a method of political reasoning to be at all fruitful, it must not misrepresent to such an extent who we ourselves are.

Nozick: Homo Economicus, Again

The same criticisms apply no less to the contractarian liberalism of Robert Nozick. Here again the legacy of Hobbes and Locke is fully apparent. Both the method of political reasoning and the assumptions about the self implicit to it are directly appropriated from the tradition's founders. The innovations that Nozick introduces occur principally at the levels of methodology – with the further introduction and modification of decision-theoretic models into the contractarian method – and political ideology – employing the method to justify libertarian politics. The doctrine of moral agency remains in all essentials that of Hobbes and Locke, particularly the latter.[21]

In keeping with the model of *homo economicus*, Nozick perpetuates the contractarian habit of characterizing moral relations in the vocabulary of utilitarian economics. Rational self-interest remains the very essence of moral/political agency. The individual's most basic, and also most valuable, trait is that of being a 'value-seeking I.'[22] Beginning from the hypothetical standpoint of the state of nature, notably in its Lockean formulation, Nozick seeks to determine what conditions of civil association rationally egoistic utility maximizers would select, and draws the conclusion that it is the minimal state that such agents would prefer. A state that makes maximum allowance for individual liberty, within the constraints of respect for the identical rights and freedoms of others, is what rational bargainers would assent to, Nozick argues. (The detailed arguments Nozick provides cannot be rehearsed here.)

Nozick supplements, and in some ways modifies, this straightforward contractarian view of the self in some writings published after *Anarchy, State, and Utopia*. Some of these writings evince at least an element of dissatisfaction with the standard Hobbesian and Lockean accounts of the self which had been assumed so unproblematically in the earlier treatise. In *Philosophical Explanations*, for instance, and in a context different from that of *Anarchy, State, and Utopia*, Nozick writes that the sort of care or interest which the self has for itself is not strictly egoistic; it is not the extent but the reflexivity of the interest the individual has in itself that makes it special.

The self's care for itself is special in being reflexive, care for itself as itself rather than as a bearer of some unreflexive property. This care need not be greater than its care for all other things. The theory of the self does not entail egoism. The self's care about itself is special, not in its unique magnitude but in its distinctive reflexiveness; each of us can say 'I care about myself simply for being me.' We care specially about our current and our future selves because they are us; we care about identity because we care about ourselves. Such caring is rather like the pride of craftsmanship, but with no external object: a reflexive act of craftsmanship.[23]

In another, again nonpolitical, context Nozick expresses a (minor) degree of dissatisfaction with the instrumental conception of rationality presupposed by contractarian and utilitarian methodology. After taking the standard instrumentalist line in his exposition of libertarianism, Nozick argues in *The Nature of Rationality* that this standard line requires supplementation. In that text and in the earlier *Anarchy, State, and Utopia*, rationality is described as the distinguishing property of human beings and that by virtue of which persons possess rights. It is spoken of in the earlier text in exclusively instrumentalist terms and primarily so again in the later work. Yet the latter text expresses the view that instrumental rationality does not exhaust the concept of human rationality. It represents the 'base state' or 'the default theory, the theory that all discussants of rationality can take for granted, whatever else they think.' Nozick adds that 'the instrumental theory of rationality does not seem to stand in need of justification, whereas every other theory does.'[24] This rather intriguing statement from Nozick does not receive the elaboration for which it so clearly calls; it is merely asserted as axiomatic.[25] At any rate, he goes on in the discussion that follows to argue that 'the concept of rationality is not exhausted by the instrumental.'[26] The theory of rational choice, he maintains, must extend beyond causally expected utility to what he calls evidential and symbolic utilities. I shall return to this.

The point to be emphasized here is that the modifications Nozick introduces to the *homo economicus* conception of the self are of a relatively minor nature, occurring sometimes outside a moral or political context altogether, and then in a manner not easily reconciled with the position defended in his political treatise.[27]

For Nozick as much as for Hobbes, the state of nature constitutes the truth of the human condition. The self remains a rationally self-interested maximizer of utility without prior moral ties and inclined to strategic action in all its dealings with human beings. It pursues its utilities, or as he sometimes expresses it, it 'tracks rightness' or 'bestness' in accordance with an overall conception or plan of life. It is able to decide what its overall conception of life will be and to regulate its actions in accordance with it. The individual governs its own life by fashioning autonomous choices. The autonomy of the individual in choosing its ends and conduct creates a natural right to liberty not to be contravened by the state or other persons unless this accords with principles the individual, if fully rational, would choose for itself in the state of nature.

What is less straightforward in Nozick's account of the self is the matter, much debated among classical contractarians, of the freedom of the will. The capacity for free choice which had been assumed unproblematically in the political context of *Anarchy, State, and Utopia*, in a later text becomes a highly problematic issue. Writing in a metaphysical context, Nozick expresses serious misgivings about the freedom of the will. Hard pressed to refute metaphysical determinism, and feeling obliged to take it seriously, Nozick remarks that what is most intolerable about determinism is the implication it seems to engender for human dignity. Like political freedom, without the freedom of the will 'we seem diminished, merely the playthings of external forces. How, then,' he continues, 'can we maintain an exalted view of ourselves?'[28] If determinism places the self 'beyond freedom and dignity' the basis of self-respect is lost. Nozick's concern in this regard, however, is not to refute the determinist thesis – this he does not do – but to remove this implication should determinism be true. It is, in his words, to 'defang determinism without denying it.'[29]

He carries this off by arguing that the intrinsic worth or dignity of persons rests not on the freedom of the will but a particular view of human action. The dignity of the self is not diminished so long as we are able to conceive of action as 'tracking bestness,' or in conventional language, as maximizing utility. Dignity stems not from our being the originators of action in a sense involving free will, but from the connection between action and value. The individual selects from among the options open to it the course of action producing the most valuable outcome. Whether the selection is causally determined or an act of free decision, the worth of the act and ultimately of the agent itself depends on the selected action's pursuing optimal utility. Human freedom and dignity are linked with outcomes, and the language of instrumentality retains its dominion. This account has the advantage of rescuing freedom and dignity from the clutches of determinism, should that doctrine prove true, yet at a stiff price. In making these traditional liberal notions contingent on value, translating them in the process into the vocabulary of instrumentality, the conception of the self that ensues is one able to claim value for itself, perhaps even the highest value, yet not dignity in the sense in which Kant spoke of it. This figure, who understood something about human freedom and dignity, insisted on the separation of dignity from mere value, a distinction of crucial importance to many liberals and Kantians, and impossible to draw in Nozick's terms.

If the worth of the individual and its actions stems from the connection of the latter to optimal utility, Nozick also possesses a theory of objective value unusual among twentieth century liberals. An idea usually greeted with scepticism by liberals whether contractarian, utilitarian, or otherwise, the notion of objective good or intrinsic value is defended by Nozick in *Philosophical Explanations* and given an unusual rendering. Objective value, according to his account, is a measure of 'organic unity.' Whether discussing the value of a human life, scientific theories, or the arts, the intrinsic value of each is a function of the degree of organic unity or integrity which is attained by it; the relative value of the item is in direct proportion to this degree of unity. Nozick maintains that it is the mark of an item possessing intrinsic value to unify discordant elements, much as Plato sought a hierarchical ordering of the soul's warring parts. So ordered, the soul takes on a higher order of intrinsic worth. The value of these items is not contingent on the pleasure or happiness that derives from such unity, but organic unity itself.

Lest liberals worry that a theory of objective value may subvert the values of individuality by prescribing authoritatively the objectively best ordering of ends or way of life, providing a philosophical ground for state action thwarting individual autonomy, Nozick in the same discussion provides a conception of individuality designed to cohere with the theory of value. Individuality, the political value *par excellence* of *Anarchy, State, and Utopia*, is translated in the metaphysical context of *Philosophical Explanations* into an affair of ordering values in particular, nongeneralizable ways to suit the person one is. Since there are a plurality of objective values and no single correct manner of ranking them, an element of individuality or creativity is introduced in determining which intrinsic values will be realized and in what manner.

A person who tracks bestness, who seeks value, will have to formulate her own package of value realization; she cannot simply 'maximize' on the value dimension. This package need not be an aggregate, it can pattern and unify the diverse values it realizes. In thus patterning value, the person may emulate a previous pattern exhibited by a value exemplar or described in some tradition, or she may create a new complex unity, sculpting the value contours of her life in an original, perhaps unique way.[30]

Although values possess an objective character, the fact of their irreducible plurality coupled with the absence of an objectively correct method of weighing such values entails that individuals must decide for themselves what mixture of values they will pursue, in what order of priority, and in accordance with what overall conception of life. As the nature of value strives for the greatest possible organic unity, the personal ends one holds must be ordered into a unified conception which constitutes the general purpose of one's life. Such overall conceptions also admit of plurality, being relative in some measure to the temperament and capacities of the individual. There is, then, a range of objectively valuable possibilities among which persons must choose, and it is in making such choices that the values of individuality come into prominence. This coupled with the separateness of persons thesis introduced in the critique of utilitarianism protects individual autonomy from perfectionist or paternalistic government action purportedly grounded on objective value.

Nozick's account of individuality, unlike that provided by classical liberals, does not entail that persons are in no fundamental sense social beings, embedded in traditions and ways of life which precede them and within which they form an identity. While the Lockean state of nature remains the theoretical point of departure for Nozick, he is not concerned to deny the fact of human sociability, nor does he need to in justifying libertarian politics. What is needed for this purpose, he believes, is the negation of not human sociability itself – something surely impossible – but the mistaken implication often drawn from it, especially by those on the left, that the person's status as a social being creates in it 'a general floating debt which the current society can collect and use as it will.'[31] Socialist politics depends on not only the premise that we are social beings or 'products,' but the inference that this fact generates a range of unchosen obligations which governments must enforce by legal means. It is the inference, not the premise, that Nozick denies. No interesting political consequences are entailed by the fact of human sociability, he holds.

Where this fact does carry consequences is in the theory of rational choice. As noted above, Nozick wholly accepts the instrumental conception of rationality while denying that it provides an exhaustive analysis of the rational. The denial is based in part on the premise that as a social being the individual is concerned in fashioning choices with not only the suitability of means to a given end but the significance or symbolic meaning of the end as well. The individual inhabits a social world rich in symbolic meaning about which it cares deeply. These meanings largely represent our cultural inheritance and serve an important role in informing rational choice. Not wishing to bracket the order of significance altogether, as is customary among decision theorists, effectively banishing it to the realm of the irrational, Nozick proposes its incorporation into the theory of rational choice. 'Symbolic utility,' as he calls it, must be incorporated along with 'evidential utility' into a broader theory expanded beyond the bounds of causal instrumentality. The symbolic and the evidential, no less than the causally instrumental, constitute legitimate modes of rationality to be incorporated into a single decision-theoretic account. Into this broader account Nozick introduces a new rule of rational decision as maximizing decision-value: 'A rational decision ... will maximize an action's decision-value, which is a weighted sum of its causal, evidential, and symbolic utility.'[32] In arguing for the ethical and political relevance of 'symbolic utility' in *The Nature of Rationality*, he takes his position beyond the conventional view of rational choice employed in the earlier *Anarchy, State, and Utopia*.[33]

At the basis of Nozick's libertarianism are two classical liberal doctrines, one Lockean and one Kantian, relating to the self. The Kantian idea, familiar to all students of moral and political philosophy, is that the individual is to be treated in all matters as an end in itself, while the Lockean idea is that the individual is the possessor of inviolable natural rights. As a student of Locke, Nozick fully subscribes to the theory of natural rights. These are held by individuals in the state of nature, or the condition of anarchy, and include the basic rights of life, liberty, and property, as well as the right to enforce these however one sees fit. Being natural, they are not contingent on the rule of law or any other form of social recognition, nor are they possessed by individuals in virtue of their participation in a political order. Rather, such rights are possessed by individuals as human beings and as natural endowments.

This medieval and thoroughly metaphysical view of human rights also receives a Kantian spin in Nozick's interpretation of rights as 'side constraints.' Respecting persons as ends expressly rules out the sort of moral balancing act (whereby the rights of some persons are 'weighed' or 'balanced' against the rights of others in the interest of an overarching social good) often favoured by utilitarian and new liberals as well as by certain nonliberal modes of thought. The rhetoric of weighing or balancing rights, Nozick observes, most often conceals the fact that particular persons are being treated as mere means while others enjoy the benefit of their sacrifice. A better interpretation of rights conceives of them as constraints on the conduct of persons and governments alike. The idea of rights as side constraints expresses a view of persons as inviolable ends in themselves as well as separate and free agents. Individuals, in this conception, are protected by impenetrable barriers – moral, political, and legal – against harmful interference. Rights are to be regarded as inviolable constraints, and removed from the calculus of social utility.

Nozick argues that taking this Kantian principle seriously, along with the principles of liberty and the separateness of persons, leads us into the vicinity of libertarian politics. The minimal state, in his view, is the only one that provides adequate protection for rights. A government whose functions extend beyond the minimal ones of enforcing contracts and protecting against force, fraud, and theft invariably sacrifice individual rights in ways that cannot be justified morally. Any state more extensive than the minimal libertarian one would fail to meet with the approval of rational bargainers, each of whom would value the protection of its rights over any overarching social good to which such rights could be subordinated. They would not consent to the kinds of coercion to which all more extensive political orders must resort.

While relatively few contemporary liberals share Nozick's ideological position, the assumptions concerning moral agency which underlie it are for the most part standard fare among neoclassical contractarians. The view of the self as a (primarily) egoistic maximizer of utility, comporting itself in its ethical and political interactions no less than in its economic relations in strategic mode, unburdened by moral ties or ends not of its express choice, is currently the dominant view among liberals in the contractarian and utilitarian traditions. Whether explicitly held or presupposed in its method of reasoning, the self of neoclassical liberalism remains firmly rooted in the tradition of Hobbes.

Communitarianism and Metaphysical Embarrassment

As noted at the beginning of this chapter, liberalism in the twentieth century has become an internally diverse and contested tradition as it has come increasingly to constitute the mainstream of political thought in the West and indeed in much of the world. Liberal politics has been upheld in recent decades by writers working within a variety of philosophical traditions by no means limited to the utilitarian and contractarian. The decline of foundationalism in epistemology and widespread scepticism about metaphysics have both had considerable effect on contemporary moral and political philosophy, prompting a similar scepticism about the need for, or possibility of, foundational justifications of moral and political assertions. This has led numerous critics of liberalism, and many liberals themselves, to abandon the foundational doctrines of utilitarianism and contractarianism and return to the traditions of Aristotle and Hegel. Liberalism is currently defended by traditional utilitarians and contractarians, by writers having a primarily economic perspective, and is alternatively defended and opposed by neoaristotelians, neo-hegelians, and postmodernists. Uniting most of these is a certain scepticism, even embarrassment, about many of the tradition's standard assumptions regarding the moral and metaphysical constitution of the self. The quest for origins, the state of nature, natural rights, the noble savage, idealism, materialism, determinism, egoism, instrumental rationality, and other assumptions conventionally upheld by liberals have fallen into disfavour among proponents and opponents of liberalism alike. Common among its proponents is the desire to bracket as many of these assumptions as is possible without dismantling liberal politics in the process.

One source of this desire, and of the metaphysical embarrassment that motivates it, is a line of argument advanced by a group of critics working within the Aristotelian and Hegelian traditions. The communitarian critique of liberalism is the most philosophically interesting and powerful such critique at present and serves as the contemporary successor to the Rousseauan, Hegelian, and Marxist critiques of liberalism on which it draws. Like the first two, the communitarian critique of liberalism presents a difficulty in classification, conceivable in some respects as a critique from within the liberal tradition and in others as a critique from without. Certain communitarian writers may accept while others reject the liberal label, a matter of less significance than the content of the critique itself. In the most general terms, communitarian writers reject many of the classical and often metaphysical assumptions that underlie liberal politics, including those that pertain to the fundamental constitution of the self. They reject all ahistorical and asocial depictions of moral agents of the kind traditionally upheld by liberals together with what they regard as the tradition's excessive concern with the values of individuality at the expense of the values of community life.

The communitarian critique of liberalism begins at the beginning:

with the state of nature. Conceived as a historical hypothesis, the state of nature is now universally recognized as a myth. The metaphysical quest for origins, for 'natural man' or the 'natural human condition' prior to all sociability is a fanciful and ultimately futile undertaking. The idea that if only we strip away all the accidental traits of the self – the socially and historically contingent, the unrepeatable and particular – we shall unearth a deep core of being describable in the language either of the metaphysician or the moralist depends on assumptions that can no longer be taken seriously, principally the essence/accident dichotomy of classical metaphysics. As a historical and metaphysical hypothesis, the state of nature may be summarily dismissed. Yet when conceived as a moral or political hypothesis, as we have seen, many present-day liberals believe the state of nature or its counterparts (the original position or the initial choice situation) to be perfectly unobjectionable when construed more modestly as a device of representation or a counterfactual thought experiment. Such a move certainly commits the theorist to fewer assumptions than the older historical conception, but it does not remove all the assumptions to which communitarian and other critics object. Construed as a moral hypothesis, the theory of the state of nature remains committed to a variant of the essence/accident dichotomy. The essence of the self, while no longer described in the language of metaphysics, remains subject to description in moral terms. It is in all essentials the Hobbesian self minus the metaphysical underpinnings: the original chooser, the presocial strategist, the instrumentally rational maximizer of utility.

As a moral/political hypothesis, the state of nature represents an impossible, ahistorical vantage point on human affairs. Far from representing the truth of the human condition or 'the moral point of view,' the condition of complete asociality and ahistoricality, of unconditioned freedom, perfect equality and impartiality is both unattainable as a standpoint for reflection and irrelevant as a perspective from which to make assertions about the world of actual human practices. It is unattainable for the reason that moral agents, and moral theorists no less, are factical beings situated in finite perspectives. 'The moral point of view' is not properly conceived as a standpoint transcending or prior to the contingent world of practice but a partial and finite perspective located within such practices. There exists no Archimedean point for practical reasoning, or indeed for philosophical inquiry in general as a number of contemporary schools of thought (including communitarianism, antifoundationalism, hermeneutics, phenomenology, pragmatism, critical theory, postmodernism, deconstruction, and feminism) have urged. Furthermore, as I argued in my discussion of Rawls, such a standpoint, supposing it were possible to occupy fully, would be of no relevance for actual moral agents who bear little resemblance to the mythical figures occupying the state of nature or its contemporary equivalents. Persons are not accidentally social, historical, or cultural beings. Particularity is no less a part of their being than universality. The standpoint of choosers without social involvements, moral ties, presuppositions, particularity, and contingency is not a standpoint of rational choosers; it is no standpoint at all. Moral questions, far from being clarified from this perfectly hypothetical perspective, are distorted by it while the course of inquiry proceeds down irrelevant avenues.

One important facet of the communitarian argument is the critique of the notion of rationality implicit in both utilitarian and contractarian accounts. That rationality should be conceived as a purely formal and rule-governed notion, in essence equated with strategic efficiency, places reason beyond any normative, cultural, or historical context. That reasoning should be presuppositionless and acontextual, that it should proceed in explicit deductive fashion from premises to conclusion without importing hidden premises or prejudices of any sort, is a mistaken epistemological ideal which overlooks the very conditions that make reasoning possible. Reason always occurs within a context and against a background of tacit assumptions, practices, traditions, language, and culture, a background that can never be fully thematized in a single act of reflection. Reason is never without a multitude of presuppositions which constitute our historical particularity. This applies as much to moral and political reason as to all other modes of reasoned reflection. The act of abstraction required by an acontextual rationality is beyond the limits of reflection, while the identification of normative with instrumental reason both decontextualizes and narrows beyond recognition anything that we would wish to characterize as moral reasoning. Strategic rationality, rather than bracketing all controversial assumptions arising from our particularity, leaves us with an impoverished conception, yet one that still retains assumptions which many would contest, principally the assumptions of mutual indifference and egoism. Instrumental reason assumes at once too much and too little. It assumes too much in supposing it possible and desirable to abstract from all context and all particularity, as well as in requiring that we conceive of moral agents as mutually indifferent utility maximizers, and too little in bracketing all assumptions relating to particular values, beliefs, and identities.

In addition to its impossible acontextuality and impoverished instrumentality, the conception of reason presupposed by conventional liberalism cannot support its own highest values of human rights and the intrinsic worth of the individual. Instrumental rationality declares the subjectivity and moral equivalency of all ends, thus placing these values on a scale occupied by all other desired ends. With only quantitative distinctions between values, there can be no exceptional reverence for any of them, including the rights and dignity of the person. Most clearly in the case of utilitarian liberalism, these values are to be tallied alongside other ends and it is their weighted sum that is to be maximized, not any particular value in the equation. Critical of this quantitative, even bureaucratic, tendency within utilitarianism, contractarians seek to establish a more categorical basis for liberalism's highest values while continuing to employ a mode of rationality that refuses all but quantitative distinctions. Neoclassical liberals, like their utilitarian and contractarian predecessors, are unable to justify categorical protection of the dignity and rights of the person so long as rationality is assimilated to instrumentality. Categorical imperatives cannot be generated by this conception of reason. Only hypothetical imperatives may be generated from an instrumentalist conception of reason, undermining contractarian liberalism's promise to justify categorical prohibitions on human rights violations.

To go along with conventional liberalism's ahistorical and decontextualized rationality are similarly ahistorical and decontextualized notions of the self, to which communitarians also object. The notion of a worldless subject coolly surveying the contingent world of human practices and looking out through the eyes of pure reason is a myth which must be entirely overcome. Handed down by the Enlightenment, the myth of the worldless subject has been in full decline in recent decades as a result of the efforts of a number of philosophical and social-scientific schools of thought. From Hegelianism to postmodernism and hermeneutics, a variety of schools have expressed the view that sociality and historicity are pervasive in the constitution of the self, whether the subject is conceived as a moral agent or in other capacities. The common liberal assumption that, in order to assert the moral priority of the individual over the collective (and likewise of the right over the good), it is necessary to presuppose its ontological priority as well causes no end of difficulty for liberal politics. The assumption is that the individual must be conceived apart from all intersubjectivity and only subsequently and contingently as belonging to a historical community, tradition, or way of life. Its moral being and identity must be detachable from all such accidents, its essence consisting solely in the capacity for rational choice. This is necessary, liberal theorists have often believed, in order to assert the primacy of individual rights. Michael Sandel expresses this point in the following terms:

> For justice to be primary, certain things must be true of us. We must be creatures of a certain kind, related to human circumstance in a certain way. In particular, we must stand to our circumstance always at a certain distance, conditioned to be sure, but part of us always antecedent to any conditions. Only in this way can we view ourselves as subjects as well as objects of experience, as agents and not just instruments of the purposes we pursue. Deontological liberalism supposes that we can, indeed must, understand ourselves as independent in this sense.[34]

The communitarian objection is that in order to defend an individualist politics, it is necessary to assume an untenable individualist ontology. It must be assumed that all traits of the self arising from its sociality are merely contingent properties detachable through reflection. There must be a deep core of being within the self describable without reference to other selves, some inner citadel or essential human nature fully beyond the vicissitudes of history, experience, and intersubjectivity. Whether it is the noumenal subject of transcendental idealism, the rational chooser, or some other core of selfhood, liberal politics must presuppose some such notion in order to advance its position. Yet such notions draw liberalism back into the region of the metaphysical which it often seeks to bracket. It draws liberalism, moreover, into debates that seem utterly fruitless and intractable. Liberalism must further conceive of the self as ontologically prior to each of its ends, including both its particular values and its overriding conception of the good. For the individual to choose these in a rational manner such ends must be held at a distance and not factor into the constitution of the individual's identity. One's moral being must be unaffected by one's view of the good. Yet, the communitarian argument continues, the self cannot be understood in such a fashion. It cannot be abstracted from the totality of social involvements, moral ends, and way of life in which it has its being. Nor can it be stripped down to some metaphysical substratum underlying experience. Distinguishing in metaphysical fashion 'essential' from 'accidental' traits of the self is a pointless exercise.

Conventional liberal notions of rationality, the self, and community are in an important respect logically wedded. In viewing them as such, the difficulties that beset the foundations of liberalism become all the more apparent. To be a moral agent in this view means to be preoccupied with the choice of means most conducive to one's subjective ends and to employ rational strategies in their pursuit, while to be a member of a political community or any other collective body means that one has determined such membership to be a useful strategy in attaining these ends. Instrumentality is the dominant paradigm underlying each of these notions. Yet it is a paradigm ill-suited to political philosophy. At home within the field of economics (although this too is contestable), the instrumentalist mode of thought that dominates much of the liberal tradition attempts to generate principles of justice in a moral, cultural, and historical vacuum. It carries out its reflections in an impossible contextless condition and without regard for the kinds of ends that are being maximized. It gives rise to a condition of rational madness: the complete domination of means over ends, and potentially of some persons by others. The instrumentalist paradigm is ultimately a vacuous, even illiberal, mode of political thought.

It is replaced in communitarianism with a return of sorts to the Aristotelian and Hegelian traditions. It is in these traditions, communitarians maintain, that the sociality and facticity of the self are properly conceived and carry a significance far greater than in conventional (utilitarian and contractarian) liberalism. Communitarianism, a school of political thought that does not lend itself to easy description,[35] replaces the instrumentalist and individualist paradigm of liberal politics with one that takes seriously the situated character of human existence. Both individual agents and their capacities of rational reflection are embedded in a lifeworld which precedes them and which may never be fully objectified in an act of reflection. Persons are social beings in a strong, constitutive sense. Not only dependent upon other human beings for the attainment of certain ends, or inclined toward others as a strategy in self-interest, individuals are socially and historically conditioned beings in every respect. Their understanding of themselves and of the good, their capacities of reflection and choice, their identity and basic mode of comportment as moral agents are all so many social inheritances making up its factical condition. So must a conception of justice arise within a community of moral agents similarly situated. The notion of political right can neither be universalized nor detached from shared understandings and practices that comprise a particular way of life. Rationality itself is inseparable from sociality. Rational discourse is embedded in social practices and always proceeds against a background of shared assumptions or within a common horizon of understanding.

Communitarianism would have us adopt a measure of historical consciousness typically absent among liberal theorists (with some exceptions).[36] It recommends that we take seriously the moral and political implications of the failure of Enlightenment individualism and foundationalism. Particularity cannot be entirely suspended in the manner required by conventional liberal and other foundationalist theory. It can never be reduced to a simple object of reflection, being itself the standpoint from which reflection occurs. Recognizing the historical embeddedness of reflection in all its forms entails that practical reason must take its departure not from formal and ahistorical methodology of the kind recommended by Enlightenment philosophy, but from the traditions, practices, and way of life that constitute our historical particularity. Communitarian politics favours a reversal of liberalism's priority of universality over particularity, methodology over tradition, and theory over practice. Since abstraction altogether from the latter values is an impossibility, political reflection must be immanent. It must forego the ahistoricality of state of nature theory and its analytical equivalents for more modest, situated forms of reflection. It must conceive of moral agents and reason itself as social constructions defined by historical particularity and inseparable from it.

The communitarian thesis assumes a variety of forms. In the work of some theorists it is argued that the self is constituted by its social attachments and moral ends. Liberal individualism, in this view, is mistaken in distinguishing the person that one is from the moral ends and social attachments that one has, a distinction that reduces the latter to the order of accidents. With no way of distinguishing accident from essence, the particular values and forms of intersubjectivity appropriated by the self cannot be separated from its mode of self-understanding. Who the person is is a function of its particularity – of the ends, attachments, and way of life which are its own – and not, as liberalism has traditionally supposed, of universality alone. In particular, as Sandel has stressed, one's moral ends must be understood as constitutive of one's identity as a moral agent. These ends do not belong to the periphery of the self but define us as the persons we are. We cannot conceive ourselves as moral agents apart from the values and interests we have by virtue of our participation in forms of community life.

If the self is not ontologically prior to its ends neither is it separable from the particular narrative history that it lives out within such communities. The self, as Alasdair MacIntyre has argued, has the structure of a narrative. The particular narrative configuration within which the self is constituted is itself a social construction, while the individual it-self is never more than the coauthor of its being. The individual becomes what it is only within particular narrative configurations, roles, and social practices that are less chosen than discovered by virtue of our social involvements. Both our self-understanding and conception of the good stem directly from the roles we occupy and the practices in which we participate with others. Who one is, therefore, is in large part an inheritance from tradition. One's identity is implicated in the final ends, roles, and narrative history which one appropriates from tradition.

Communitarianism sometimes takes a more explicitly Hegelian turn, as represented in the work of Charles Taylor. This critic of liberal individualism, or 'atomism' as he prefers to call it, faults liberal doctrine for its lack of historical consciousness and failure to recognize the profoundly social character of human existence. The self cannot be understood in a social and historical vacuum but becomes what it is within practices of intersubjectivity. It assumes an identity that is inseparably linked with an interpretive framework or historically contingent horizon of understanding. Individual identity emerges from a 'fundamental orientation' toward social reality which is handed down through tradition. This fundamental orientation is the standpoint from which items gain significance, including our own lives. It is inseparable from both our forms of self-understanding and a view of the good. Taylor's formulation of this Hegelian idea is worth quoting at length:

> To know who I am is a species of knowing where I stand. My identity is defined by the commitments and identifications which provide the frame or horizon within which I can try to determine from case to case what is good, or valuable, or what ought to be done, or what I endorse or oppose. In other words, it is the horizon within which I am capable of taking a stand. People may see their identity as defined partly by some moral or spiritual commitment, say as a Catholic, or an anarchist. Or they may define it in part by the nation or tradition they belong to, as an Armenian, say, or a Quebecois. What they are saying by this is not just that they are strongly attached to this spiritual view or background; rather it is that this provides the frame within which they can determine where they stand on questions of what is good, or worthwhile, or admirable, or of value. Put counterfactually, they are saying that were they to lose this commitment or identification, they would be at sea, as it were; they wouldn't know anymore, for an important range of questions, what the significance of things was for them.[37]

A crucial premise in the communitarian argument is that much or all of what constitutes the self is a social inheritance rather than an object of choice. The individual is the inheritor of a wide variety of social involvements and conditions, including everything from its tacit understanding of the world to the practices and roles it takes up, the values and moral categories that it appropriates, the customs and relationships that are constitutive of moral identity. Its moral being – not only the values and principles that it explicitly holds, but its fundamental mode of comportment as a moral agent – is largely or entirely an appropriation from a particular historical community. This is taken as a key premise in the critique of liberalism since the latter presupposes that individuals are choosers in a rather strong sense – that they choose their own values in accordance with criteria of rationality and in a free and autonomous fashion. Liberal politics assumes that individuals are not so profoundly situated that they cannot determine their own ends through autonomous acts of reflection. Yet such a view, communitarians argue, ignores the embeddedness of both the self and its own allegedly autonomous choices. According to the communitarian premise, many or all of the factors that enter into the constitution of moral agents belong to them while being unrelated to acts of choice. Individuals find themselves already claimed by these. The individual is never a moral *tabula rasa* selecting its ends in the presuppositionless fashion described by utilitarian and contractarian liberals. It is more accurate to characterize the acquisition or appropriation of moral ends as an act of self-discovery than as one of rational choice. Explicit acts of choice are preceded by a fundamental moral orientation which is less chosen than discovered.

What becomes of the foundations of liberal politics when the pervasiveness in subjectivity of intersubjectivity is fully recognized? What becomes of the politics of individuality without the ontology of individuality – without metaphysical essentialism, ahistorical selfhood, and ahistorical rationality? When both the content of rational choice and the capacity itself are thoroughly socialized, must not justice itself be socialized? Communitarians, socialists, and others frequently reply to this in the affirmative. Being bound by traditions and ends not of our choosing, a political morality founded on unconditioned choice is ill-suited to beings like ourselves. The capacity to abstract from our historical particularity is exaggerated by liberal doctrine, and it is this exaggeration that underlies the high value liberals place upon individual choice. A historically conscious politics would replace the values of individuality with the values of community since it is only within communal practices that individual selfhood is fashioned. If community is ontologically prior to individuality, then it must be morally prior as well.

The idea of community commonly accepted by communitarians is the virtual antithesis of the instrumentalist view common among liberals. Community comprises common purposes, shared understandings, and an assortment of values, attitudes, and norms that make up a particular way of life. Founded on a shared history, culture, and language, community is what provides its members with a moral orientation in terms of which they may fashion individual identities and pursue particular ends. It is, moreover, a unity in a sense more profound than liberals have conventionally realized (again, with exceptions). Reminiscent of romanticism, Rousseau, Hegel, and the new liberalism, communitarian writers often gesture toward organicism as a model of communal life in direct contrast to neoclassical liberal instrumentalism. Social life is no mere contingency, nor the product of a real or hypothetical social contract between presocial atoms, nor is it merely an arrangement of mutual accommodation. Rather, community in its several forms, both political and otherwise, connotes a unified body neither artificial, contingent, nor instrumental. It is a collective body with intrinsic value and a unified will. Moreover, it is a body whose members share allegiance to a common moral framework. While not always agreed on particular judgments, the members of a community are in consensus about the underlying norms and values of social life, about the import of communal ties, and so on. Thus understood, community life is not only misconceived by liberal doctrine but effectively undermined by its abstract principles of justice and by its moral vocabulary of individuality, human rights, and instrumentality. Liberalism exaggerates the degree of antagonism that exists between individuals and between the individual and the state, thereby exaggerating the need for and value of impartial principles of right. Socialized selves are less inclined to appeal to such principles than to the common good and the agreed upon norms of community life. So goes the communitarian argument.

It is an argument that, from a liberal perspective, contains a surprising lack of concern about the possibility of majoritarian and repressive government as well as a lack of suspicion about appeals to consensus and tradition. It contains ambiguities with respect to rights which liberals also find troubling, specifically how much weight in a communitarian order individual rights would carry in comparison with other values with which they may conflict, or even whether such rights would exist.

In assuming a critical posture, communitarian writers direct the thrust of their argument (frequently the whole of it) against the liberal vocabulary of rights and take time to document its failings while leaving altogether unclear whether such rights nonetheless warrant protection, and if so – and equally important – how much weight they carry in comparison with other moral and political considerations. Rather than confront such questions directly, the common communitarian stance is merely to remark upon the shortcomings of liberal individualism while extolling a quasi-collectivist political morality. Communitarians such as Sandel, MacIntyre, Taylor, Roberto Unger, Michael Walzer, and numerous others speak in ambiguous terms about both rights and the various obligations individuals are asserted to have toward the communities to which they belong. We hear mention, for instance, of obligations 'to belong to or sustain society, or a society of a certain type, or to obey authority or an authority of a certain type'[38]; we hear of 'obligations of solidarity, religious duties, and other moral ties that may claim us for reasons unrelated to a choice'[39]; and that 'what matters at this stage is the construction of local forms of community within which civility and the intellectual and moral life can be sustained through the new dark ages which are already upon us.'[40] In short, what we hear from communitarians is the insinuation, rarely altogether explicit, that the norms and ends commonly upheld within communities are in fact morally binding. Whether individuals grant or withhold their assent, these values have already claimed their allegiance, and the question of assent is moot.

A note of caution is called for here. As mentioned, the main thrust of the communitarian position is 'negative' or critical of liberal doctrine, and a satisfactorily detailed articulation of its 'positive' stance still awaits. It is therefore difficult to state precisely in what a communitarian political order would consist and what sort of departure from liberalism this would represent. One thesis that does seem clear is that the common good is to assume greater importance than what liberalism traditionally recommends. The liberal primacy of justice thesis – or the principle that individual rights are to outweigh all other values, including the common welfare – would be reversed on the communitarian view and replaced with a politics of the common good, however this may be conceived. Neutrality with respect to competing conceptions of the good would be replaced with official recognition of one such conception, namely the one able to characterize itself as the 'common good' or as constituting our collective way of life. A rough and ready distinction may be drawn between liberalism as a politics of rights and communitarianism as a politics of the common good, however the precise contours of the distinction are far from clear. The communitarian vocabulary is one of quasi-organicism and quasi-collectivism; it speaks of the general welfare, the preservation of tradition, the cultivation of communal ties, and so forth, albeit in terms that typically lack specificity. Were it to call unambiguously for a collectivist political morality the contrast with liberalism would at least be clear. Alternatively, if liberalism did not maintain a commitment to the principle of the common good the contrast would again be clear, yet neither of these conditions holds. As a consequence, the matter of what precisely is at stake in the debate between liberals and communitarians is not readily discernible.

I must therefore resort to stipulation, with all due trepidation and apology to those communitarian writers who do not fit my characterization. The liberal theory of justice, as I shall continue to speak of it, gives priority to the rights and freedoms of individuals over all other kinds of normative considerations in fashioning public policy, and insofar as it is possible remains neutral with respect to competing conceptions of the good life. Conflicts between the values or aspirations of the community and the rights of the individual are resolved in favour of the latter on the liberal view and in favour of the former on the communitarian view. Communitarianism rejects the neutrality thesis while recognizing in one manner or another the value of justice and individual rights. The latter values, however, communitarianism refuses to privilege over the shared ends that comprise a communal way of life. Rather, these shared ends are awarded primacy. As a consequence, the communitarian view frequently favours a sizeable turn toward the political left. A socialized self requires a socialized politics, prodding liberalism still further in its renunciation of limited government and its general ideological shift during the twentieth century toward a politics of welfare egalitarianism. Communitarianism carries this historic turn still further, sometimes following it around the bend into the region of socialist politics.[41]

If this rendering of the distinction is not wholly false, the question becomes whether properly acknowledging the social character of the self requires not only a renunciation of classical liberal theories of subjectivity, but a further renunciation of the liberal theory of justice with which they have been traditionally aligned. Do socialized selves require a socialized politics? In the following (and final) section of this chapter, I argue that both questions should be answered in the negative. Liberalism, I maintain, would be well served by ridding itself of the theories of the self that it has traditionally presupposed. What is more, it never needed such theories as a metaphysical backup for its conception of justice. What it needs, instead, is to work through and finally overcome the metaphysical embarrassment that currently plagues much of liberal philosophy.

Working Through Metaphysical Embarrassment

Historically, the liberal theory of justice has presupposed metaphysical assumptions concerning the self that increasingly and rightly are falling into disfavour in many contemporary philosophical circles. Whether conceived as the transcendental subject of Kantian idealism, the materialistic *homo economicus* of contractarian and utilitarian accounts, an appendage of the social organism in the new liberalism, or the strategically rational chooser of contemporary decision theory, the human subject has traditionally been viewed by liberals as possessing an underlying and determinate nature – a deep core of being – describable in the language of the metaphysician. With some exceptions, liberals have typically held that the individual is not only morally prior to the society or community in which it lives but ontologically prior as well. It is ontologically prior both to the practices and forms of life characteristic of the community to which it belongs, as well as to its own autonomously chosen ends. Liberalism's traditional conceptions of subjectivity are thoroughly metaphysical and essentialist at a time when essentialist theories of the self are increasingly on the wane. Theories that underscore the facticity and sociality of the self have carried the day in recent years, forcing liberalism to modify much of its classical posture and to concede either a total or partial victory to the political left, which so often is thought to be alone in awarding due recognition to the pervasiveness in subjectivity of intersubjectivity.

To communitarians liberals owe a debt of gratitude for reminding us of important lessons taught by Aristotle and Hegel above all, and for helping restore a sense of historical consciousness in political philosophy. The criticism that liberal theorists all too often have been lacking historical consciousness in their thought concerning justice and the individual is well taken. It is, moreover, a criticism of no small importance. Yet for all that, it is not a criticism that subverts liberal justice. It is a line of argument that compels liberalism to overhaul radically the philosophy of the self on which it relies, however, it does not force liberalism to abandon any of its political theses. In order to do so, the communitarian argument would have to demonstrate not only the failings of individualist ontology – which it succeeds in doing – but also the logical dependence of liberal politics on this false ontology. It would have to demonstrate the logical inseparability of the politics and the ontology of individuality, and this it cannot do. For any of liberalism's principles of justice to be unseated by the communitarian critique, the latter would have to incorporate several strong assumptions which cannot withstand examination, assumptions pertaining to the fundamental constitution of moral agents. I shall examine these assumptions presently and contrast them with the set of related theses on which liberalism, as I conceive it, properly relies.

As communitarians rightly point out, liberal philosophers have exaggerated the kind and degree of distance from particularity and facticity that is possible for moral agents. The idea that rational beings, in order to determine their ends or formulate judgments, must retreat to a presocial condition wherein they possess powers of absolute self-determination is a metaphysical and epistemological fantasy. Moreover, it is a fantasy that liberalism never needed to assume. That reason affords total distance, elevates itself above all contexts and all facticity, and reflects without presuppositions are common Enlightenment doctrines which were in the air at the time of liberalism's inception. The founders of the tradition being thoroughly enamoured with Enlightenment philosophy, it is no surprise that liberalism was established on its basis; yet that the connection between liberal politics and these Enlightenment assumptions is not only historical but logically necessary is wholly assumed by the communitarian critique.

There is in fact no logical dependence of liberal principles on these untenable Enlightenment assumptions. Liberal theorists never needed to suppose that individuals and their rational capacities are antecedent to all social contexts and capable of total distance from them. No hyperbolic, quasi-Cartesian powers of abstraction are needed in order for liberalism to defend its principles of justice. What is needed, more modestly, are capacities of critical reflection, judgment, and imagination. These capacities are finite and situated within particular horizons of understanding which represent our inheritance as social and historical beings. Indeed all reflection is situated and operates against a background of tacit evaluations. Reasoned critical reflection always 'begins,' so to speak, not at the 'beginning' but *in medias res*, joining a conversation that is always already begun and enjoying the luxury of neither the first nor the last word in it. Even in its radical forms, critical reflection attains only a partial and limited distance from the lifeworld and tradition within which it stands. Yet while it may be said that, as situated selves, we belong to traditions of understanding – that both our comprehension of phenomena within the social world and our modes of self-understanding are preceded, made possible, and limited by a particular hermeneutic framework – such belonging does not constitute captivity. We are never trapped within any given framework or horizon of understanding. Like language, such horizons always remain malleable, porous, and in some measure open to the possibility of novelty and difference. Belonging is never without a measure of distance. It is this distance that opens a space for critical reflection – for the various modes of oppositional thinking, reasoning, novel signification, and imaginative utterance. It is this element of critical distance from tradition that prevents situated selves from becoming mere 'social products' of the kind spoken of by the more positivistic and deterministic schools of social science. Situated selves do not lack a capacity for refashioning traditions from within, or transforming what is given into what is questionable. Nor are these reflective capacities the mysterious and private domain of 'expertise.' They are capacities shared by all competent speakers of a language and all moral agents.

Associated with the capacity for critical reflection are the related capacities of autonomy, choice, judgment, and imagination. Again, each of these capacities is situated within an historical context, finite, and limited in its operations. Moreover, liberal philosophers have frequently erred in conceiving of these capacities in asocial and ahistorical terms, losing sight of both their conditions of possibility and their limits. And again, liberalism never needed such assumptions. What it requires are premises far weaker and more plausible than those appropriated from the philosophy of the Enlightenment. Liberalism depends on what we may call the revisability thesis: the thesis that moral agents, while situated beings with situated capacities, are nonetheless capable of revising their moral ends, questioning convention, reasoning about norms, reflecting on practices, refashioning their identity, reconstituting traditions, and unseating consensus. It supposes that each of these capacities, like all human capacities, is finite yet sufficiently robust as to make it possible for individuals to revise the ends that they inherit from tradition. Otherwise stated, liberalism asserts that while individuals are social beings they are not for all that mere social products. Persons are social yet separate beings. They are factical selves, yet their facticity underdetermines their being.

The crucial difference separating the revisability thesis from the much stronger set of Enlightenment assumptions noted above is that the former thesis remains mindful of both the social and historical conditions of possibility of our reflective capacities as well as their limits. This thesis contains an important element of historical consciousness of the kind recommended by the neohegelian critique, while refusing the political implications some writers draw from that critique. It recognizes that 'particularity,' as MacIntyre has stated, 'can never be simply left behind or obliterated,' and that there is no way of abstracting ourselves from our history 'into a realm of entirely universal maxims which belong to man as such.'[42] Yet it denies the inferences drawn from this by many of liberalism's critics. It denies that because we are social and factical beings our capacities of reflection are so attenuated as to render us incapable of revising our judgments on the basis of reason. It denies that our socialization so hard-wires our being that all talk of individual autonomy is impossible or so thoroughly circumscribed as to remove the value liberals attribute to it. It denies as well that ends that are shared and passed down through tradition are for that reason morally binding. Yet communitarianism, insofar as it represents a departure from liberalism, appears to depend on each of these inferences, none of which is persuasive. Liberals need not accept the premise implicit in the communitarian argument that we must choose between a view of the self as perfectly unconditioned, presocial, essentialist, and autonomous on the one hand or a view of it as entirely conditioned, socially constructed, hard-wired, and nonautonomous on the other. There are situated forms of autonomy, reflection, and reason, and the fact of their situatedness and finitude does nothing to undermine the value and import that liberals attribute to them.

The revisability view has been represented in recent liberal thought by such figures as Rawls, Gauthier, and Will Kymlicka. Rawls's brief reply to Sandel's critique includes the assertion that individuals who may indeed be constituted by certain of their moral ends and attachments are fully capable nonetheless of revising these ends and attachments, and hence of being personally accountable for them. Much the same sentiment is expressed by Kymlicka. As he writes: 'What is central to the liberal view is not that we can *perceive* a self prior to its ends, but that we understand our selves to be prior to our ends, *in the sense that no goal or end is exempt from possible re-examination.*'[43] Gauthier expresses a similar view. 'What matters is that [moral agents's] preferences and, within limits, their capacities are not fixed by their socialization, which is not a process by which persons are hard-wired, but rather, at least in part, a process for the development of soft-wired beings, who have the capacity to change the manner in which they are constituted.'[44] Undertaking changes of this kind, revising our moral ends or even our identity, need not be an unproblematic or simple affair, nor is it likely to be accomplished with equanimity, leaving persons unchanged in the process. Such exercises in self-creation may well be carried out, as Soren Kierkegaard would say, 'in fear and trembling.' It may be a matter of the most profound, even existential, import while in other instances it may be somewhat more mundane.

That the liberal revisability thesis possesses at the very least an intuitive plausibility is difficult to deny even by communitarian writers who sometimes offer statements that appear to support this thesis. Not wishing to assert that persons are utterly trapped by the ends and conditions they inherit from tradition, Sandel for instance grants the view that 'as a self-interpreting being, I am able to reflect on my history and in this sense to distance myself from it.'[45] While immediately adding that the distance thus attained 'is always precarious and provisional,'[46] this is all that the revisability view requires. It assumes not complete but partial distance. Similarly, MacIntyre writes that while moral agents are always embedded within traditions, these traditions are by no means the determinate and static entities for which we often mistake them, but exist in a state of perpetual reconstitution. A tradition may be refashioned from within just as a narrative history may be refashioned by the self who lives – or is – it. Taylor as well, after convincingly disposing of liberal atomism, has defended an ethics of authenticity whose affiliation with liberal doctrine is readily apparent. What all such views have in common is an important element of reservation preventing the move toward a stronger social or historical determinism of the kind defended by many of those on the far left, including some Marxists, socialists, and feminists. The communitarian critique coupled with a rejection of the revisability thesis seems to lead us into the vicinity of political collectivism in one form or another, a collectivism likewise dismissive of the capacities, values, and rights of individuality. Were communitarians to take this further step of rejecting the revisability view, a move that most all of them seem reluctant to make or to follow consistently, then the contrast between communitarian and liberal politics would be considerably more clear than it appears at present. Communitarians who refuse to make this move, or to do so in a consistent fashion, leave liberals to wonder on what grounds they ought to abandon their theory of right.

Two possibilities that immediately present themselves are that the noted capacities of reflection, judgment, reason, imagination, revision, and so on, together with the distance that makes them possible, are so highly circumscribed that the strength of the capacities is negligible in comparison with their limits, or alternatively that their moral value is negligible in comparison with the collective will of the community. Either view, again, takes us into the region of collectivist politics, yet communitarian writers typically are less than eager to make this move and instead offer a vague gesture toward a more moderate stance whose contrast with liberal politics is unclear. Moreover, both possibilities seem plainly mistaken. Changes in belief, ends, and attachments, including those of a profoundly constitutive nature, are not unknown or even uncommon occurrences particularly in large and pluralistic communities. Even radical conversions are not unheard of, even if they typically are less radical than they appear at first glance. Persons may reject any given doctrine, role, or norm into which they are socialized and substitute or invent another even if they do not reflect themselves into some presuppositionless and presocial retreat in order to do so. The moral value of these capacities stems from the value of people determining in some measure the course of their own lives rather than conceding this task to others or to the community in general. The authority of custom, in the liberal view, takes second place to individual judgment.

Were the revisability thesis to suggest any sort of heroic stance, one allowing individuals to suspend all their beliefs Cartesian style and abstract themselves from history, the communitarian reply would quite properly be to remind us of the limits of reflection and the heroic stance itself. Taylor provides this rejoinder in a passage not dissimilar to many others found in the communitarian literature:

> It goes on being true of such heroes that they define themselves not just genetically but as they are today, in conversation with others. They are still in a web, but the one they define themselves by is no longer the given historical community. It is the saving remnant, or the community of like-minded souls, or the company of philosophers, or the small group of wise men in the mass of fools, as the Stoics saw it, or the close circle of friends that played such a role in Epicurean thought. Taking the heroic stance doesn't allow one to leap out of the human condition, and it remains true that one can elaborate one's new language only through conversation in a broad sense, that is, through some kind of interchange with others with whom one has some common understanding about what is at stake in the enterprise. A human being can always be original, can step beyond the limits of thought and vision of contemporaries, can even be quite misunderstood by them. But the drive to original vision will be hampered, will ultimately be

lost in inner confusion, unless it can be placed in some way in relation to the language and vision of others.[47]

The same sentiments are expressed by other communitarian writers and provide an important corrective to conventional liberalism and indeed to Enlightenment philosophy generally. Where the latter are inclined to emphasize, and exaggerate the radicality of, departures from tradition, communitarians insist on changing the emphasis toward the conditions and limits of unconventionality. Departures from convention are limited and piecemeal in nature, communitarians correctly observe. This change in emphasis may well be instructive, as I believe it is, yet whether this in itself carries political implications troubling for liberalism is doubtful. Our possibilities of thought and action are enframed within shared understandings, but they are no less valuable for that; our reflective capacities and autonomy are limited by the conditions that we inherit as historical beings, but this does not lessen their importance to us as moral agents.

The communitarian emphasis on the limits and the underlying social conditions of the reflective capacities too often runs into a kind of quasi-determinism according to which individuals are not only embedded in social contexts but are to an important degree passive as well. Situated selves are passive selves, at least for the fundamental matters of our moral lives. Our moral categories and identity are not chosen but inherited, the life histories we live are those into which we have been drafted, our ends are those that stem from traditions which have claimed us, and our attachments are those that we have not chosen but discovered. Yet why should this be so? Why is passivity so often linked with sociality and historicity? This is surely the legacy of Hegel, who argued that full autonomy is an illusion and that it is through socialization that persons acquire their ends and identity. Yet the fact that persons cannot choose their socialization does not entail that they cannot choose to amend any given element of it. It is a common and mistaken assumption of many who speak of socialization, historicity, and the limits of reflection to suppose that the fact of human finitude entails either that we are compelled by virtue of our finitude or socialization to accept the judgments, ends, etc. that we have inherited or that we are morally obligated to do so (and all too often that it is for the state to determine how such obligations shall be met). Yet the claim that tradition makes on us is not of this nature. A tradition does not resemble an iron cage without exit; it neither compels nor obligates our allegiance but delimits in the fashion of a language the terms within which reflection proceeds. These terms themselves, again like those of a language, are modifiable. Innovation in thought and action is no less possible than semantic innovation. Refashioning a tradition is as much a form of participation within it as simple conventionality.

A series of false dichotomies is frequently apparent in the literature of communitarianism. Either the self is a social and historical construct or it is an asocial Hobbesian atom; either its aims and attachments constitute its being or they are merely so many accidental properties detachable at will; either it is totally encumbered or totally unencumbered by its ends; either unsituated and naive voluntarism or situated conformity. It ought to go without saying that we are compelled to choose between none of these options and it is entirely possible to conceive of the self as a profoundly social being without viewing it as a hapless and incapacitated social product.

Also implicit to communitarianism is a certain 'myth of the given,' in Wilfrid Sellars's phrase. Determining – more accurately, discovering – our moral ends and identity is essentially a matter of consulting established conventions and settled traditions. Like such conventions, they represent the given of our moral lives. Any considerations that factor into the self's own identity are simply given, like nature or God's commands. The implication is that among all the traits of the self, those of a constitutive nature are unchosen while those amenable to personal choice or revision are mere accidental properties peripheral to our true identity. That the act of determining our ends is properly conceived as one of discovery rather than choice is given the lie by ordinary experiences we have all had of deliberating on, or deciding, which values we shall pursue and in what manner. Unless we are the unwitting victims of false consciousness, we appear at liberty to decide upon reflection what ends we shall pursue, and while it is likely that most persons most of the time will opt to follow convention, that they must do so is by no means an inescapable fact. There is remarkably little that is truly and finally given in human existence, including in our moral lives. Our ends and identity as moral agents are typically complex; we may inherit a variety of roles, stand within different communities, adopt conflicting ends and conflicting identities, and reflect from the standpoint of a 'fundamental orientation' that is at odds with itself, open-ended, fragmented, rooted in conflicting traditions, or confused. We must decide which ends, roles, or traditions from those we may inherit in a complex and pluralistic society will continue to hold our allegiance and which will be modified, subordinated, or abandoned entirely. Deciding such matters constitutes a large part of our moral experience, and it is not settled by consulting the settled convictions of a community.

These settled convictions, moreover, are typically far less settled than some communitarians suppose. It is far less at the level of explicit judgments and consciously articulated convictions than at the level of pre-reflective and tacit assumptions that anything resembling consensus reigns within modern societies. Fundamental understandings and pre-understandings (what Hans-Georg Gadamer terms 'prejudices') very often underlie and even make possible the disagreements we have concerning 'issues' both ethical and political. These debates frequently take the form of hermeneutic disputes over the exact manner in which these basic preunderstandings may best be interpreted or applied to practical contexts. Yet communitarians frequently underestimate the difficulty of such interpretive disputes or, more troublingly still, mislocate solidarity at the level of reflective convictions rather than at the more fundamental level of tacit preunderstandings. Either way, the result is a disturbing underestimation of diversity with respect to persons and judgments alike. Communitarianism too often resembles a kind of quasi-romanticism inclined to celebrate convention and the attachments that precede reflection, and which sometimes has recourse to the metaphors of organicism. The principal danger of this and all other forms of political romanticism, as a brief glance at history quickly reveals, is to underestimate grossly the extent of disagreement that exists within all forms of community life – the conflicts of belief and interest which give rise in the first place to the need for political reflection – and, related to this, to overlook the separateness of persons. Community is as much the site of conflict as of consensus. It is the site of individuals with private pursuits no less than of collectivities with shared aspirations.

Moreover, as the critics of political romanticism in its several forms have frequently observed, inherited roles, ends, conventions, and even identities are sometimes experienced as deeply oppressive or insulting to one's dignity as a distinct individual. Situated selves all too often experience their inheritance as not only an identifying orientation but the dead weight of the past or a call to conform to the old ways. Subtle forms of indignity are occurrences familiar to many inheritors of convention. This obtains more in the case of some conventions than others to be sure, and is by no means restricted to those long decried by the so-called 'emancipatory movements' of the left. Solidarity is all too often a mask for intolerance of dissent and for a thousand other forms of oppression both subtle and unsubtle. As Amy Gutmann has noted:

> A great deal of intolerance has come from societies of selves so 'confidently situated' that they were sure repression would serve a higher cause. The common good of the Puritans of seventeenth-century Salem commanded them to hunt witches; the common good of the Moral Majority of the twentieth century commands them not to tolerate homosexuals. The enforcement of liberal rights, not the absence of settled community, stands between the Moral Majority and the contemporary equivalent of witch-hunting. The communitarian critics want us to live in Salem, but not to believe in witches.[48]

Communitarians appear remarkably untroubled by the language of solidarity, convention, and 'our' way of life, as if the prospect of a slide from this to the darker forms of political collectivism were utterly remote.

More troubled are liberal philosophers who react, or overreact, to considerations of this kind by stating categorically the irrelevance of communal ends, identities, ways of life, and conceptions of the good from the discourse of justice. Particularity in all its forms is not only to be subordinated to universality in instances of conflict but banished entirely from the realm of the political. Of these two distinct claims, only the first is required to satisfy liberal concerns about human rights while the second represents a bit of unnecessary hyperbole. Particular conceptions of the good, liberals maintain, place second to universal human rights while governments are to assume a neutral stance toward competing views of the good. The reasons offered in support of these principles are several, and include scepticism concerning the possibility of determining authoritatively in what the good life consists, the value of autonomously fashioning or refashioning one's own ends, and the fact of reasonable disagreement. No recourse need be had to the classical doctrine that one's good is fully knowable prior to all social involvements. The most compelling justification of the priority of right and neutrality toward the good stems from the revisability thesis: that persons are capable of revising their ends, critiquing their inheritance, learning from different perspectives, modifying an established way of life, and further that there is no reason to believe that rational persons will or ought to agree on these matters. Indeed, it is the norm that they will not agree unanimously over a sufficiently broad range of issues. While communitarians typically underestimate or regret such disagreement, liberals do neither, and even celebrate heterogeneity and the virtues of tolerance and *rapprochement*. Plurality is not a symptom of the breakdown of community but the normal outcome of reasoned reflection. Liberalism is alone among political philosophies in recognizing at once the 'essential contestedness' of reason, the presence of the capacities of reflection in the constitution of the self and the fundamental import of these capacities in our moral lives. It is by means of the capacities of reflection that persons fashion their own lives and in so doing make their lives their own, something for which they may legitimately be held to account.

The principles of neutrality and the primacy of justice reflect a better appreciation than the communitarian alternative of not only individuality but sociality and belonging as well. Liberalism understands all forms of belonging as distanced belonging and all sociability, to use Kant's apt phrase, as 'unsocial sociability.' It captures the tension that exists between collective participation and individual separateness. It recognizes that while many of our social involvements are of a constitutive nature, pervading subjectivity, so do the capacities for distancing and reflection, producing a permanent tension within the self between fellowship and detachment. The unceasing dialectic between social involvement and reflective withdrawal is never perfectly or finally resolved by the self. Providing for its resolution is an unending project which calls for a profoundly personal or existential choice relating to the ultimate significance of one's life.

Liberalism recognizes that choices of this nature are not without certain political conditions of possibility, not least of which is individual liberty. State neutrality and the full range of individual rights and freedoms traditionally defended by liberals make it possible for persons to determine not only their particular ends and the means conducive to them, but the manner in which questions of social belonging will be resolved: whether they will appropriate unrevised the ways of the community, modify certain of its conventions in piecemeal fashion, or seek a more radical revision. Whether one's overall conception of the good draws one closely into fellowship with others or lies in more solitary projects is not a matter that permits of a single authoritative answer, nor does the question of which ends, roles, conventions, or identities among those we inherit are more worthy than others and which would be better abandoned entirely. The neutrality thesis accepts without regret the plurality of perspectives concerning the good. It requires neither an outright value subjectivism nor even respect for the ends that persons voluntarily adopt or the choices they make, but respect for the persons themselves who make such choices. Neutrality provides the fairest procedure by which individuals and collectivities with incompatible conceptions of the good may arrive at political decisions in ways that do not involve the imposition of the will of some on the actions of others or even the 'way of life' of a majority on a minority. Neutrality is a procedure of political accommodation that refuses to become partisan in disagreements about the nature of the good life, and brackets such considerations (or those conceptions of the good, at least, that are contested by sane and competent persons in a given community) from deliberations about public policy.

Liberalism is rightly regarded as an 'art of separation' or a philosophy of right that insists on drawing distinctions typically not drawn by non-liberal modes of thought, including that between our identity as persons and our identity as citizens. It recognizes that while distinguishing *citoyen* from *homme*, the public from the private, or the domain of the political from the nonpolitical is far from unproblematic, such distinctions must be drawn for political purposes. No end of difficulty obtains at the theoretical level in separating the political from the nonpolitical, but at the level of practical reason distinctions of this kind are imperative in order to prevent all matters of a 'social' nature from falling within the province of the state. Communitarians, socialists, and others on the left too often assume, as Kymlicka observes, 'that whatever is properly social must become the province of the political. They have not confronted the liberal worry that the all-embracing authority and coercive means which characterize the state make it a particularly inappropriate forum for the sort of genuinely shared deliberation and commitment that they desire.'[49] Society is not an organic whole of which the state is the head and the individual is an appendage, or of which the separateness between persons is the separateness of an arm and a leg. All the ingredients of authoritarian politics are contained in such holistic metaphors and in modes of thought that refuse liberal distinctions between persons and citizens, privacy and publicity, nonpolitical and political. The roughness and readiness of each of these distinctions is surpassed only by their usefulness in counteracting the possibility of political authoritarianism.

In sum, it can be said of much of the history of liberal doctrine from Hobbes to the present that it has incorporated assumptions that are both untenable and unnecessary as metaphysical underpinnings for its conception of justice. The most conspicuous of these assumptions pertain to the self and, as the communitarian critics rightly argue, these assumptions must be largely rejected. Individualism conceived as an ontological and metaphysical doctrine is neither plausible nor necessary as a foundation for political individualism. The moral priority of the individual as citizen does not depend on the ontological priority of the individual to the forms of community life in which it is situated. We are all situated selves, constituted by no ahistorical essence or deep core of being but by a wide

array of social involvements and inheritances which comprise our facticity as moral agents. We are profoundly historical beings, yet beings capable of critical distance from the histories that we ourselves are.
Although it has been customary for liberals to characterize the self as
prior to its ends and social inheritance, this need only be the case in the
sense that we are capable on reflection (situated reflection at that) of rejecting any given element of our inheritance and replacing it with values
or beliefs of a different kind. That our identity as persons is constituted
by our moral ends and our sociality does not imply that we are captives
of any particular configuration of these, or that any are beyond the
bounds of critical reflection. Liberalism need assume neither that the self
enjoys unlimited autonomy in fashioning its ends, nor that its identity is
not constituted by these, nor even that it is necessarily their most competent judge (all of which assumptions are false), but only that were it
not their final judge, its life would not properly be its own.

Justice represents the first virtue and warrants priority over the good
for the reason that it is justice that guarantees that persons shall be at liberty to pursue not only a good life, but a life that is of one's own autonomous making. It provides the conditions whereby our lives may become
our own, and ensures that individuals shall not be compelled to follow
a path that is not their own. It is within these terms that we may lend
support to liberal doctrines regarding the primacy of justice, the inviolability of the individual, and the universality of human rights. Without
having recourse to ahistorical or essentialist conceptions of the self, liberalism maintains that persons, in order to pursue any given conception of
the good in an autonomous fashion, must first have guaranteed to them
a designated jurisdiction within which they are free to fashion their lives
and to pursue a self-chosen conception of the good life. Justice is what
makes it possible for moral agents to determine what they shall become,
and is the necessary condition of autonomous selfhood. Justice warrants
priority over the good not because the self is radically autonomous by
nature, but because the self properly becomes an agent only within a
framework of individual rights and constraints on the power of the
state. It is only within such a framework that moral agents may determine, and be held responsible for, the direction of their lives.

There are many ways in which the self may fashion a meaningful existence from among the various ideals of the good life which are possible
for it given the set of social circumstances which it inherits. A multiplicity
of such conceptions, whether these are personal or shared views of what
is worth pursuing in life, must be regarded from the standpoint of public

policy as equally legitimate. That there is legitimate disagreement concerning the good, and that individuals must be at liberty to fashion their lives by choosing among a plurality of such possibilities, are insights that liberalism alone properly heeds. Liberalism may be viewed as a form of institutionalized scepticism since it incorporates the belief that there is no available knowledge of a uniquely and supremely authoritative conception of the good, even one that is alleged to represent 'our' common way of life.[50] In a liberal order, it is less important from a political vantage point which values I choose than whether it is I who choose them and whether I do so autonomously. This contrasts with communitarian and other less sceptical views that would single out a particular view of the good as having a privileged claim on our loyalties, with potentially ominous implications for individual freedom.

There is, accordingly, no need for liberalism to continue to presuppose essentialist conceptions of subjectivity as a metaphysical backup for its principles of justice. It does not require a self that is ontologically prior to either society or its own ends. Liberalism would be better served by replacing such assumptions with a conception of the self that fully recognizes its social and historical nature as well as the fact that moral agents, while indeed socially constructed beings, are not for all that mere social products. The self is always underdetermined by its facticity and is capable of refashioning its ends and identity in and through re-consideration. While it does not enjoy unlimited autonomy in determining the moral agent it shall become, it does possess the capacities of critical distance, reason, judgment, and imagination through which it may contribute to its own (re-)constitution.

Those of us who wish to place liberalism on a more defensible philosophical basis must undertake a fundamental reformulation of its understanding of moral selfhood, one that properly reflects the ubiquity of the social in the constitution of identity while preserving classical liberalism's commitment to individual self-creation. Such an undertaking must navigate around classical metaphysical assumptions while preserving the moral and political insights such assumptions were intended to support. This is my task in the following chapter. The account that I shall offer stems primarily from the tradition of phenomenological hermeneutics, a tradition typically regarded as at some remove from liberal individualism. I shall defend a conception of the self as a narrative construction at once situated within a lifeworld while possessing capacities of autonomous and rational agency.

PART TWO:

THE POLITICS OF INDIVIDUALITY

4

Changing the Subject,
Refashioning the Liberal Self

The communitarian critique serves as a reminder of the pressing need for the liberal tradition to overcome in a more thoroughgoing and radical fashion the legacy of Hobbes in conceiving liberalism's fundamental unit of analysis, the individual agent. While the inference frequently drawn by communitarians and those on the political left that a historicized and socialized conception of the self entails a socialized, collectivized, or otherwise illiberal conception of justice fails for the reasons mentioned in Chapter 3, it would be a mistake for liberals to reject outright the substance of the communitarian argument, thus failing to appropriate important lessons articulated by such figures as Aristotle, Rousseau, Hegel, or even Marx. The communitarian accentuation of human embeddedness and sociality provides an important corrective to neoclassical liberal doctrine which fully restores the Hobbesian legacy with embarrassing metaphysical consequences. The neoclassical school provides a ground for liberal justice at a prohibitive cost; it abandons any sense of historical consciousness of the kind that the new liberalism began to incorporate (without great success) and which communitarianism in a more radical gesture seeks to establish as a new foundation for political discourse. Once liberalism divorces itself from Enlightenment assumptions and works through the metaphysical embarrassment from which it continues to suffer, the way will be clear for a refashioned liberalism, one that is both mindful of the intersubjective and situated nature of the self and yet remains wedded to an individualistic politics. Then it will be possible to conceive of individualism as a political, not a metaphysical, doctrine.

It is the main argument of this study that a liberal politics of individuality – a politics of individual rights and freedoms, of state neutrality and the primacy of justice – is fully justifiable without a metaphysics of individuality. Liberalism may be defended without conceiving of the self as ontologically prior to the lifeworld, culture, social practices, and forms of community life in which it lives and has its being, and without the standard metaphysical assumptions to which conventional liberalism has long subscribed. Liberal justice relies not on these standard assumptions but what I have called the revisability thesis – the idea that while many of the individual's moral ends, attachments, and so on are indeed constitutive of its being, they do not fall beyond the bounds of revision and personal choice. That they are not selected in a presocial vacuum or in naive voluntarist fashion is undeniable and even truistic. Yet that a thorough renunciation of classical liberal views of the self spells trouble for liberal politics, a central premise of the communitarian critique, is an assertion that is altogether false. It is false, that is, on the condition that liberalism incorporates a conception of moral agents that accords with the revisability view. Our task, then, is to provide a fundamental refashioning of the liberal theory of the self. It is to provide a theory of the person as a situated agent, a theory which represents a philosophical articulation of the revisability thesis. Like previous liberal theories, it incorporates a strong conception of agency and sets out from the standpoint of the individual, yet not from the standpoint of an individual conceived as altogether removed in its being from the configuration of social and historical circumstances that it inherits or as essentially antagonistic toward other persons. Rather, it begins with the individual conceived in the language of phenomenology as a concrete 'being-in-the-world' as well as a 'being-with-others.' It recognizes that while neither the state of nature nor the state of war represents the truth of the human condition, social reality encompasses individual persons and the actions in which they engage. All else in political morality is derived from this.

A conception of justice that begins with the individual being-in-the-world and being-with-others, represents a departure from the classical view which in its zeal to establish the moral priority of the individual asserted its ontological priority as well, creating an opposition between self and others, or self and world, which the political order had to mediate. In the view taken here no such oppositions are asserted, nor are they presupposed by taking as a starting point for political reason the perspective of individual persons. In conceiving of the self as a concrete being-in-the-world the question of ontological priority does not arise, self and world being equiprimordial realities. I begin from the standpoint of the individual not because it is prior in its being to all social realities, nor because in carrying out its reflections it stands above such realities, but because it stands out from them, and the fact of its standing out carries far-reaching significance. Facticity, historicity, and sociality underdetermine our being or our fundamental mode of comportment as moral agents, and the fact and manner of our standing out as particular beings is of the most fundamental importance in our moral lives.

Liberalism would be better served by renouncing the paradigm of instrumentality as concerns both the relation between self and others and the nature of rationality (the latter is our focus in Chapter 5), as well as any notion of an underlying core of selfhood meant to serve as the deep metaphysical source of human freedom and dignity. There is no need for liberalism to defend its political principles by making implausible appeals to outmoded and essentialist notions of subjectivity, including the atomistic self of contractarian and utilitarian theories. It need not and ought not engage in metaphysical debate concerning whether the self is properly described within the categories of idealism, materialism, or evolutionary biology, but must undertake an inquiry of a different kind. Phenomenologically, there is no basis whatever of the metaphysical belief in an underlying substance or essence of the human being unifying its disparate actions and experiences. Positing an ego substance or noumenal entity of any sort is not only dubious phenomenologically but altogether unnecessary for the purposes of moral and political philosophy. The metaphysical fiction of the subject – be it the abstract subject of modern epistemology or the equally worldless moral subject of conventional liberalism – would be well lost. Of the subject we may say, following Nietzsche, that it 'was only invented as a foundation for the various attributes,'[1] or as a unifying principle for human experience. Unity, according to this fiction, has to be presupposed as a condition of experience and is only possible given a metaphysical substrate of some description. The subject must possess a determinate nature prior to its attributes and impervious to the contingencies of history and culture.

While a principle of unity of one description or another is indeed an indispensable ingredient of a philosophy of the self, conventional liberalism errs in articulating this principle in the metaphysical vocabulary of the subject, substance, essence, noumena, and so on. A principle of unity may be conceived without invoking a substance ontology and while appreciating fully the socially constructed, historically situated, and decentred character of the self. We may conceive of the person as constituted not only by certain of its moral ends and attachments but more fundamentally by the language, conventions, texts, and modes of self-understanding that characterize a particular historical setting. Such a conception recognizes that self-knowledge never resembles an originary presence of the self to itself but is always mediated through a variety of interpretive structures from symbols to narratives to human action. Without invoking any notion of a self *an sich*, it is possible and desirable to conceive of the moral agent as a decentred and situated being-in-the-world yet one that possesses the capacities of individual agency.

In developing this argument I situate my view within the tradition of phenomenological hermeneutics, particularly as represented in the thought of Paul Ricoeur, while incorporating premises as well from the pragmatism of John Dewey and certain continental philosophies of existence. I propose to defend a hermeneutical or narrative theory of moral selfhood and to demonstrate how this conception of subjectivity may be incorporated into liberalism in a manner that neither undermines nor compromises the philosophical legitimacy of the latter as a political morality. Liberalism should rid itself of the theories of the self that it has traditionally presupposed and replace these with an understanding of the individual as a situated agent possessing a narrative identity.

Navigating around classical liberal assumptions about the person, I defend a conception of the self as an essentially unfinished construction, a being continually in the process of becoming itself in the course of experience and, most importantly, in its actions. While constituted by a configuration of social involvements, the self is capable of contributing to its own constitution through autonomous acts of reflection and choice, and through self-chosen action. How the individual comes to be constituted as a moral agent and what role, given its social embeddedness, it plays in fashioning its own identity are the principal questions with which I am concerned in this chapter. Does this view of the individual as a social construct entail any kind of semi-deterministic thesis for which it is a social product with an attenuated capacity for autonomous choice (a view attributable to some of the more extreme exponents of the left), or is it capable in significant measure of constituting and/or reconstituting itself through its own choices? A liberalism that upholds the primacy of individual rights clearly must defend a version of the latter view, and one that wishes to avoid metaphysical embarrassment must do so in a manner that does not depend on outworn theories of the self.

The Decline of the Worldless Subject

As mentioned in Chapter 3, theories of the self that accentuate its embeddedness within a configuration of social and historical conditions have essentially carried the day in recent decades owing to the combined efforts of several philosophical and social scientific schools of thought from phenomenological hermeneutics to poststructuralism, deconstruction, postmodernism, communitarianism, socialism, feminism, and so on. The notion of an abstract, ahistorical, or worldless subject is currently in full retreat, a fact that should not be regretted even for a conception of politics that awards moral priority to the individual and its associated values and rights.

Within the hermeneutical tradition in particular, in which my account of the self is largely situated, it is maintained that the human being's most fundamental mode of comportment, including in its capacity as a moral agent, is not that of utility maximization but understanding and self-understanding. With the ontological turn initiated by Martin Heidegger in *Being and Time* and carried forward in the works of Hans-Georg Gadamer (principally *Truth and Method*), Paul Ricoeur, and others, hermeneutics was transformed in the twentieth century from a discipline concerned with understanding and interpretation as methodological problems within the humanities and social sciences to one that conceived of understanding as the fundamental mode of being of human existence itself. As the basic mode in which the human being orients itself and finds its way in the world, understanding constitutes more than a faculty of cognition but belongs to the elementary constitution of human existence in general. The ontological condition of the self is to comport itself toward phenomena understandingly and self-understandingly, interpreting significance and fashioning order out of the chaotic array of phenomena confronting it in consciousness. In this manner human beings reflectively cope with their experience of the world in general, gaining familiarity with and orienting ourselves within the world by articulating it in language. The elementary search for coherence is implicit within and underlies our experience of the world in general, while the most basic and 'universal human task' (as Gadamer describes it) is to bring to speech the phenomena that confront us, enabling us thereby to gain an orientation toward, to cope reflectively with, and to comprehend what confronts us in the world. Understanding, in hermeneutics, is not merely what we do but what we 'are.'

To be human, in this view, is to be situated within a particular configuration of meanings, language, possibilities, and relationships that comprise a lifeworld (*Lebenswelt*), the preconceptual setting which forms a background against which human existence is played out. A human being is always already a being-in-the-world (to cite Heidegger's famous expression), a radically historical, social, and also linguistic being which never exists in a worldless condition but within a world of objects and, more importantly, of meanings. Human life unfolds within a meaningful totality of relations, a configuration of linguistic and cultural conditions into which it is 'thrown' and in which it orients itself understandingly. The hyphenated expression 'being-in-the-world' indicates that the self and the world in which it exists constitute a unitary phenomenon such that the being of the former is not analysable apart from the lifeworld in which it is embedded. The self, environed by being prior to reflection, cannot stand apart from its world in the manner presupposed by Descartes and the Enlightenment philosophy that followed in his wake.

As a historical being, the self projects itself into a finite set of possibilities of what it may become in the course of its existence. Following Heidegger, the human being is viewed within hermeneutics as a radically noncartesian, nonsubstantial entity, a being that is never altogether determinate or finished but which exists both in the modes of actuality and possibility. What it is, is ultimately inseparable from its possibilities of becoming. Hence it is a futural as much as a present being, one oriented by its past, existing in the present and projecting itself into an anticipated future. The possibilities which it has (which it 'is') are inherited from a particular historical tradition and are to some extent circumscribed by the previous self-understandings of that tradition. This is Heidegger's statement of the radical finitude of human beings – that what we are is a function of what we may become, while what we may become is fundamentally limited by what we have been. Already constituted by a past, the human being reconstitutes itself in comporting itself toward a possible future.

As well as dwelling in a world of meanings and possibilities, the human being is always already a 'being-with-others' and, related to this, a speaker of a language. The virtual antithesis of the Hobbesian atom, the hermeneutical subject is a profoundly social being whose existence is played out within a space of intersubjectivity, a space that comprises language, conversation, social practices and relationships, and modes of political and community life. There is no inner retreat of the soul protected from the vicissitudes of history and social reality, no metaphysical item prior to all social involvements. The public and private, outer and inner, lives of the individual are entirely taken up with projects, preoccupations, values, and attachments which are inconceivable apart from our involvement with other selves. The self's innermost cognitions, iden-

tity, and moral 'preferences' are articulated within a conceptual framework that it inherits, rendering impossible the kind of ahistorical and
rationalist evaluation of the good presupposed by conventional liberalism. A being by no means self-sufficient or fully constituted in its being
apart from intersubjectivity, or 'prior' to its 'entry' into social relationships, the individual self is constituted by a multitude of factors which
make up its 'essential' sociality. Uppermost among such factors is its elementary linguisticality drawing the self into a web of significations and
conversations passed down to it through tradition. Within a particular
horizon of understanding, objects in the world acquire a significance
that is contingent on, and specific to, a given hermeneutic framework.
Linguisticality, as Gadamer in particular has shown, is far from a contingent feature of human existence. To the primordial constitution of the
human being belong language, shared understandings, traditions, and
forms of association that comprise our being-in-the-world.

At present these premises concerning human historicity and social
embeddedness hold considerable currency in several philosophical circles, and they are perhaps sufficiently familiar that they do not require
more detailed exposition. The premises on which my account of the self
as a moral agent rests pertain to this set of phenomenological-hermeneu-
tical observations: that the human being is invariably a being-in-the-
world and a being-with-others; that it is situated within a lifeworld from
which it inherits a particular horizon of understanding; that it exists in
the mode of possibility no less than that of actuality; that it appropriates
a finite set of possibilities into which it continually projects itself; and
that its most fundamental mode of comportment toward its world is that
of understanding and self-understanding. Prior to all maximization of
utility or moral bargaining, persons are oriented toward social reality
and engaged in the task of comprehending it in language and finding
their way amid networks of significations. They are interpreting and
self-interpreting beings characterized by a fundamental historicity and
linguisticality. Social involvement is neither a mere strategy in self-interest nor a contingency of any sort, as liberalism has been accustomed to
asserting. Nor does the paradigm of instrumentality afford a proper understanding of the relation between the individual and society. The relation is better conceived as one of mutual constitution, the social whole
being comprised of individuals alone (without any overarching social
whole distinguishable, except metaphorically, from the sum of persons
composing it) and the individual being constituted by its (distanced)
participation in social relations. The self belongs to a lifeworld prior to

reflection and assumes its identity within a particular moral ethos, captured in the Hegelian notion of *Sittlichkeit*. As complete autonomy is a myth of Enlightenment philosophy, it is untenable to conceive of the self as a being of unconditioned objectivity in its knowledge of the world or in its evaluative judgments. Reflection always presupposes a background of tacit understandings and attitudes which characterize the subject's facticity. No power of abstraction or method of reasoning makes it possible for reflection to transcend history or attain the perspective of unconditioned objectivity. This entirely fictional standpoint was never a possibility for finite beings belonging to a lifeworld and inseparable from a meaningful totality of relations.

In this view there is nothing objectionable in the hypothesis that the self is a social and historical construction whose identity and being are contingencies, a being without a metaphysical centre or core of selfhood. That it is a creature of language, intersubjectivity, and history is an observation that has become increasingly apparent since Hegel, Nietzsche, Heidegger, and others have succeeded in debunking the myth of the worldless subject. In its theological, rationalist, materialist, idealist, utilitarian, or contractarian forms, the worldless subject is a demolished abstraction currently in its final death throes. That its plug may at long last be pulled is not to be regretted by liberals committed to a political morality of individualism. Nor should its decline prompt communitarians, socialists, and others on the left to announce liberalism's collapse, yet it does compel liberalism to jettison its metaphysical baggage beginning with its fundamentally essentialist and ahistorical conceptions of the self. It counsels a rejection of the premises that the individual, complete and ready-made in its identity and view of the good, confronts social reality as an external barrier to its gratification, as something over and against itself and toward which it comports itself in strategic fashion.

Rejecting conventional liberal ontology means giving up once and for all the asocial and ahistorical self which in its several manifestations has been too often presupposed by liberal theorists. As a being whose basic mode of existence is to be oriented toward a world of meanings by understanding it in language, the human being takes on an interpretive orientation which marks its particular way of being human. It learns a manner of being human in the same gesture that it acquires an orienting framework in terms of which phenomena within the world gain significance. Both the capacities of understanding and self-understanding as well as the forms in which they occur constitute so many inheritances from the lifeworld in which we are embedded, as is our basic mode of comportment as moral agents. Our tacit evaluations and, more significantly, the particular moral language or family of ethical categories that we appropriate from tradition are brought with us in fashioning judgments about the good and in all ethical relations. To speak a moral language is to comport oneself toward social phenomena in a particular way. It is to identify saliences in human action, to comprehend significance, to invest with importance, or otherwise to gain a moral orientation in some measure specific to a particular time and place. If language furnishes a worldview for understanding then the specific moral vocabulary we speak by the same token furnishes a perspective on social reality, an orientation that constitutes us as the kind of moral agents we are.

Abandoning individualist ontology involves accenting the role that convention plays in fashioning our existence and identity. Convention affords patterns which we may choose to follow from among the myriad possibilities open before us or a basic structure which we may adopt or depart from in the course of our lives. Whether we opt to follow convention or depart from it, either course gains intelligibility only with reference to convention itself and against a backdrop of further conventions and traditions. Our existence and identity are conceived either as following a set pattern, as a partial departure from it, or as a radical repudiation. In each case the sense of our lives is understood in relation to tradition, even if only in negative terms as its contravention.

Critics of liberalism are correct in charging its proponents, particularly utilitarians and contractarians, with underestimating the pervasiveness of intersubjectivity in subjectivity and exaggerating the degree of antagonism that obtains between individuals. That our moral being and identity are constituted by our attachments and ends, reflective and tacit appraisals, shared understandings and by an array of practices, concepts, relationships, and traditions are premises whose truth value is becoming increasingly difficult to contest. The basic hypothesis that the self is constituted within a space of intersubjectivity has been articulated in several forms in recent decades. Spelling out the specific form of this hypothesis which liberalism properly incorporates and demonstrating its coherence with liberal doctrine is my present task.

A Hermeneutical-Pragmatic Philosophy of the Self

If self-knowledge does not resemble an originary presence of the self to itself or an introspective apprehension of some kind of internal *eidos*, self-knowledge would more plausibly be viewed as a reflexive act that is mediated by interpretive structures of one kind or another. The 'I' is misconceived as a substantial entity, but is an event of linguistic utterance or an 'implicate of language usage.'[2] It comes into being in the act of asserting itself as a subject of action or a bearer of predicates and is thus inseparable ontologically from the linguistic event in which it is constituted. The 'I' is the implied subject of a series of predicates, where it is the predicates alone that constitute it as the particular 'I' that it is. Otherwise stated, it is the predicate that possesses ontological priority over the subject rather than the reverse, the subject being nothing over and above the multiplicity of predicates attributed to it over the course of time. The metaphysical assertion that there 'must' be a determinate and substantial subject for the act of predication to be possible, a subject given prior to its predicates, lacks entirely the necessity metaphysicians typically presuppose. Phenomenologically, there is no greater necessity in supposing the self to be ontologically prior to its predicates than in positing a noumenal realm lurking behind the phenomena of consciousness. Both are disposable metaphysical fictions which conceal from view the eventual (or event-like) nature of the 'I.' Indeed it is not stretching the matter too far to say that the subject is simply its predicates, or an implied configuration of these without an ego substance underlying and unifying them.

'Knowing thyself' is knowing the series of predicates by which one is constituted as a particular self. It is a reflective act mediated by structures of interpretation the most fundamental of which is language itself. The self comes to understand itself and be understood by others through the medium of language and texts, among which may be counted the various signs, expressions, and conversations which mark one's factical condition. (I shall argue later in this chapter that the self comes to understand itself as a moral agent specifically through the medium of text-analogues, including in particular its own actions and through a vocabulary of ethical concepts.) As a social construct, the self is constituted in the interplay of linguistic utterance and the various forms of interaction in which it is immersed. Language – what hermeneutics characterizes as 'the social medium par excellence'[3] – represents the principal medium through which the identity and being of the self are disclosed, for it is in this medium that the assorted predicates which constitute a subject are integrated into a coherent interpretive structure. In opposition to classical liberal assumptions, the self is nothing (no thing) prior to the multifarious acts of linguistic expression and to the social interactions and practices in which it becomes involved. It is ontologically prior to neither language nor social reality, but is constituted as the subject that it is through a myriad of social – and above all linguistic – practices. It is as a product of language that the self comes to understand itself indirectly or through a medium of historically contingent signifying practices and interpretive conventions. The human subject is a speaking subject, one that comports itself within the lifeworld or language that it inhabits by engaging in practices of signification which make it possible to fashion an understanding of the world and its own identity. Far from being a mere instrument of expression, language belongs to the fundamental constitution of the self and the social world to which it belongs.[4]

One form of speech is especially significant to the constitution of the self. This is the practice of narrative interpretation. This form of linguistic utterance is so pervasive a phenomenon of human existence that it would be no exaggeration to characterize the human subject as not only an understanding and speaking subject but more specifically as a storyteller. This species of interpretation underlies, often in rudimentary form, so many of our perceptions, evaluations, affects, choices, and other cognitions that it could be described as ubiquitous to human experience. No culture or community is without a (usually vast) repertoire of narratives by which it understands itself and recounts its experience of the world, whether they assume the form of cultural or national histories, biographies, fictional texts, moral tales, religious myths, creation stories, fables, or parables. The universality of narrative in its multiple forms and its ubiquity in experience are testament to the storied nature of human existence. The self continually narrates the phenomena it apprehends, configuring disparate experiences and relating objects or events in intelligible sequences with a before and an after. Phenomena are illuminated by being arranged into meaningful patterns, drawing connections and pulling together disparate events in an ongoing effort to escape the 'blooming, buzzing confusion' of experience. Narrating our experience of the world is not a primitive effort of understanding but a universal practice of arranging into meaningful and ordered configurations previously disparate experiences, events, and cognitions.

Human experience in general is characterized by understanding, and narrative is one of the principal forms that it assumes. From understanding empirical events to written texts, cultures, or actions, the hermeneutic art of arranging phenomena into ordered temporal sequences best exemplified by the narrator, biographer, and historian has advanced far beyond the rudimentary narratives and proto-narratives of everyday life.

The fundamental structure of the latter, insofar as it is experienced as meaningful, conforms to that of the narrative. As Theodore R. Sarbin writes:

> Present two or three pictures, or descriptive phrases, to a person and he or she will connect them to form a story, an account that relates the pictures or the meanings of the phrases in some patterned way. On reflection, we discover that the pictures or meanings are held together by the implicit or explicit use of plot. When the stimulus material depicts people, the story will reflect recognizable human sentiments, goals, purposes, valuations, and judgments. The plot will influence the flow of action of the constructed narrative figures.[5]

By situating an utterance, event, or experience in a narrative structure, it takes on a significance transcending particularity, is comprehended together with other utterances, events, or experiences with which it may be related and in the process of being recounted assumes a larger significance. It gains intelligibility and coherence in being placed within a narrative frame. The search for narrative coherence which we associate with the storyteller and historian is embarked upon by persons generally in the course of everyday life, albeit normally in less articulate and sustained forms. It is a reflective act so fundamental to experience that it is typically undertaken without express awareness. Frequently prereflective, narrative serves to synthesize scattered events into meaningful sequences which exhibit a semblance of direction and development.

As Heidegger observed, the self is a temporal being caught up in a chain of past, present, and future. It is always ahead of itself in being taken up with projects orienting it toward an anticipated future and in a continual state of becoming. It possesses a dynamic state of being, constituted as much by its future possibilities as by its present actuality. The human subject experiences its life as unfolding over time and, to the extent that such a life is experienced as meaningful, as displaying an important element of directionality and teleology in the same way that a narrative develops over time and contains a sense of direction. While lacking absolute beginnings or endings, human life includes a multiplicity of narrative unfoldings, large and small, with approximate and overlapping beginnings and endings, and varying degrees of directionality. By configuring an individual's past, present, and future in the form of a meaningful thread of development, narrative captures both the temporal and the teleological character of human life. The configuration of a plot structure introduces into a life history a thread in terms of which that life may be understood. It is disclosed, as with any history, as more than a merely empirical chronicle of events or series of unrelated episodes, but as the development of a story line with a coherent beginning-middle-end structure.

Narrative and temporality have been prominent themes in the recent work of Ricoeur. He identifies a reciprocity between narrative and human time according to which 'time becomes human time to the extent that it is organized after the manner of a narrative; narrative, in turn, is meaningful to the extent that it portrays the features of temporal experience.'[6] Our experience of the present is entangled within a 'dialectic of remembrance and anticipation.'[7] The present not only arises from the past and anticipates the future but takes on whatever significance it has by virtue of its temporal structure. It is understood as a continuation, modification, or departure from the past, as setting in motion a new sequence of action or putting an end to an old one, as breaking a habit, or following convention. How I am situated is how I have come to be situated and also how I am on the way to becoming situated. The present is structured in terms of projects initiated in the past and to be completed in the future.

Human experiences, for Ricoeur, are not altogether discrete events but episodes that call for narrative recounting. Temporal experience becomes intelligible – becomes 'human,' as Ricoeur puts it – as scattered events take on the character of episodes comprehended within a larger plot structure. He writes:

> My basic hypothesis ... is the following: the common feature of human experience, that which is marked, organized and clarified by the fact of story-telling in all its forms, is its *temporal character*. Everything that is recounted occurs in time, takes time, unfolds temporally; and what unfolds in time can be recounted. Perhaps, indeed, every temporal process is recognized as such only to the extent that it can, in one way or another, be recounted.[8]

Narrative recounting serves to hold past, present, and future together within an intelligible configuration or plot structure. It affords a perspective from which it is possible to gain an understanding of past experience from the standpoint of events that followed or may be projected to follow after them. The provision of an ending enhances our understanding of the past, now construed as a beginning rather than an isolated and possibly meaningless occurrence. From a retrospective standpoint we may return to the beginning of a temporal sequence in order to observe how it led to an end or to the present, and thereby to comprehend its significance.

The function of the plot is to convey intelligibility and meaning on the multifarious events, actions, relations, and cognitions of ordinary life through an act of creative synthesis. Synthesizing heterogeneous events in the interpretive act of emplotment makes for an understanding of those events by taking them out of their isolated particularity, a particularity in which the significance of an event is likely to be minimal or absent altogether. The meaning of an event in human experience is not inherent to it or determinable in abstraction from its temporal and narrative context, but gains significance for the first time in being recounted or comprehended within a larger synthesis. To be understood as a meaningful occurrence it must be interpreted or seen as contributing to a larger structure. The interpretive function of emplotment is summarized by William Lowell Randall as follows:

> As regards matters of meaning ... plot does more than merely connect the events of the story like so many beads on a string. Rather, it constructs them. It rescues them from randomness by conferring on them a relevance – a purposefulness – because of the role they play in relation both to each other and to the story overall. Each event 'means' something not in terms of itself, that is, but of its place within a developing narrative context. As the story 'unfolds' into its future, then, fresh events possess increased meaning potential over those preceding them. As we say, the plot 'thickens.'[9]

Plots thicken not only in getting longer but in synthesizing new elements previously unrelated to the original story line, by taking unexpected turns, integrating new subplots, or combining old story lines with new ones, thereby adding depth and complexity to the account. In the thickening of the plot and the interweaving of subplots the meaning of events may be altered considerably as they are reconfigured into different narrative constructions. What had been viewed as a decisive action to initiate a sequence of events comes to be viewed as a failed and abandoned venture when comprehended together with later events which followed or failed to follow them. A minor occurrence comes to be seen from the perspective of later events as decisive to the course of a life. It is a commonplace of experience that it is best understood in hindsight. The reason for this is that the retrospective glance is capable of integrating a larger range of experience in a broader synthesis than is possible in the present. Interpretation of the present moment is limited on account of its merely anticipated grasp of future events while retrospective narration grasps the moment together with its then-future consequences. Events take on correspondingly different meanings by being synthesized differently with, and hence comprehended in light of, other events. Their significance is altogether contingent on the narrator's art.

If it belongs to the constitution of human existence to display an inescapably temporal and narrative structure, then we have identified a unifying and organizing principle for human experience which presupposes no metaphysical substratum or noumenal realm of any kind. Experience possesses unity not on account of its connection with a unified and underlying ego substance but its narrative structure. Unity is not an a priori presupposition of experience but an outcome of hermeneutic reflection, and specifically of narrative emplotment. It is an achievement of cognition rather than its presupposition. Nevertheless, the unity and coherence that characterize human experience are far from seamless and are typically shot through with discordances and incoherencies of various kinds. The narrative unity of a life rarely matches the unity and organization of a fictional narrative. The coherence of the former is not without disruptions or contradictions, elements that resist incorporation in a unified narrative account and interrupt the continuity and elegance of a well-constructed history. However, human experience is unified by virtue of its temporal and narrative structure, and to the extent that it is understood, its heterogeneous elements are synthesized in the hermeneutic act of recounting. The unity of experience is neither given nor grounded on a metaphysical foundation but is an achievement of the hermeneutic art.

A hypothesis equally central to the hermeneutical conception of the self is that it is in narrative form that subjectivity is properly constituted. The self is constituted as a moral agent by a configuration of actions, experiences, ethical commitments, and practices emplotted into a biographical account. As Ricoeur states:

> Our own existence cannot be separated from the account we can give of ourselves. It is in telling our own stories that we give ourselves an identity. We recognize ourselves in the stories that we tell about ourselves. It makes very little difference whether these stories are true or false, fiction as well as verifiable history provides us with an identity.[10]

The moral identity – indeed the very being – of the self is constituted as a narrative unity (to use MacIntyre's expression) in the sense that the identity of the self as a moral agent is comprehended through the synthetic act of configuring a narrative history out of the disparate episodes of a life. The unity that characterizes the self is very far from being a determinate fact about the individual and is more properly viewed as a product of hermeneutic configuration. It is a historical construction, the history of its becoming and the predicates attributed to it. Its being consists in what it has become and what it is on the way to becoming as both moments are synthesized in a recounted biography.

Hermeneutics, as Anthony Kerby expresses it, defends 'a model of the human subject that takes acts of *self-narration* not only as descriptions of the self but, more importantly, as *fundamental to the emergence and reality of that subject.*'[11] As an ontological thesis, the narrative conception of subjectivity pertains to the subject's most fundamental mode of being. It is as a character in a narrative history that the self is constituted as the being that it is. In fashioning our morally significant actions and experiences into a meaningful succession of events – a coherent ordering of the scattered episodes of a life into the structure of a plot unfolding over time – the self is given the identity of a character in a narrative. It has the identity of both the principal character in its own biography as well as a supporting character in the life histories of other individuals, whether this is in a major or minor capacity. We play a supporting role in the narratives of all those with whom we form relationships of one kind or another, and it is as a character in such histories that the identity and being of the self take the form that they do.

There is no need to posit something 'deeper' or more essential in human subjectivity than the layers of narrative interpretation that are fashioned in discourse, the plot structures that provide a sense of both our own identity and the meaning that our lives have for us. A being that comports itself understandingly in a lifeworld composed of social meanings is never without a degree of self-understanding as well. We gain an understanding of ourselves both individually and collectively precisely by telling our own stories. The autobiographical act is paradigmatic of the attempt to make sense of our lives just as recounting the history of a nation provides an understanding of national identity. Providing a narrative account of events affords the broadest, most encompassing structure in which a sense of personal identity may be articulated. This is evident from the ordinary phenomenon of getting to know a person. Becoming acquainted with a person, and similarly gaining an understanding of a nation or a people, turns on our learning the

story of their life. It turns less on an enumeration of personal characteristics – and not at all on the description of a personal essence – than on
a history in which these traits came to characterize the person. We learn
the manner in which a person came to be in their present circumstances,
what configuration of events, choices, and accidents led to the present
and what future they envision for themselves. In the case of a nation,
culture, or people, we learn the history of their struggles, their sufferings
and triumphs, their founding and sustaining myths, their achievements
in the arts and sciences, the history of their political thought and practice, the history of their internal struggles and foreign conflicts, and their
national heroes or outstanding personages. Merely empirical descriptions of present characteristics abstracted from historical context lack
both the breadth and depth of a narrative history which encompasses
such traits while viewing these within the larger context of their historical unfolding.

The narrative structure of the self is closely linked with the structure
of human action. As an event dependent for its intelligibility on interpretation, especially hermeneutic acts of narration, meaningful action
becomes understood in light of its before and after, or the configuration
of circumstances which prompted the action and the consequences
which followed from it. A human action is not an isolated occurrence
with a determinate meaning but depends for its intelligibility on a larger context or sequence of events of which it constitutes a part. As Ricoeur in particular has demonstrated, the meaning of human action is a
reflection of its significance to the development of not only a succession
of actions and events but a narrative succession. It is above all in the unfolding of a plot that the meaningful character of action is disclosed. Like
our actions, the more significant of which become key episodes, human
life as a whole lends itself to narrative recounting. Both a life and the actions of which it is composed display a proto-narrative structure, one
which may take rudimentary form but which, if it is to be understood,
strives for reflective articulation in the form of a story.

The human subject is equally far from being metaphysically given and
epistemologically transparent to itself. For self-knowledge it is dependent on the mediation of interpretive structures from metaphorical and
narrative constructions at the most general level to the particular signs,
cultural works, values, experiences, beliefs, relationships, practices, and
actions of which our biographies are composed and which, for this reason, are constitutive of identity. They belong to our identity on account
of their incorporation as episodes into the larger frame of a personal his-

tory. A human being is understood only in being recounted and is the implied subject of the recounting. Randall describes the affinity between human existence and narrative as follows:

> A life has a beginning, middle, and end, like a story. A life is about someone doing something, as is a story. A life has a main person in the middle of it, as a story often has. A life can be fraught with conflict, can be seen as manifesting a set of recurring themes, and can even be divided into certain chapters – again, as can a story. A life is a sort of world within itself, as is a story. Finally, a life is never simply given, but always in part composed, constructed, created – as is a story, even a supposedly 'factual' one.[12]

That experience should take on a narrative configuration is by no means an automatic or given fact of our existence. While our being-in-the-world is never without a degree of self-understanding, the latter comes to fruition only within reflection and optimally within the hermeneutic practice of narration. As any story-teller, biographer, or historian knows, the fashioning of a narrative is no simple affair of stringing together or chronicling isolated events, but is an interpretive art requiring imagination, discrimination, and judgment. A meaningful rendering of events is made possible by a process of selective attention and emphasis, discrimination between relative significance and insignificance, judgment concerning what events or episodes are to be comprehended together with or read in light of other events, interpretation of what constitutes the beginning of a sequence, or a turn within it or an ending to a particular chapter or act within a larger configuration. Like that smaller unit of imaginative predication, the metaphor, a well-fashioned narrative provides an original and possibly insightful mode of seeing-as, disclosing events and experiences in a particular, and by no means self-evident, light.

In the constitution of the self there is remarkably little that is altogether evident or determinate. Neither the individual occurrences that make up our personal history nor the manner of their configuration are without need of the narrator's art. Like historical events, the events of our personal past are not raw data, determinate and unchangeable in their significance. Only the fact of their having occurred, and not their meaning, is given. This is because the latter is contingent on the larger history of which an event is interpreted as being a part, a history which may continue to unfold in the present and is therefore modifiable, or a configuration which like any interpretation may be reinterpreted in a different and perhaps more illuminating fashion. As an interpreted history, the being of the self is inseparable from the process of its becoming, and with respect to both the past (what it has become) and the future (what it is on the way to becoming). The self is a being in process of becoming itself, or as Nietzsche says, it is 'the *as yet undetermined animal*'[13] which must 'become what it is.'

A being that is constituted by interpretive structures may be reconstituted through a creative modification of these structures. However a note of caution is called for in this matter. To assert that the constitution of the self is not a metaphysical given but a product of narrative configuration is by no means to suggest either that there are no limits to the analogy between understanding a life and story-telling or that the narrator's art permits unrestricted poetic licence in a kind of interpretive free for all. The alternative to metaphysical seriousness is not free-wheeling frivolity but the interpretive faithfulness to phenomena characteristic of the biographer, historian, or phenomenologist. That there are episodes in our experience that possess a certain gravity and definiteness about them which limits the poetic licence of the narrator need not (indeed cannot) be denied, nor is it entailed by the analogy between story-telling and the recounting of a life. Moreover the affinity between human experience and the unfolding of a narrative is not without limits in another respect. The various threads that make up a human life are rarely tied together in the elegant fashion of a fictional narrative. However, as David Carr puts it:

> [A]re we justified in concluding that, since the events of our lives do not fit together as neatly as those of a good story, they occur randomly, simply one after the other? Or that our lives are scrambled messages, a hubbub of static and noise? Because we experience no neat, absolute beginnings, and no ultimately satisfying and all-explanatory endings, is it correct to say that we have none at all?[14]

Like all analogies, that between narrative and the self is not perfect. However, it does provide an account of subjectivity that is both comprehensive and phenomenologically adequate.

The hermeneutical-pragmatic conception of the self, accordingly, sets out from the premise that subjectivity is not properly characterized as having a determinate and essential nature discoverable through metaphysical, scientific, or economic investigation but is a historical and social construction fashioned by layers of interpretation. As morality concerns practice, it is to the realm of the practical that a theory of the self as a moral and political agent must finally turn. The self is not only a concatenation of interpretations and experiences occurring over time but an agent as well. It is the implied subject of not only its experiences, sufferings, and inherited circumstances but its own self-chosen actions. As a narrative construction, it is fashioned by layers of interpretation which take as their primary object not an underlying core of being (of which such interpretations could be said to be either accurate or inaccurate representations) but a collection of actions voluntarily undertaken by the subject. Moral agency must be understood from the point of view of practice.

A theory of the self as both the author and product of action involves uncovering an important area of common ground between hermeneutical philosophy and pragmatism. This point of convergence is expressed in John Dewey's thesis regarding 'the *essential unity of the self and its acts.*'[15] Dewey understood that the constitution of the self as a moral agent is properly conceived with respect to its mode of comportment toward practice. Moral identity is inextricably linked with conduct, particularly that which is habitually undertaken. Moral action is related to the self both as an expression of the latter and as part of a continual process of reconstituting the self as the kind of agent it is. Dewey's articulation of this view is worth citing at length.

> Now every such choice sustains a double relation to the self. It reveals the existing self and it forms the future self. That which is chosen is that which is found congenial to the desires and habits of the self as it already exists. Deliberation has an important function in this process, because each different possibility as it is presented to the imagination appeals to a different element in the constitution of the self, thus giving all sides of character a chance to play their part in the final choice. The resulting choice also shapes the self, making it, in some degree, a new self. This fact is especially marked at critical junctures, but it marks every choice to some extent however slight. Not all are as momentous as the choice of a calling in life, or of a life-partner. But every choice is at the forking of the roads, and the path chosen shuts off certain opportunities and opens others. In committing oneself to a particular course, a person gives a lasting set to his own being. Consequently, it is proper to say that in choosing this object rather than that, one is in reality choosing what kind of person or self one is going to be. Superficially, the deliberation which terminates in choice is concerned with weighing the values of particular ends. Below the surface, it is a process of discovering what sort of being a person most wants to become.[16]

In freely choosing a course of action, one is doing considerably more than merely expressing a preference or maximizing utility. One is actively determining one's moral identity.

This is achieved by simultaneously pursuing, opening up, and closing off possibilities of further action. As a being that exists not only in the mode of actuality but in the mode of possibility – hence, as Heidegger saw, as a projective or futural being – the moral subject is inseparable in its being from the possibilities that are open before it, and these possibilities are continually modified in light of choices made and actions taken. In committing oneself to a course of action, one is not only pursuing the ends that one prefers but putting one's moral identity in question and giving shape to oneself as a moral agent. This is most evident in cases in which the choices one makes are of momentous significance in determining the general direction life will take, choices pertaining for instance to a vocation or a set of ethical values to which one will become committed. The course undertaken derives its significance from its contribution to one's self-understanding as well as from the further possibilities for action that it in turn generates. Over the course of a life, particular actions and experiences are singled out in consciousness as crucial in the fashioning of an identity. One sees such events as crucial episodes in the unfolding of a life history.

Such is the case, as Dewey noted, not only in confronting choices of momentous significance but in all decisions made by the subject that are of moral interest. All actions freely undertaken, from those that provide a life with its fundamental direction to the relatively undistinguished actions of everyday life, are of constitutive importance to one's moral identity. In moral action, the agent puts itself at stake in the pursuit of its ends. An identity is fashioned in the succession of actions and the formation of habits. Action often takes on an habitual character, introducing a measure of continuity into our moral lives. Such continuity, Dewey suggests, is best captured in the concept of 'conduct,' a word that connotes more than a succession of actions and indicates a meaningful series of these leading in the direction of further action. Conduct exhibits a certain directedness analogous to the unfolding of a plot, and is quite unlike a mere succession of unrelated episodes. In displaying a continuity of direction, conduct fashions a meaningful sequence out of disparate actions and experiences. What is at stake, then, in moral conduct is the kind of self that is being fashioned and refashioned in the choices it makes and in the habits of action and thought which it forms.

A literary illustration may clarify Dewey's thesis. The character of Jean Valjean in Victor Hugo's *Les Misérables* may be taken as a paradigm case of an individual whose moral identity is entirely contingent on his choices and actions. Valjean is very much a self 'in the making,'[17] in Dewey's phrase, and aware of himself as such. In undergoing profound personal transformation from the barbarous existence of an imprisoned convict to the character who gradually takes shape as a result of his experience with the Bishop of Digne and in the course of involvements with a series of other characters, Valjean becomes what he is in the realm of practice. He emerges in the course of the narrative as a character inseparable in his being from his comportment toward other persons and from a long succession of self-chosen actions. It is a pointless metaphysical exercise to ask whether Valjean, the convict whom we encounter in an early part of the narrative, is the same self whom we read about in later chapters, a question that turns on the precise description of a metaphysical core self underlying and persisting throughout the course of a personal history. Such a question, in the account I am offering, is unanswerable and without purpose. (It is, of course, the nature of a question to contain presuppositions, and when one or more of these presuppositions is false the question as formulated will impede the course of inquiry or lead it down pointless and irrelevant paths. This state of affairs has characterized metaphysical discussions of personal identity and its persistence through time. The result has been a fruitless quest for the necessary and sufficient conditions of personal identity or the concrete substance that underlies our being and makes us the entity we are. It is a quest that should be abandoned and replaced with an inquiry of a different kind: not a metaphysical inquiry but a hermeneutical and ethical inquiry into the manner in which the self comes to be constituted as the being it is and what role it plays in fashioning its own constitution.)

In Valjean we comprehend the unity of the self and its acts of which Dewey speaks. Hugo presents a character mindful of the contingency of his own moral identity and the manner in which he is himself at stake or in question in the course of deliberation and action. Faced with the recognition that his identity as a moral agent could be otherwise – indeed that it has been otherwise – Valjean becomes the moral agent he is through an arduous process of reform in the space of intersubjectivity and in the course of a succession of freely chosen actions. What emerges in the course of the narrative is a configuration of habitual action and a continuity of direction marked by key episodes, decisive events, turning points, new beginnings, and habit formation. Over the course of time and in the formation of habits of thought and action, a self and its actions are unified.

The moral identity of the self, then, is its identity as the subject of the actions that it performs over time. As conceived along hermeneutical lines, the self emerges in and as the course of a narrative history; along pragmatic lines, it is the subject's actions that constitute the most compelling and decisive episodes of the history that it itself is. The self is not ontologically prior to its actions and choices, but is dependent in its identity and being as a moral agent upon these. It is contingent on an emplotted configuration of conduct, deliberations, judgments, affirmations, and commitments governing its involvement in social reality. Its involvement in the world of practices, both discursive and moral, make up its being-in-the-world and being-with-others.

The thesis that 'what the subject *is, is the series of its actions*'[18] originates with Hegel in *Elements of the Philosophy of Right* and finds expression in the writings of Nietzsche, Jean-Paul Sartre, and other continental philosophers of existence. It receives its most satisfactory expression, however, in Dewey's pragmatism, a philosophy that well understands the primacy of practice in various facets of human existence from the moral and the political to the domains of knowledge and truth. Dewey's view of the self as implicated in its actions provides a useful complement to the hermeneutical account which runs the risk of overemphasizing the embeddedness of subjectivity within discursive practices at the expense of nondiscursive or moral practices as well.[19] Both linguisticality and action hold centre stage in a philosophy of the self that accentuates the idea of narrative unity, understood as the unity of the self and its actions.[20]

Nietzsche is correct in writing: 'there is no "being" behind doing, effecting, becoming; "the doer" is merely a fiction added to the deed – the deed is everything.'[21] In contrast to essentialist conceptions of the self, the hermeneutical-pragmatic view is of a being that is without a determinate metaphysical nature. It is interpretation and practice that belong to the most fundamental constitution of the self as a moral agent. There is no need to posit any manner of substance underlying the actions, cognitions, and experiences of the self as Nietzsche pointed out over a century ago and as the narrative conception presupposes.

I shall now provide a more detailed and thematized account of the idea, central to liberal politics, of the self as an agent. Liberalism has long presupposed a strong conception of individual agency, and it remains to describe how the individual conceived in narrative terms comes to be constituted as not only the implied subject of a narrative history but an agent as well. What does it entail both philosophically and politically to speak of the self as an agent or the author of its actions?

The Self as a Situated Agent

Drawing attention to the social and interpretive character of the self, whether in the manner that I have described or in another fashion, is often taken as a problem of some importance for a theory of justice that traditionally has insisted on not only the moral but the ontological priority of the individual to the society or lifeworld in which it is situated. As we have seen, liberals – particularly those working from utilitarian or contractarian premises – commonly presuppose that reasoning from the standpoint of the individual agent or rational chooser means reasoning from the standpoint of a worldless subject whose identity and mode of being are determinate prior to its 'entry' into a social world or to its choice of ends, attachments, and practices. If the latter is not a tenable theory of the self, does not replacing this with a conception of subjectivity that properly recognizes the factical, social, and interpretive character of the self – one that recognizes that moral ends, practices, relationships, and forms of life are indeed constitutive of moral identity – undermine liberal doctrine, as communitarians and other critics of liberalism assert? Picking up where the argument of Chapter 3 left off, I propose that an acknowledgment of the ubiquity of the social in the constitution of identity does not lead inexorably in the direction of communitarianism, and furthermore I shall argue that it is precisely the hermeneutical-pragmatic conception of moral selfhood that places liberal principles on a more defensible philosophical basis. This argument hinges on the possibility of the self becoming a part-author, and indeed the principal author, of its own being. Liberal morality rests on the premise that while individuals are social beings in a constitutive sense, we are not for all that mere social products, nor are we morally obligated to act as if we were. It presupposes that we are capable of refashioning the narratives that we ourselves are, and that it is in so refashioning ourselves that the meaning that our lives have for us is authentically created. Liberal morality, in other words, presupposes a capacity of personal agency understood in narrative terms as the possibility of self-authorship, or the capacity of individuals to fashion – or, more accurately, refashion – themselves through self-chosen action.

Understanding the pervasiveness of the social in the fashioning of moral identity neither entails that we are thereby placed under an obligation to belong to or perpetuate the customs and traditions that we inherit nor commits us to viewing the individual as a hapless social product or essentially unfree 'conditioned' being with little or no capacity for autonomy. The thesis that moral selfhood is socially constructed or, more precisely, linguistically constituted must not be confused with the view that the self is a mere product of social conditioning or its environment. As a being-in-the-world, the self is indeed a participant in practices not entirely of its choosing and is possessed of possibilities which are inherited from history, including possibilities of narration. What we may become has been circumscribed to some extent by the previous self-understandings that have taken root in our lifeworld. As Heidegger argued, what we are is in part a function of what we may become, while what we may become is fundamentally limited by what we have been. What is more, the self is already constituted as an object of narration prior to its developing a capacity for self-narration.

Considerations of this kind force us to acknowledge that our autonomy in choosing the self we shall be or become is not without limits. A myriad of inherited roles, practices, and narrative forms inevitably precede our efforts to fashion an identity for ourselves and limit our possibilities of self-creation. 'In life,' as MacIntyre writes, 'we are always under certain constraints. We enter upon a stage which we did not design and we find ourselves part of an action that was not of our making.'[22] However, the social roles, practices, and narratives that fashion our identity are appropriated, it must be emphasized, as possibilities of being. History furnishes us with a set of possibilities in terms of which we may understand ourselves, but such interpretive possibilities underdetermine identity for the reason that the narratives we inhabit are never altogether prewritten. Moral agents possess the capacity to rewrite, perhaps radically, the narratives that they themselves are.

Self-respecting human beings rebel at the thought of being mere social products conditioned in either their actions or their identity by considerations over which they have little or no control. While it is true that we are factical beings, it is no less true that we are always more than this. We are not only what we have become (the point that communitarianism accentuates) but what we aspire to be, the possibilities of becoming toward which we continually strive. We are, as Nietzsche realized, actors of our own ideal,[23] and while it was with derision that Nietzsche made this observation of human beings, it is precisely here that we find a primary source of human freedom and dignity. It is in the realization that the self is always more than a product of social forces, an outcome of environmental conditioning, or an unimaginative character in a story of someone else's telling that it becomes possible to conceive of the self as a proper object of respect and oneself as an object of self-respect.

It is in becoming simultaneously the principal character and author of its own life that it becomes an agent in the full sense of the term. Phenomenologically, we experience conduct as being genuinely our own, as freely authored in large part by the self and decidedly not as the outcome of causal forces beyond our power to control. It is only our possibilities that are determined, and this only in a weak sense for they are continually modified by virtue of the choices that we make and the actions that follow them. Our possibilities of self-understanding are inherited, potentially at least, through acts of creative appropriation. We take up roles in such a manner as to adapt these to suit the character we wish to be, and while it is the case that the self finds itself already inhabiting roles and living out a narrative history prior to reflection, there is absolutely no necessity for the self being or remaining any given character or within any particular narrative configuration. Moral agents are free, and are even under an obligation, to assume responsibility for their own narrative history as well as for their particular actions.

The self assumes responsibility for the narrative that it itself is by undertaking a transition from being the lead character in a narrative history to being its part-author as well. It becomes coauthor of its own biography both in taking responsibility for the narrative configuration of its past and present as well as through its actions. As Ricoeur writes, 'By narrating a life of which I am not the author as to existence, I make myself its coauthor as to its meaning.'[24] As an imaginative and self-interpreting being, the self possesses the capacity to reconstitute its identity by reinterpreting its own life history, making itself part-author of the meaningful configuration that is its life. As a moral agent, it refashions its identity by comporting itself in a manner of its choosing in its social relations and assuming responsibility for its conduct. Through both its understanding of the past and present and its orientation to the future, the self takes on the role of coauthor of its own being. With Ricoeur, I place some emphasis on the notion of the self as coauthor rather than sole author for the reason that the self has always already been narrated prior to acquiring a capacity to narrate itself, and the story lines it lives out are not wholly of its choosing. It is as a contributor to a story long under way that the self fashions or refashions its own being. Yet while it may never become sole author of its own life history, the self may assume the role of principal author.

It is well known that it is always possible to reconfigure a narrative history, and that just as it is possible for historians to construct competing accounts of the same historical events, it is possible for individuals to recount the story of their lives in multiple ways. We are both socially constituted and self-constituting beings with the capacity to reinterpret the significance of our individual actions and experiences as well as our life history as a larger configuration. The self, like anything that is interpreted, may be reinterpreted, and in being reinterpreted, both the significance of its life and its moral identity may be radically recast. Lacking an essential nature, the human being is undetermined in its most fundamental mode of being. It is, furthermore, undetermined – or underdetermined – by what it has been and continually awaits further determination through its future actions. Individuals often engage in writing or rewriting their own narrative histories, and sometimes in radical form. We modify our autobiographies in both reinterpreting the significance of our personal past and deliberating about our projected future. The significance of past events is often reinterpreted in light of events in one's present. We may be led to revise our understanding of the past, for instance, in psychotherapy or as a result of such momentous experiences as confronting our mortality or undertaking a fundamental change in beliefs. A conversion in beliefs may occasion a profound revision of one's self-understanding, leading one to view past events in a wholly new light. Events no longer have the meaning they once had. Episodes from childhood take on an altogether new meaning in being recounted anew. What had been viewed, for instance, as an ordinary and trifling occurrence in one's youth may in time come to be understood as a key episode in the formation of an identity. From the perspective of the present we may come to view as a naive and juvenile pursuit what had been understood in our youth as dedication to an ideal or selfless devotion to a cause. Hindsight, as is well known, introduces a degree of perspective on the past that is never available in the present and which may radically modify the significance of past events in light of events which follow them. With the benefit of hindsight and associated changes in perspective, one's personal past may be recounted in significantly different ways, and with changes in narrative recounting come potentially radical modifications in the identity of the self.

Self-understanding bears little resemblance to the simple act of discovery for which it is often mistaken. It is not 'self-discovery' if by this is meant an apprehension of some ready-made material or an introspective exploration of the inner recesses of our being. While the introspection that aims at self-understanding must often endeavour to penetrate beneath the 'surface phenomena' of conscious life, what it encounters there is not an inner core which might lend itself to metaphysical description.

It encounters what the historian and biographer encounter: a multiplicity of signs, cultural works, memories, events, experiences, actions, and other phenomena which display no given mode of configuration. It encounters material that has in most cases already been integrated in some fashion by oneself or others; however, the point to be emphasized is that there is absolutely no necessity to read the present configuration as a final or 'accurate' representation of the truth about the self. It is one possible mode of seeing-as, one interpretation among a host of possibilities, and of which more than one may be informative. In fashioning a self-interpretation or autobiography (and, obviously, one's autobiography need not take an explicitly crafted or written form), the material with which one deals largely takes the form of what is called 'second nature' – a phrase that captures the intuitive plausibility of the notion of self-authorship. 'Human nature' is primarily, and perhaps entirely, second nature if by this phrase we understand a product of artifice highly malleable and lending itself to alternative interpretations. As mentioned above, the meaning that attaches to any given element in our personal history is contingent on its inclusion in a sequence of events and actions. It is highly interpretable given that it is always possible to abstract that episode from the plot or subplot in which it has been understood and reintegrate it in a different subplot. In being alternatively recounted, an alteration in perspective and meaning is the result.

The process of self-understanding permits such revisions and in principle is never closed to interpretive reassessments, disruptions, variations, and inventions. The self remains as open to interpretation as an historical event and may lend itself to as many competing accounts, none of which is definitive of our true being or identity. Indeed, the category of truth – if taken in its traditional metaphysical sense of correspondence – does not lend itself to the art of self-understanding, as if there were a single definitive mode of recounting a life history. To understand oneself is to become one's own principal author. It is to recount a story in the midst of its unfolding, to write and perhaps rewrite its personal past by arranging episodes in a particular fashion, viewing one event in the light of another, emplotting an action or experience in a particular sequence, selecting and arranging elements in a fashion that is coherent and perhaps compelling. Above all, the self interprets itself behaviourally. As Randall writes: 'Through our conduct in relationships, through our reactions to the forces and factors impinging upon us, through our responses to the events that happen to us daily, and through the decisions we make and the actions to which those decisions lead – in all of these ways we determine, more or less, for better or worse, the direction our development takes.'[25] The self is an essentially unfinished being, one continually in the process of becoming itself. As Nietzsche and the existentialists realized, the self becomes what it is in the course of a life and never acquires an identity that is altogether determinate. Existing in the mode not only of being but of becoming, its identity is inseparable from its possibilities. In choosing among the possibilities of what it may become, the self acquires a definition that is forever provisional and contingent on its future choices, actions, and experiences. It is, as Dewey noted, nothing apart from 'the thread of continuous development'[26] that links together all the significant occurrences of a life into a unified identity. This is an identity that remains subject to self-modification as long as choices are available to it, and modification by others as long as it remains an object of discourse.

To maintain that the self is nothing apart from a 'thread of continuous development' is to refuse to be drawn into metaphysical speculation concerning the nature of the substance that must allegedly underlie experience. While, as we have seen, it is undoubtedly the case that there is and must be a principle of unity in human experience, it is a mistake to identify this with any kind of substance. Narrative is able to serve as a principle of unity since it is precisely its function to beget self-understanding by integrating a multiplicity of experiences into a unified life history. Thus conceived, the unity of the self is the virtual antithesis of a metaphysical given and is misconceived in the vocabulary of substance ontology. A product of narrative integration and moral action, it is an achievement in self-creation both on an interpretive and a behavioural level. In Deweyan terms, the unity of a human life is the unity of the self and its actions or the correlativity of character and conduct.[27] Dewey maintains that the self is constructed through moral action, particularly that which is habitually undertaken. Continuity and consistency of action give rise to a persistent sense of self. It is through a willed integration of our actions into identifiable patterns and sequences that a self comes to be constituted and a measure of virtue is normally achieved. Indeed, for Dewey, it is often the mark of an unethical action to fail to cohere with one's more habitual courses of action. So closely, in his view, is moral selfhood tied to continuity in conduct that he proposed the view that moral temptations 'usually take the form of fancying that this particular act will not count, that it is an exception, that for this just one occasion it will not do any harm. His "temptation" is to disregard that continuity of sequence in which one act leads on to others and to a cumulative result.'[28]

It would be instructive to add emphasis to the word 'usually' in the passage cited. Here Dewey assumes that one's habitual patterns of action are not harmful for others. Of course, it remains a possibility in principle that the thoroughgoing immoralist could act in a way that is consistent and well-integrated. This kind of unity neither constitutes nor guarantees moral virtue. What it constitutes is an intelligible sense of self and a persistence of identity over time.

To this pragmatic conception, hermeneutics adds that the unity of the self and its actions is a unity that is fashioned in terms of a narrative structure. The individual endeavours to understand itself by integrating its actions into a coherent and unified narrative account, one consisting perhaps of a variety of subplots, yet which in some manner hang together to form an intelligible and meaningful whole. Synthetic unity is the mark of a human life that is meaningful and thereby capable of being understood. Mature selfhood is properly viewed as an achievement in self-creation which fashions all morally significant actions and experiences into a narrative unity displaying coherence and directionality. It is in the quest for narrative unity that the meaning of a life and its conception of the good largely reside, as MacIntyre has convincingly argued.[29] The moral agent understands itself by appropriating roles that belong to the narratives endemic to a lifeworld, and transforming these to suit the character it wishes to be. It seeks meaning through the myriad of choices it makes and integrating these choices into a coherent, non-contradictory self. Narrative coherence is something that we continually strive for not only in our pursuit of the good but more fundamentally in our pursuit of meaning and self-understanding. A life experienced as a series of unrelated episodes is one in which meaning is elusive and self-understanding is forever beyond one's grasp. Such an existence is characterized by a fundamental disunity between the self and its actions and an alienating absence of direction.

The non-contradictory self is the product of a willed configuration of elements each of which is constitutive in the fashioning of identity. Making sense of who we are, our place in social reality, and the meaning that our lives have for us all depend on the achievement of synthetic unity and narrative coherence. This kind of integrity is an integration of the various plot lines, projects, values, relationships, and practices which make up our private and public lives. The unity of purpose, valuation, and action that provides the individual with an identity is continually at stake and demands an effort directed against the threat of contradiction, narrative incoherence, and meaninglessness. A self continually at stake in its actions is at risk as well of having its identity compromised through action that is ill-chosen or, as we say, 'out of character.' Contradictions that emerge within conduct between one's various roles or subplots threaten to make one's existence a series of unrelated episodes devoid of meaning and ultimately devoid of a self.

The philosopher and psychologist who most profoundly conceived the idea of a dynamic, integrated, and non-contradictory self is undoubtedly Nietzsche. A self that seeks unification of its values, actions, purposes, and character traits in an integrated and non-contradictory framework of its own fashioning is precisely the sort of character Nietzsche held up as worthy of the highest admiration. The self that becomes what it is through an effort of will possesses both integrity and 'style.' Nietzsche expresses this in a famous passage from *The Gay Science*:

> *One thing is needful.* – To 'give style' to one's character – a great and rare art! It is practiced by those who survey all the strengths and weaknesses of their nature and then fit them into an artistic plan until every one of them appears as art and reason and even weaknesses delight the eye. Here a large mass of second nature has been added; there a piece of original nature has been removed – both times through long practice and daily work at it. Here the ugly that could not be removed is concealed; there it has been reinterpreted and made sublime. Much that is vague and resisted shaping has been saved and exploited for distant views; it is meant to beckon toward the far and immeasurable. In the end, when the work is finished, it becomes evident how the constraint of a single taste governed and formed everything large and small. Whether this taste was good or bad is less important than one might suppose, if only it was a single taste![30]

For Nietzsche, the self is a dynamic and coherent configuration of traits, actions, and valuations, while the self to be admired – the one possessing 'style' – achieves a willed reconciliation of powerful and conflicting elements, a sublimation of instinct and an overcoming of the weaknesses and recalcitrant elements of its nature. The latter sort of character identifies itself with every one of its actions and sees all the episodes of its life as essential to its present constitution.

While the liberal self need bear no more than a passing resemblance to Nietzsche's *Übermensch*, it is an individual agent involved in the constitution of its identity in the following respects. First, on an interpretive level, the self assumes (or is capable of assuming) the role of principal author of its narrative history through retrospection and personal reflection. Although the self-interpretations it constructs are by no means authoritative or definitive (indeed they may be quite the contrary: they may be self-serving, false, or even pathological), it is through engaging in acts of self-interpretation that the self unifies within itself the roles of principal character and author of its existence. It becomes an agent in becoming an author true to itself and true to its history after the fashion of the historian who remains faithful to the phenomena and integrates them all in a coherent and complex configuration. The self becomes an agent in a second respect at the level of action. In choosing and assuming responsibility for its conduct, identifying itself with the sum of its actions and the habits and plot structures that they compose, it contributes to its constitution as an agent. It is within the categories of practice, interpretation, and self-creation that the concept of moral agency is properly articulated.

It has been a guiding intuition of liberal morality that the self possesses a capacity for autonomous agency and self-creation which is of ultimate moral importance. Liberals traditionally have defended the right of the individual to become its own author, or to determine the direction its life will take and the meaning that life will hold for it since these represent principal sources of the self-respect without which human life would be intolerable. Although the individual's capacity to make autonomous determinations and become its own author is not without limitations, it is nonetheless sufficiently robust (or capable of becoming so) that liberalism is justified in positing individual self-creation as a worthy ideal. It is an ideal that concerns the most basic manner in which individuals make their lives their own by becoming the principal author of their own lives.

These sentiments are familiar to not only the liberal tradition but romantic and existential thought as well, especially the notion of authenticity. An idea with roots in Rousseau and the romantic tradition, it was revived in the twentieth century by Heidegger and other continental philosophers of existence; authenticity affirms a view of the self as a distinct, inward, self-directed, and potentially creative individual. Rousseau, as we have seen, lamented the manner in which human nature had been corrupted through its involvement in lasting forms of community life, as well as the domination of convention and the constant comparison of self with others. Upon entering society the individual lost its 'natural' moral independence and even its self-love came to be contingent on social recognition. It became corrupt through alienation from its spontaneous nature – a nature that had to be recovered, precariously and imperfectly, through political means. Part of Rousseau's legacy to romanticism was the notion of an original, presocial, and inner core of selfhood which was to be recovered through the celebration of our individual natures. With Heidegger and other existential philosophers, the idea of an originary core of selfhood existing somewhere in the inner regions of our being was rejected, while the ideal of authenticity was reinstated without this metaphysical assumption. Apart from their metaphysical commitments or lack thereof, the various advocates of authenticity held in common an affirmation of the conditions of personal individuation and a critique of the various social obstacles to their fulfilment.

The ideal of authenticity stands opposed to all types of vapid conformity, uniformity, and conventionality, as conditions that inhibit the free expression of individuality. In the existential literature it is the insipid tendency of modern culture, technology, and institutions to so overwhelm the 'existing individual' or '*Dasein*' that its existence is not properly its own. It fails to be true to itself in surrendering to the authority of convention or '*das Man*' (to use Heidegger's expression). Authenticity is a refusal to relinquish responsibility for one's choices to convention. While distinct from simple unconventionality, it refuses all unthinking acquiescence to established modes of thought and action, and celebrates the vital, spontaneous, and inward character of the self. It calls on the individual to recognize and cultivate a sense of its separateness from other persons and to concern itself actively with the elements that make up its personal being. In calling on the individual to be true to itself, the ideal of authenticity need posit no 'inner self' or core of being as that to which one is to be true. Instead it calls on one to be true to, and indeed cultivate, one's originality, separateness, and individuality.

In narrative terms, the ideal of authenticity celebrates the act of taking upon oneself the challenge and responsibility (perhaps the burden) of becoming the principal author of one's life. In stating that authenticity is essentially a matter of freeing oneself from the nameless authority of *das Man*, Heidegger maintains that authentic selfhood is fundamentally a question of authorship. What is in question for the self is whether it has taken upon itself the task of being the principal author of its life or has evaded this responsibility. Its life becomes authentically its own – it becomes an agent – in assuming the role of author. It becomes accountable for its life history and refuses to remain in the state of perpetual drifting characteristic of the inauthentic self. As Carr points out: 'This drift is the evasion of responsibility: I am, it seems, responsible for my own life only if I am its author. Or, more precisely, I *am* responsible whether I realize this or not; the question is whether I accept or evade this responsibility.'[31] What is in question is whether the actions and story lines that constitute my life as a moral agent are self-chosen or merely acquiesced in unthinkingly. The mark of authentic human existence is that it has taken upon itself the role of principal author of its life rather than conceded this task to others.[32]

The self takes up the task of refashioning its identity in freely choosing the plot lines in which it will become or remain involved, the roles and practices in which it will participate, and the judgments and values it will uphold. In making determinations of this kind and integrating these into a coherent and non-contradictory framework, the self contributes to its constitution as both an interpreter and author of its being. It refashions itself by forming a narrative unity out of scattered episodes, making these hang together in light of a certain self-understanding and set of values which make up its moral identity. In unifying the roles of principal character and author, an agent takes possession of itself, affirms its separateness and individuality, is fully present in its actions and choices, and in so doing becomes responsible for them. It also gains in the process a measure of self-respect and self-esteem – what Ricoeur describes as 'the most advanced stages of the growth of selfhood.'[33]

To speak of existential authenticity as an ideal is to presuppose neither that the self invents itself *ex nihilo* nor that it creates its values in radically voluntarist fashion, whether in a state of nature or some other presocial fiction. It presupposes what in Chapter 3 I referred to as the revisability thesis: that no one of our moral ends or attachments is immune to criticism and possible revision by the self. It presupposes that the assigned roles, practices, conventions, and valuations which make up our 'moral starting point' are experienced – or experienceable – as contingent, provisional, and questionable. It is characteristic of authentic individuality to encounter and comport itself toward its facticity in a particular manner. It perceives the 'given' conditions of its existence as being not altogether given, but as capable of being otherwise. It sees the possibility of alternative modes of interpretation and action, the questionablenessof received values and self-understandings, and the contingency of human affairs generally. It experiences its facticity not as belonging inescapably to the natural order of things but contingent and revisable elements of its existence. In gaining an awareness of the narrative history that it already lives prereflectively, and of the roles and story lines that others have assigned it, the authentic self is able to gain an explicit comprehension of the story that it already is, to perceive the possibility of its being otherwise, and engage in its reinterpretation by way of acceptance, modification, or refusal.

As various philosophers of existence have insisted, authentic selfhood is a matter of the individual exercising its capacity for choice in all matters open to it. So much of human existence is subject to personal decision, from our choice of values and beliefs to the meaning that our lives have for us, or whether we will continue to exist at all, that this group of writers was correct in making personal choice, freedom, and responsibility the central themes of its philosophies of human existence. That 'human beings,' as Karl Jaspers puts it, 'are what they are, not simply through birth, breeding, and education, but through the freedom of each individual upon the foundation of his self-existence'[34] is a sentiment frequently expressed by the authors of this school. That human existence lacks a blueprint and is confronted with the necessity of choosing who and whether it will be is expressed well by José Ortega y Gasset in the following concise and representative text:

> We are not launched into existence like a shot from a gun, with its trajectory absolutely predetermined. The destiny under which we fall when we come into this world – it is always *this* world, the actual one – consists in the exact contrary. Instead of imposing on us one trajectory, it imposes several, and consequently forces us to choose. Surprising condition, this, of our existence! To live is to feel ourselves *fatally* obliged to exercise our *liberty*, to decide what we are going to be in this world. Not for a single moment is our activity of decision allowed to rest. Even when in desperation we abandon ourselves to whatever may happen, we have decided not to decide.[35]

The radical gesture by which existential philosophy advances a view of the self not as a mere subject, as it has been conceived for so much of modern philosophy (the abstract 'knowing subject' of modern epistemology), but as an agent and author of its existence represents perhaps its most significant and lasting contribution to philosophy. Its accentuation of the themes of human freedom, authenticity, choice, commitment, and responsibility is its legacy to the present, and one with which any contemporary philosophical account of the self must come to terms. In particular, it is the principle that while human existence is situated within a lifeworld and conditioned by a finite set of possibilities, the individual must decide with freedom and responsibility the manner and terms of its existence rather than surrender this task to others. If the human being is without a fixed nature and identity, and must choose these within a network of social involvements and constraints, it faces a task the difficulty of which must not be underestimated. Recognizing the extent to which it is at stake in its actions and choices, as well as the responsibility that this recognition entails, may be greeted as a liberation or experienced as a burden, or perhaps both. In any event it is a task of profound difficulty and one at which the self may easily fail. The attainment of authenticity and narrative coherence, as Carr writes, 'is a constant task, sometimes a struggle, and when it succeeds it is an achievement. As a struggle it has an adversary, which is, described in the most general way, temporal disorder, confusion, incoherence, chaos. It is the chaos and dissolution represented, paradoxically, by the steady running-off of mere sequence.'[36] Inauthenticity and the failure of self-understanding display a common tendency toward a mere succession of experiences without direction, development, or coherence of any discernible kind. Rather than lending themselves to a particular narrative account, experiences trail off into nothingness with alienation the inevitable consequence.

In narrative terms, inauthenticity is describable as the failure to become the principal author of oneself either through unreflective conformity or more cognizant forms of deflecting responsibility for one's existence onto other persons or circumstances beyond one's control. All too frequently the privilege and burden of self-authorship is transferred to others imagined to possess capacities superior to one's own, whether they are persons of authority, parents, clergy, therapists, educators, tradition, public opinion, or the gods. Inauthenticity is a refusal to take possession of one's being-in-the-world, the surrender of the capacity for self-narration. The inauthentic self is a character of someone else's invention, an actor in a story of someone else's telling, uttering lines others have written, repeating what it has overheard, going through the motions of a human life, and taking care not to turn a discerning eye to its uninspired existence. In surrendering its agency it seeks to relinquish responsibility in the same gesture, an action – or inaction – frequently unburdened by reflection. When it is accompanied by reflection, the relinquishing of the self may occur on the grounds of a philosophical or theological belief – that one is bereft of liberty and compelled to act as conditions beyond one's control determine, or alternatively that the true meaning of one's existence lies in some promised land of religion, and that entry into the happy land must be purchased at the price of surrendering to the gods the principal authorship of one's life. This transfer of authorship and responsibility may be either witting or unwitting, reflective or unreflective. When the former, the self has usually been seduced by a fiction passing for the truth, as in the instances mentioned above. Surrendering the capacity for self-authorship must in some instances be forced while in others persons are eager to unburden themselves even (or perhaps especially) of the gravest and most elementary aspects of their existence. 'We are eager,' René Muller writes, 'to relinquish ourselves because it is a difficult and painful matter to become a self, and because we long for the rewards that our culture is only too ready to give us in exchange for that self.'[37] That freedom for many is a burden they are anxious to be rid of is an observation that Dostoyevsky and the philosophers of existence ably brought to our attention, and for which the contemporary evidence is overwhelming.

If inauthenticity consists of a surrender of personal authorship and responsibility it is frequently accompanied by an ahistorical, congealed, and self-deceptive worldview as well. According to this view, one's mode of comportment as a moral agent along with one's identity, values, beliefs, and categories of thought are given facts of one's existence. They are neither contingent historical constructions, objects of individual choice, nor subject to personal revision, but have the character of strict necessity. Were it to become self-reflective, this worldview would be positively medieval in its dogmatism: the various elements of human existence belong to a natural or quasi-natural order transcending mere individuals and their capacities and choices. Our ethical commitments and categories are congealed into given and fixed objects, as if transcendental deliverances from a metaphysical realm of values. Yet the usual condition of this worldview is to remain unreflective, the believer being content to assume that what is has always been and must forever remain. It forgets the contingency of its existence, that its fundamental understandings and evaluations are constructions which have a history (or, as Nietzsche says, a genealogy), that its view of the world is an interpretation, and that the conventions it inherits belong to no natural order but to human artifice. The self-deceptiveness of this worldview stems from its pretension that individuality, with its attenuated capacities, is incapable of achieving significant modifications of existing conditions (or that such conditions never require significant modification), as if the latter were entirely given while the self is bereft of liberty.

The imperative for individuals to assume the role of principal author of their lives becomes the more pressing when the grand narratives of previous ages have reached their present state of collapse. The grand narratives of human existence associated with the major world religions have lost their capacity to provide universal and ultimate answers to questions concerning the significance of human existence. Indeed, the very notions of ultimate significance and ultimate answers have fallen on hard times of late, and rightly so. That there is no single path that all should follow hardly permits serious questioning, even if the message has perhaps not filtered through to the pharisees of our age and their devotees. The myth of 'the way' – the sacred narrative, universal blueprint, or ultimate meaning of human life – has met its demise, at the hands of Nietzsche and the philosophies of existence that he inspired. That the self is thrown back on its own resources and 'forced to be free' to fashion a life of its choosing without the metaphysical comfort of metanarratives or other grand blueprints of life is a lesson taught by Nietzsche: '"This – is now *my* way: where is yours?" Thus I answered those who asked me "the way." For *the* way – does not exist!'[38] Authentic human existence no more conforms to a 'one size fits all' model than does a well-told tale or a work of art. It assumes the form that it gives to itself, and without the reassurance of cosmic mythologies.

Individual agency, thus conceived, is a task and achievement of self-creation, and it is one that presupposes certain political conditions of possibility. As liberalism has recognized, it is self-chosen values, actions, and narratives that make autonomous individuality possible. Its traditional valorization of universal freedom and human rights are indicative of a certain understanding of the conditions of both human dignity and the manner in which the individual comes to constitute itself as an agent. Liberalism recognizes that the meaning and dignity of human life are inseparable from the possibilities of autonomous choice that are available to us, possibilities of thought and action without which our lives would not be our own. More so than alternative conceptions of justice, liberalism recognizes – and awards considerable importance to the recognition – that it is in creating and protecting jurisdictions of autonomous choice that governments make it possible for the individual to become the principal author of its life. In insisting on the need to place limits on the rule of collective opinion in governing individual lives, liberalism endeavours to maximize the sphere of autonomy that belongs to the self, for it is in establishing these limits and ensuring spheres of autonomous choice that we guarantee that the integrity of the self will be respected. Liberal principles of justice ensure that a system of rights and obligations will make it possible for the individual to fashion itself in the manner of its choosing within the constraints of recognizing the identical liberty of others. Since it is only in a political order of human rights and constraints on state power that it is possible for the self to become an agent in the full sense of the term, protecting the freedom and integrity of the individual is the foremost responsibility of government in a liberal order. Individual self-creation is possible only in a social order in which all citizens are guaranteed equal and wide spheres of autonomy, and it is only in creating these jurisdictions that we give meaning in practice to the abstract idea of respecting the integrity of the self as the principal author of its existence.

This argument, it must be emphasized, does not presuppose that as an author the individual enjoys anything approaching complete moral independence, if by this is meant the capacity to fashion itself or its ends *ex nihilo* or in a presocial condition (a myth that classical liberalism never needed to assume), but only that the story lines that one lives and the ends that one pursues are subject to revision by the self, and that it is in this way that our lives become authentically our own. We author our lives by authorizing a particular set of commitments in terms of which we shall understand ourselves as moral agents. The notion of self-authorship presupposes the full range of liberal freedoms. The individual becomes the principal author of itself only when it can claim the right both to act as it wishes and (perhaps more importantly) to resist doing what others would have it do, no matter their number.[39] Our lives become our own only within a fabric of self-authorized practices, roles, relationships, and institutions, and it is only insofar as a life is authentically self-chosen that it is properly characterizable as belonging to the self. It is in contributing to its constitution through its actions and self-interpretations, by integrating the disparate episodes of its life history into a unified and non-contradictory framework that the self comes to assume the role of author and fashions a moral identity. Undertaking this process represents perhaps our most basic task as moral agents. It is liberalism alone that places this task at the centre of its concerns in insisting upon the creation of jurisdictions of autonomy in which individuals may fashion a sense of identity in relative freedom from the overbearing reach of state power.

It is one of the ironies of our age that at a time when the sacred masterplots of the past have at last run their course, and have been replaced in part by the ideals of authenticity and individuality, a whole new set of socio-political obstacles to their attainment have also come into being. This set of conditions compounds the difficulty already inherent to the task of becoming an agent and represents the very negation of the political conditions of agency and authentic individuality (a topic to which I shall return in Chapters 5 and 6). At the very time when the discourse of human rights enjoys broad appeal, we have entered a period in which individual agency is threatened by mass society, mass politics, and mass alienation. 'The individual,' as Jaspers writes, '... is today annihilated by the mass-man'[40] or by a configuration of powers, institutions, and socio-economic conditions over which it perceives itself as having very little control. It feels itself 'disempowered,' to use a fashionable expression, by enormous and impersonal structures of economic production, political power, and technological control. As human beings in contemporary society are herded together in an anonymous mass, supplied with their basic needs as these are determined by political structures acting on their behalf and in their name, they are absorbed into an order of technology, rationality, and political power defying ordinary comprehension and in which the individual feels itself lost. Economically, a replaceable cog, scientifically, an object of explanation and technical mastery, and politically, a unit of calculation, organization, and manipulation, the individual in mass society is at a loss even to understand its condition much less to direct its course, with an alienating loss of agency as its main consequence.

That we are living at a time of political, cultural, and economic levelling, a period in which liberties are subordinated to the calculus of social utility and the requirements of a socio-political order of technical efficiency, instrumental rationality, and 'progressive' equality of distribution was already observed by the existential philosophers of the early and middle twentieth century, and it is an observation that still more accurately reflects the conditions of the present time. There being no such thing as levelling up, we have opted to level down in the direction of a common denominator that prizes security over liberty, outcome over opportunity, and sameness over difference. We have chosen dependence on government, uniformity of communication and conduct, and virtual imprisonment in systems of technology in exchange for guarantees that we shall receive our daily bread and the small comforts with which so much of our existence is occupied. 'As soon,' Gabriel Marcel observes, 'as a preoccupation with security begins to dominate human life,' as at present it has, 'the scope of human life itself tends to be diminished. Life, as it were, tends to shrink back on itself, to wither.'[41] The capacity to author our lives is surrendered in permitting ourselves to be made over in the image of technical and mass man. We come to live in a condition at once safe and storyless, one in which meaning and self-understanding elude our grasp and for which we substitute small gratifications and material comfort. As it is no longer possible to surrender to the sacred and comforting mythologies of the past, we surrender to the mythology of technical progress and the instrumentally rational order of the present.

Whether a way out of our current impasse may be found is a matter I take up in Chapter 6. There I examine the consequences for public policy of the philosophy of the self I have articulated in this chapter. First, however, I turn in the following chapter to consider a line of questioning raised by the hermeneutical-pragmatic conception of the self concerning the concept of reason. Since the time of the Greeks, it has been customary for philosophers to speak of the human being as a rational animal, and this tradition is one from which the account offered here does not depart. It does depart, however, from the particular formulation that this hypothesis has received since the Enlightenment. The modern conception of reason as instrumental rationality, a premise that continues to underlie liberal theory particularly in its standard utilitarian and contractarian formulations, is one I propose to reject. If the self is not only an agent but a rational agent, what precisely does this mean, and what sort of departure does this account represent from standard liberal doctrine?

5

Rational Agency

Zoon logon exon: In these words Greek philosophy defined the human being as the being that possesses the *logos*. As beings that 'by nature desire to know,' as Aristotle famously expressed it in the opening sentence of the *Metaphysics*, human beings are endowed with rational natures which constitute our defining characteristic and elevate us above the order of nonhuman nature. Reason has from the time of Plato been understood as a faculty of cognition – the 'eye of the mind' – which ascertains the truth about the world either directly or through the mediation of mental representations.

In modern times the conception of the human being as a rational animal has remained foundational to the disciplines of metaphysics, epistemology, philosophical anthropology, ethics, and politics. Yet the notion of reason in both its theoretical and practical variants underwent in the philosophy of the Enlightenment a profound transformation which continues to underlie the moral and political thought of our time and indeed contemporary culture as a whole. Beginning with Descartes, reason was wedded to the notion of method or technique. Philosophical rationality became a matter of rule-governed inference from foundational principles and its proper abode was the realm of logical propositions, abstract generalities, ahistorical theorizing, and formal methodology. The mathematical and natural sciences became paradigmatic of rationality in general owing to their apparent certainty, methodological rigour, and practical efficacy.

In the specific domains of ethics and politics, reason at the time of the Enlightenment was also circumscribed to the order of the instrumental. Practical rationality was transformed into an entirely technical affair of determining the most efficient means of securing ends either given by nature or subjectively chosen. The foundationalist project of ascertaining first principles and correct means was nowhere more apparent, as we have seen, than in the liberal tradition. Within liberal doctrine the notions of reason, self, and community were similarly translated into the vocabulary of mechanics and instrumentality, and integrated into the original liberal problematic of determining the optimal means of securing individual felicity. Instrumentality became the *sine qua non* of practical reason from the inception of the tradition to its contemporary utilitarian and contractarian formulations. Both variants presupposed the same Enlightenment epistemological ideal of formal certainty and rationality that is entirely ahistorical, procedural, and without presuppositions, and which proceeds in explicit deductive fashion from incontrovertible premises to objective conclusions. In the conventional liberal view, instrumental rationality displays the virtues of methodological objectivity and impartiality in bracketing all controversial assumptions stemming from our particularity and in rising to a higher order of abstraction. Like its theoretical counterpart, practical rationality is conventionally understood in express opposition to intuition, passion, faith, and imagination, all of which values resist incorporation into the order of instrumentality.

Scepticism has arisen in recent decades concerning the foundationalist project in philosophy generally, a scepticism that extends to the standard conception of reason at the heart of conventional liberalism. That practical reason should emulate the mathematical and natural sciences and be narrowed to the instrumentalist and strategic paradigm has come under criticism on grounds of its reductionism, its excessive rationalism and formalism, its ahistorical and acontextual character, and for its rather arid, even bureaucratic, humour. Scientific-technological rationality may not be paradigmatic of reason in general; on the contrary, it may merely be one form of reason among others and perhaps an impoverished form at that: this argument has been suggested by several of the same schools of thought that voiced objections to traditional liberal conceptions of the self, and on related grounds. That there is something more to rational agency than mere cleverness or shrewdness in attaining our ends, and more to rational discourse than the correct application of technique, possesses intuitive plausibility and causes us to inquire into the nature of this something more. What precisely does it mean to speak of the self as a rational being as philosophers since the Greeks have described it, and specifically in the realms of the ethical and the political? The hypothesis defended in this chapter is that the instrumentalist conception of rationality, dear to conventional liberals, must be placed within limits and situated in a broader and more adequate conception of practical reason. This view further develops the conception of the self presented so far and is a key premise in the reconstruction of liberal politics.

The Regime of Instrumentality

Since the Greeks, it has been customary for philosophers to separate theory from practice, yet it was not until the modern Enlightenment that the realm of practice was subordinated entirely to that of theoretical methodology. No sooner had the school of rationalism declared that rationality was to consist in method alone than the founders of liberalism followed suit in subordinating practice and practical reason to method. The age of rationalism that Descartes initiated had succeeded in declaring certainty the sole aim of reasoned inquiry and method the only avenue by which it may be attained.

The dawn of modern science witnessed the introduction of the experimental method based on the mathematical model as a technique for the explanation and prediction of events in the natural world. The method of scientific experimentation was a technique that had met with astonishing success in generating predictions and securing control over the natural environment, and the fact of its practical efficacy in combination with the apparent certainty, necessity, and universality of its conclusions prompted philosophers to follow suit in declaring method the *sine qua non* of rational philosophical discourse. Rationality became restricted to technique. Based on the model of scientific investigation, philosophy was to proceed in the monological fashion of the solitary thinker – *solus ipse* – deriving conclusions either deductively or inductively, but in either case in strictly methodological fashion. Judgments formed were to be verifiable by others employing identical procedures of thought, thereby removing all elements of prejudice and bias from the course of inquiry. In the spirit of modern science Descartes had separated *res cogitans* from *res extensa* and declared the former the source of all certainty and method the means by which it was to be achieved. In declaring the primacy of technique and the dichotomy of subject and object Descartes ushered in an age of modernity which in time would draw all areas of knowledge within the sphere of technique.

In the process the idea of practice was radically transformed from its older and broader Greek connotation as *praxis* to the rarefied notion incorporated from the sciences. In conceiving of the human being as an epistemological subject set in opposition to the world as *res extensa* over which it presided, practice was also transformed by the philosophy of the Enlightenment into an object of technological management. The domain of practice belonged to the environmental pole of the subject-object dichotomy and as such became an object of scientific inquiry and technical mastery. The natural and social environment was a field of resistance for the subject, a collection of objects to be comprehended in thought as a means toward their prediction and control. The idea of practice was transformed into one of applied science and technology as the purview of method was widened still further.

In time no other form of reasoned inquiry was to be characterizable as such unless it could demonstrate its scientific or methodological credentials before a tribunal of epistemic certainty. In its essence, rationality was a truth-seeking and problem-solving capacity which operated *more geometrico* or in accordance with methodological principles comprehended in advance of their application. Within the domain of ethics and politics, rationality was conceived as a quasi-scientific and formal notion, in essence equated with strategic efficiency, operating in abstraction from all normative and historical context. Like scientific rationality, practical rationality professed to operate without presuppositions, from a foundation of incontrovertible first principles, and in accordance with formal procedures which if correctly implemented guaranteed reliable knowledge concerning the nature of justice.

As modernity progressed, methodological and instrumental rationality came to pervade human experience of the world in general and delimited in the most fundamental manner the basic mode in which human existence is understood. Instrumentality became a regime of power/knowledge (to use Michel Foucault's expression) constituting our most fundamental mode of practice and discourse. This regime of knowledge is characterizable by the complete domination of means over ends, theory over practice, quantitative calculus over qualitative perception, and so forth. It produced the technological imperative to expand ever more widely the reach of scientific knowledge and instrumental rationality, and an insatiable demand for systems of technology capable of coordinating means to ends with optimal efficiency. The cardinal intention of dominating the natural environment succeeded in marginalizing nonmethodological and nontechnical modes of thought from the domain of rational discourse. As modernity witnessed the unprecedented reduction of truth to method, rational thought to calculation, and the wholesale expansion of scientific-technological thinking to all areas of human life, technology came to be viewed as an end in itself as means increasingly took on the character of ends. The imperative to invent ever more efficient machinery and means of production to manage ever more perfectly the practical circumstances of human life elevated efficiency and convenience to the status of quasi-ends. Having been banished from rational discourse, ends were displaced by means which in turn became increasingly indistinguishable from ends themselves.

In the twentieth century, the regime of instrumental and scientific-technological rationality was not without critics who had become increasingly troubled by dangers they perceived to be implicit to this mode of knowledge. At a practical level, this mode of rationality produced a dehumanizing effect in direct proportion to its expansion into ever more areas of human life. As these came to be shaped and reshaped in accordance with the latest technology, the meaningful character of human existence had seemed to diminish. This was profoundly disturbing to critics of the instrumentalist paradigm from Max Weber to the Frankfurt School to members of the phenomenological movement. These thinkers carefully documented the growing domination of the instrumentalist paradigm in all regions of experience and culture; for example, the growing mathematization of human knowledge, the extension of the natural scientific model to the study of social life, the bureaucratization of social practices and institutions, the proliferation of rules for the regulation of all aspects of social life, and the widespread disenchantment and loss of meaning which were their consequences. The modern world, Weber observed, had become an 'iron cage' of purposive or means-ends rationality. Both human beings and their world had been made over in its image: the former as egoistic consumers of utility and the latter as a set of resources for, or a field of resistance to, the subject's gratification. Objectification of subject and object alike, and of human thought generally, had become the norm. In modern society, as Max Horkheimer and Theodore Adorno write, 'thinking objectifies itself to become an automatic, self-activating process; an impersonation of the machine that it produces itself so that ultimately the machine can replace it.'[1] An ideal previously unthinkable took shape in the twentieth century that scientific-technological rationality would perhaps one day eliminate the need not only for traditional forms of economic production but indeed for thinking itself; the notion that one day computers may do our thinking for us has dawned on not a few minds in recent decades, while others rightly regard such an idea as a nightmarish scenario of science fictional proportions. The dangerous absence of limits on instrumentalism and methodologism threatens to create – if it has not already – a condition of rational madness encompassing all areas of human experience, knowledge, and culture.

The danger inherent to scientific-technological thought has been remarked on as well by members of the phenomenological movement, in particular Martin Heidegger and Hans-Georg Gadamer. Both figures eloquently remind us of the reduction and idealization that occurred in the philosophy of the Enlightenment culminating in the regime of knowledge that presently holds sway in Western culture and indeed much of the world. That modern technology had far surpassed its original status as a mere instrument for the prediction, control, and manipulation of entities to become an all-pervasive conception of the world was correctly observed by Heidegger.[2] For Heidegger modern technology is not a means but a way in which the 'truth of being' is revealed, comparable in this respect to a worldview or a language. It constitutes our dominant mode of understanding the natural and social world and indeed of ourselves, one in which subject and object are radically opposed while the world of entities is revealed entirely in the mode of instrumentality or in terms of its utility for the subject. The world assumes the form of a 'picture' or an enframed representation presided over and placed at the disposal of the cognizing subject. Conceived scientifically, the human world loses its character as lifeworld (*Lebenswelt*) or as an enveloping context of significance, language, and practice in which human beings 'dwell' and have their being, and becomes an idealized construction, a collection of resources for human disposal. The subject itself is reduced to a functionary of the technical apparatus, a resource manning the machinery for an uncertain purpose. The danger of which Heidegger speaks is that modern science-technology (no longer two distinct items) may, and perhaps already has, become the only mode in which phenomena are revealed and that every other mode of revealing will be abjured at the cost of losing a more primordial and authentic relation to the world, oneself, and other human beings. In tending toward totalization, modern science-technology reaches into areas of human existence which exceed its capacity and with which technical thinking is ill-equipped to cope.

Continuing Heidegger's observations, Gadamer has recounted the manner in which modernity proclaimed science-technology the *sine qua non* of rational inquiry and reduced the domain of truth to the methodologically verifiable.[3] Method became the sole avenue to truth, relegating all other modes of discourse to the status of illusion and misunderstanding. The need for countervailing modes of thought to the reigning scientism and methodologism of our age has become imperative and motivated both of these thinkers to speak anew of the truth of art and aesthetic experience, of practice and the capacities of practical (non-methodological) reflection. That science-technology cannot substitute for philosophical reflection and that there are modes of understanding and of truth that transcend the order of technique has been a prominent theme in the works of these and other phenomenological writers.

The regime of instrumentality which has governed the sciences and humanities had its origins in the natural sciences whereupon it spread to the humanities and social sciences. The latter, anxious to establish their credentials as thoroughgoing sciences, sought to mirror as closely as possible the procedures and categories of the natural sciences. Appearing to have found a home in the field of economics in particular, instrumental rationality was believed to map successfully the general conditions of the marketplace as well as the behaviour of individual economic agents, all of whom were assumed to comport themselves in the fashion of Hobbesian maximizers. Other human sciences followed suit in importing wholesale assumptions and methods from the natural sciences in an abiding spirit of positivistic rationalism. Recent years have witnessed a growing discontent in the social sciences with rationalistic modes of thought, and debate concerning the conception of rationality that properly presides over these disciplines is ongoing.

Presently no field of knowledge is untouched by the all-embracing spirit of science-technology stemming from the Enlightenment. Philosophy, of course, has been the most profoundly affected of the humanistic 'disciplines.' There rationality has assumed methodologistic and instrumentalist forms, nowhere more so than in moral and political philosophy (and there nowhere more so than in liberal doctrine). Both the form and content of modern philosophy are thoroughly pervaded by technical modes of thought. The formalistic and foundationalist project stemming from Hobbes has directed the course of modern normative theory to the present day, although discontent with the foundationalist paradigm has become increasingly widespread in recent years. In conventional approaches the principal task of ethical and political theorizing is to determine what is required of us by subsuming particular cases under general principles in a meticulous and rule-governed fashion. Conflicts are to be resolved through the conscientious application of decision procedures formulated in advance of particular cases, principles that function as major premises in a practical syllogism. In each instance one proceeds in accordance with formal algorithms and generates a well-founded judgment about the course of action to be pursued, eliminating any significant reliance on the personal responsibility of the judging subject. Rational choice, particularly within the contractarian and utilitarian traditions, is a matter of placing the particular case under the tutelage of fixed principles and is assimilated to mathematical and scientific models of derivation and quantitative calculus.

The general scientification and technification of cultural discourses is a leading cause of their present deterioration. The ideal of scientificity is so thoroughly ensconced in all areas of contemporary discourse, both academic and nonacademic, that qualitative discriminations are presently viewed with unprecedented suspicion along with the capacities of practical judgment and reflection, perception and imagination, and the practice of ordinary (rhetorical) dialogue. Nontechnical communication aimed at persuasion and consensus rather than methodological veracity is commonly viewed as a subaltern mode of discourse, prompting scholarship (or 'research') always to display its scientific credentials and often to overplay them amid the drive for technical perfection. Within the discipline of philosophy technical disputes and micro-disputes beyond the comprehension and interest of the nonspecialist have long been the norm. That philosophical scholarship normally addresses itself to a small audience of specialists is only partially explained by the legitimate imperative toward precision and clarity to which most of us subscribe. The impression, as mistaken as it is widespread, that our discipline is a merely technical one of hair-splitting minutiae rather than the classical love of wisdom which we assure our students it is, and the mixture of bewilderment and indifference that results, is not wholly incomprehensible. That philosophical language should become petrified into technical vocabularies is itself nothing new in the history of our discipline, yet its modern condition of quasi-scientific technicity is certainly without historical precedent, nor is this fact entirely a cause for celebration. Contemporary schools of thought that claim to have attained a degree of clarity and rigour superior to what was previously thought possible often pay a stiff price for their technical virtuosity. Amid the zeal for analytical rigour a certain absence of profundity, subtlety, complexity, imagination, and genuine human relevance is frequently detectable. Technically competent yet insipid and voiceless prose currently fills our libraries, a fact that has understandably prompted Heidegger to pose the question anew, 'what is called thinking?' and to lament its decline in the age of science-technology.

That 'thinking,' perhaps even 'wisdom,' should take a back seat to technical precision was already lamented a century ago by William James who regretted the tendency of philosophers in his time to subordinate the pursuit of knowledge to the fear of drawing mistaken inferences. Descartes's evil demon haunts us still, compelling us to seek metaphysical comfort in the arms of science-technology, or failing this, in the arms of a methodology imperfectly modelled on scientific rationality. The mantle of scientific respectability is currently, and has long been, eagerly contested in numerous areas of philosophy, including in the areas in which one would least expect to find it – within what the Greeks called 'practical philosophy.' The study of politics is steadily encroached on by political 'science,' as is evaluative utterance by description – or, more disturbingly, by straightforwardly evaluative utterance masquerading as scientifically neutral description, a common and ultimately dangerous phenomenon. (The danger stems from the dogmatizing tendency associated with claims to scientific authority and objectivity within what are primarily normative fields of discourse. One is easily tempted into the belief that the study of politics, or indeed social phenomena generally, could be delivered from the contested and troubled land of evaluative judgment to the promised land of scientifically neutral description.)

Whether in the final analysis the present quasi-scientific technification of philosophical language will deepen our knowledge of human existence or on the contrary render it capable only of grazing its surface (albeit a surface which is comprehended with near certainty) is perhaps a matter for which it is too soon to pronounce a verdict, although ample room for skepticism exists particularly within the field of practical philosophy. Whether we shall ever ascertain conclusively what the instrumentally 'rational chooser' would decide on, and if so whether such knowledge would possess any significance whatever to our understanding of morality, invites a sceptical response. What disappears amid the technical virtuosity of much contemporary theory, best represented in game theoretic contractarianism, are ordinary capacities of moral discernment and critical reflection, the perception of significance and an understanding of the manner in which our practices constitute our identity as moral agents. As 'the philosopher disappears into the technician,'[4] depth of insight and understanding are exchanged for mere micro-reflection and technical 'correctness.' Reason and reasonableness disappear into 'rationality.'

The deterioration of communication brought about by technification – whether scientific, instrumental, or methodological – is detectable within not only academic discourse but in various cultural discourses as well, including ordinary public debate regarding morality and politics wherein the language of utility has become dominant. That deliberation could involve something other than a merely quantitative calculus of utility, a 'tallying of preferences,' or a 'weighing of pros and cons' appears to many minds an utterly mysterious proposition (unless, of course, one has recourse to religious language, the only perceived alternative to technical seriousness). The view that scientific-technological rationality is paradigmatic of human reason in general, and that practical reasoning in essence is instrumental rationality alone, has pervaded all aspects of contemporary culture. This is observable from the proliferation of technical manuals governing virtually all aspects of human life, from the technological machinery and gadgets which increasingly control our lives to diet and exercise, personal relationships, sex and psychological well-being, each of which has become a matter for which one need only identify the proper technique to determine its 'proper functioning' and 'optimal utility.' Each of these areas of human life is a 'problem' in need of a 'solution,' where the latter is understood as an identification of correct means to fixed ends. Increasingly one relies on learned treatises and mass produced manuals setting forth how the experts have decreed one must conduct one's affairs. The sphere of personal responsibility is restricted to the choice of which expert's advice to rely on and which technique to employ.

The regime of instrumentality is observable as well in the formation of public opinion, particularly that which is politically motivated. As Gadamer observes; 'The modern technology of information has made available possibilities that make necessary the selection of information to a heretofore unimaginable extent. Any selection, however, means acting in the name of everyone else; that cannot be otherwise. Whoever does the selecting withholds something.'[5] Public officials, academics, news editors, and other 'public opinion makers' reveal and conceal in the same gesture, disclosing and withholding 'information' in accordance with particular interests and competing amongst themselves for the privilege of putting the final and authoritative 'spin' on whatever matter is before its view. The manufacturing of public opinion through 'educational' or 'information campaigns' designed to control the information that reaches public view is a disturbing reality of the present day, particularly when practiced by governments acting ostensibly on behalf of the citizenry and in their name. Informational technologies make possible a type of manipulation never before possible in addition to imposing an unprecedented uniformity of communication at various levels of public discourse.

The extension of technical knowledge from the realm of natural science to the social sciences and humanities, or from the study of natural to social phenomena generally, is accompanied at the institutional level by wholesale additions to state planning and rationalization efforts. Once comprehended scientifically, social forces invariably become subject to direct planning by political, economic, and other institutions. This is due to a logic inherent in all technological modes of knowledge, an imperative to secure increasingly efficient means toward ends which are given in advance and virtually immune to reflection (except, of course, to purely technical reflection concerned with the arrangement of ends which will guarantee their optimal enjoyment). As the march toward scientific totalization advances, the life of the individual becomes subject to ever-increasing rationalization: governments charged with the task of guaranteeing human happiness (not its pursuit but its attainment) embark on projects of social engineering directed to this end; the calculation of social utility is extended without limit to all areas of human life, relegating all nonutilitarian and qualitative discourse to the margins of rational thought; economic activity becomes subject to state intervention and regulation extending beyond the prevention of harm to the micro-management of prosperity; the growth in scientific knowledge in combination with the division of labour produces micro-experts whose sphere of competence is restricted to the performance of a narrow range of tasks; the proliferation of professional schools produces graduates whose horizons of reflection are restricted to the single-minded pursuit of technical competence and profit. Individuality becomes absorbed into the bureaucratic machinery of government, institutions, and corporations which paradoxically seem to demand more and more of us in their pursuit of optimal efficiency while providing less and less. The regime of instrumentality reaches into every corner of human existence, increasingly rendering the life of the individual the planned outcome of rationalization procedures, social engineering projects, information campaigns, and a thousand deployments of power/knowledge having the combined effect of enclosing the individual within an 'iron cage' of technical rationality. Old liberal scepticism about the possibility of determining authoritatively the contours of the good life is increasingly replaced with new liberal optimism fortified by scientific knowledge.

That few obstacles appear to stand in the way of the complete reign of instrumentality is one of the principal dangers of our time. The subordination of liberal values to the requirements of the technical apparatus and the calculus of social utility – both offsprings of liberalism – currently represents the most formidable obstacle to individual freedom in Western industrialized societies. The individual has been conscripted into an administrative order wherein the contents of its being are channelled into an ever-expanding series of files documenting and governing nearly all aspects of its existence from the economic to the medical, judicial, educational, familial, and so on. Presuming to know the will of the individual, institutions – by no means limited to the state – determine on the individual's behalf the correct means of securing its ends, relieving the individual of the burden and responsibility of choice. The danger exceeds that spoken of by Heidegger to concern the very survival of liberty itself. The danger is more pronounced in proportion to its invisibility. Within this regime of thought liberty is surrendered not 'at one fell swoop' but in minute increments none of which alone constitutes a significant threat to autonomy and each of which promises some small gratification or convenience. Nor is liberty delivered over to a centralized and tyrannical state but to a vast network of administrators, technicians, regulators, and experts, all acting on the individual's behalf and with a presumed knowledge both of the latter's ends and of the correct means thereto. The right of choice is surrendered to a greater utility, not only the common welfare (usually conceived in narrow economic terms) but the individual's own welfare (also conceived in narrow economic terms), be it economic stability or employment security. The right and capacity of self-authorship are surrendered at once voluntarily and unwittingly, a condition made possible by the totalization of instrumental rationality and the narrowing of horizons which it brings about.

In accordance with the logic of technical rationality, liberty and all other moral values are translated into the vocabulary of utility, evaluated in terms of their effects, and effectively subordinated to the requirements of the order of instrumentality itself. Like all values, freedom is conceivable exclusively as either a means or an end; not being an end (except perhaps for eccentrics), the only question concerns whether it is an efficient or inefficient means; being less efficient than social planning measures undertaken on the individual's behalf, liberties become contingent privileges and in the end inefficiencies to be eliminated for the individual's benefit and the benefit of the social order. Individual liberty becomes an unpredictable and unstable variable in the organization of mass society, a wild card and an anachronism working in contravention to rational organization and tending toward anarchy (the political counterpart to irrationality).

What becomes of the self in this scheme of things is nothing so manifestly nightmarish as that depicted in George Orwell's fictional scenario.

The individual does not become a sacrificial object for a state of monstrous dimension and intent. Instead it becomes a 'well-adjusted' and normalized being, accommodating to whatever comes its way, well-informed if not wise, and comfortable if uninspired. While its life unfolds according to predictable patterns and is highly conformist, it is not unhappy for all that, nor is its existence manifestly oppressed. Its freedom having been surrendered voluntarily, even rationally, it has no centralized authority or institution to hold responsible for the discontent it experiences. Its discontent is typically directed toward the very institutions to which it has relinquished so much of its freedom, yet not on account of any restriction in choices but the perceived extent of return on its investment. It imagines that others are gaining a greater share of utility and that it is falling behind in the competition for resources and consumer goods. If permanently suspicious about whether it has received its just (meaning equal) share in the distribution of social goods, in other respects it remains largely content with its fate on grounds of the security and predictability which the order of instrumentality makes possible.

Self-estrangement and a loss of authentic identity is the price paid by the self which allows itself to be absorbed into the instrumentalist order. It settles into a condition of normalized dependency while its sphere of expression as an individuated agent is progressively circumscribed. Its thoughts and actions are increasingly mechanized and routinized. It searches for rules in all cases of uncertainty, and it is sure to find them provided it fills out all the necessary forms and directs them to the relevant headquarters of administration. With others the self becomes absorbed into a mass of human 'resources' awaiting orders to follow and techniques to implement, or into what Heidegger calls the 'standing-reserve': 'Everywhere everything is ordered to stand by, to be immediately at hand, indeed to stand there just so that it may be on call for a further ordering.'⁶ The individual is transformed into a resource ready to be pressed into service at a moment's notice. If it fails in its duties it is readily replaced by another 'unit' from the vast 'labour supply' eager to replace it. A replaceable cog, it is swallowed up into the technical apparatus, uncertain whether it is manning the apparatus or a part of it.

Since it is the nature of technique to transform all qualitative into quantitative considerations and to deal exclusively with generalities, regularities, averages, probabilities, and other quantifiable abstractions, the individual itself is stripped of all elements of recalcitrant subjectivity which refuse to conform with statistical norms. It learns to separate normalcy from deviancy, proper functioning from disorder, equilibrium from disruption, and to identify rationality exclusively with the former. If the individual is to be a rational agent and secure its preferences with optimal efficiency, its self-understanding must be transformed to suit the requirements of the instrumentalist order. It must become the objectified abstraction of the scientific technologist: in the marketplace it must become the egoistic consumer of utility of economic science; in the workplace it becomes an efficient resource and profit-maximizing service provider; in its personal relations it searches for objects capable of satisfying its emotional needs; in its political dealings it holds a share in a massive voting block involved in permanent competition with other blocks for a larger share of power and government services; when it is sick it visits the physician from whom it receives a regimen of instructions and pharmaceuticals to which it dutifully submits; and if at the end of the day it is unhappy it visits the psychiatrist's office where it learns new ways of being normal.

It is not to be wondered at if in this storyless condition the self finally becomes estranged from itself. As all reasoned utterance and action are conscripted into a regime of instrumentality and confined to the search for efficient strategies for adjusting means to ends, the self which comprehends itself as a rational being is estranged from its own identity. Self-understanding is either confined to the thin one-dimensionality of rationalist categories or driven out into the dark night of the irrational. Either the self possesses a secure and scientific knowledge of itself or it is a construction of arbitrary fancy; either form without substance or substance without form. If the rational self has achieved remarkable success in mastering its environment and gratifying its desires, still it does not understand who it is nor the meaning of its existence. Its identity is its function in the scientific-technological order while the meaning of its existence is the consumption of utility. Hobbes's belief in the self as an appetitive machine has made it so.

One of the principal dangers of modern life, in light of which many others may be understood, is the restriction of human reason to the paradigm of instrumentality carried over from the natural and mathematical sciences. The present domination of technique over virtually all aspects of human life threatens to restrict our horizons of reflection as ordinary capacities of perception, practical judgment, understanding, imagination, and deliberation are ceded to the myth of expertise. The sphere of personal autonomy will continue to diminish as the capacity to decide with freedom and responsibility is progressively unlearned. The individual will become a normalized and insipid nonagent, anxious to follow orders provided only that they are issued by trained professionals and successfully conduct the individual to its unreflective ends.

Communicative Reason

Discontent with this general state of affairs or with particular aspects thereof has prompted a variety of thinkers to undertake a more profound questioning of the concepts of reason and rational agency. That the concept of the *logos* should be so thoroughly reduced from its original Greek connotation to the methodologistic and instrumentalist conception that we have inherited from the thought of the Enlightenment – including classical liberal doctrine – is viewed with regret by several contemporary schools. That the concept of reason should be conceived analytically in close connection with science, method, and truth is itself unobjectionable, yet that it should be so entirely reduced to the order of technique impoverishes not only the concept of reason but – for as long as the human being continues to be spoken of as *zoon logon exon* – our understanding of human existence itself, and most especially of moral experience. There is considerably more to the hypothesis that the defining characteristic of human beings is their reason than the modern assertion that they are capable of shrewdly appeasing their desires. It is the reductionism of the traditional liberal conception of moral reason as instrumental rationality and more generally of the methodologism brought into being by the Enlightenment that must at long last be put aside in making room for a broader and more satisfactory conception of rational agency.

Proposing to conceive of reason in a more Greek manner than is customary in modern thought, Heidegger drew attention to the essential connection of *logos* or reason with language. Not only, or even primarily, a cognizing faculty dwelling in the region of propositional knowledge and logical inference, *logos* means language, discourse, a bringing to light, and an offering of accounts. It is an affair of intersubjectivity no less than of inference, and of Being itself more than formal reckoning. Since understanding is the person's most fundamental mode of comportment and of being-in-the-world, *logos* names both the ground of understanding and the linguistic articulation which brings the phenomena to light. Reason is less an affair of rule-governed inference than one of language itself; it is fundamentally a saying which allows entities to be brought into view. Rationality is inseparable from linguisticality, as phenomenologists and hermeneuticists since Heidegger have remarked.

In particular, Karl Jaspers, Hans-Georg Gadamer, and Jürgen Habermas have in different ways argued for not only the circumscription of methodological and instrumental rationality but an alternative conception of reason. This is communicative reason or reason as 'boundless communication.'[7] It is as a practice of open and undogmatic communication, an unending process of questioning and responding, interpretation and reinterpretation, justification and critique, that the hermeneutically rich concept of reason is most adequately conceived. Reason is inseparable from the will to reason, or the 'boundless will to communicate'[8] characteristic of the cooperative search for reasons. Reasoned utterance searches for persuasive grounds, ultimately for accounts that will be found compelling by all speakers – not only those claiming the title of experts but all inquirers of ordinary capacity interested in a given field of investigation. Reason is opposed less to the passions or intuition than to dogmatism in all its forms – including the scientific and quasi-scientific. It stands in opposition to all self-certainty which would assert the right to bring the course of inquiry to an end on account of a speaker's uncontroverted possession of the truth.

A condition of any properly philosophical account of reason or rationality is that it is capable of saving the phenomena by incorporating the multiplicity of connotations issuing from this hermeneutically rich concept. It must encompass not only the technical connotations of reason in the sciences and humanities but its nontechnical, nonmethodological, and noninstrumental connotations found in ordinary language. It must explain why we speak of not only rationality as the proper employment of technique but reasonableness, having good reasons, standing to reason, and so on. As well, a philosophical account of reason must explain why we continue to speak of reason as the defining characteristic of human existence. Here the reductionism of technical and instrumental rationality fails. In insisting on the reduction of reason to technique, the paradigm of instrumentality brackets precisely that which constitutes the defining trait of human existence. To speak of the person as a rational being means far more than that it is able to follow procedures in the pursuit of ends, whether the ends be happiness or truth. It is to speak of reason in a far broader connotation as at once a capacity of cognition, a disposition, an attitude of mind, and perhaps a virtue as well.

The rational or reasonable person is characterized by a disposition to believe and act with good reasons, entertain alternative reasons, exercise sound judgment, be open-minded, fair, and mindful of proportion. The rational subject is no less the *phronimos* of Aristotle than the utility maximizer of Hobbes, the self-certain ratiocinator of Descartes, or the technician of modern science. Its overriding characteristic is openness to communication and learning, a willingness to engage in argumentation, provide reasons, justify, criticize, question, and reexamine all matters before it. The communicatively rational speaker is prepared to have its most heartfelt convictions called into question and learn from opposing perspectives. It is prepared to test its convictions in dialogue with others and admit its own fallibility. Never certain of the ground on which it stands, its beliefs are contingent and revisable in light of future inquiry. While such inquiry may generate consensus on occasion, or even succeed in fashioning a true belief, in principle it remains open to further inquiry. This is the case not only in order that false beliefs may be demonstrated as such but in recognition of the possibility of future discovery and modification of what currently passes for the truth. Its discoveries are provisional and its consensus temporary. It does not rest secure with its methods, themselves inventions of a previous time, or with the conclusions reached thereby but subjects these conclusions to a test of reasonableness beyond the scope of technique. It is characteristic even of the rational technician not to follow methods wherever they may lead and let the chips fall where they may, but to inquire whether conclusions methodologically derived pass a test of reasonableness – whether they 'ring true' or cohere with our sense of what is reasonable, probable, or fitting. The most technically scrupulous argument or experiment does not pass for truth before it has been taken up into intersubjectivity and pronounced true by a body of competent and independent inquirers.

Rationality in its broadest and most philosophically adequate connotation is inseparable from the practice of communicative understanding the primary exemplar of which, as Gadamer has argued, is the Platonic dialogue. Here the course of inquiry is a cooperative search for compelling arguments and reasoned consensus unconstrained by force. No speaker enjoys special authority within the conversation or privileged status on account of technical mastery or expertise unavailable to other interlocutors. On the contrary, all speakers share the burden of expressing their views and defending them in confrontation with other views. The possession of expertise or technical mastery never exempts one from the need for conversation; at most it narrows the field of competent interlocutors without limiting the need for argumentation aimed at persuasion. The discourses of expertise are no less contested than ordinary discourses. In no case does a speaker rise above the fray of rhetorical communication. At most, it moves within a relatively small circle of conversational partners, none of whom enjoys the privilege of the last word.

So conceived, rationality is an essentially agonistic and rhetorical affair, one aimed at consensus yet a consensus that is never altogether final. As Jaspers states: 'Reason has no assured stability: it is constantly on the move. Once it has gained a position it presses on to criticize it and is therefore opposed to the tendency to free oneself from the necessity for all further thought by once and for all accepting irrevocably fixed ideas.'[9] Reason's antithesis is not only the unthinking dogmatism which refuses all challenges to its beliefs but the self-certain methodologism which, convinced of the soundness of the techniques it employs and the correctness of inferences generated thereby, refuses all further conversation except as a means of educating less informed minds. In all unreason a note of intellectual arrogance is visible, a disregard of the limits of knowledge and due proportion. As Jaspers continues, reason 'demands a careful thoughtfulness – it is therefore the opposite of mere capriciousness. It leads to self-knowledge and knowledge of limits, and therefore to humility – and it is opposed to intellectual arrogance. It demands a constant listening and it is able to wait – it is therefore opposed to the narrowing furies of the passions. Thus reason works itself out of the chains of dogma, of caprice, of arrogance, of passion.'[10]

Among the principal conditions of rationality so conceived are the renunciation of force, a willingness to be led by the dialogue itself, and a degree of good will. The renunciation of force is a refusal of not only physical violence but subtler expressions of power as well. This is the power spoken of by Foucault – the power of scientific knowledge, technical expertise, and administrative authority. It is the form of utterance that is forever setting itself up as an epistemic court of appeal on grounds of its scientific credentials or technical expertise. The final authority in all conversation, it forever has the last word and inspects the credentials of its would-be interlocutors.[11] Communicative reason necessitates a renunciation of dogmatism in all its forms, a willingness to give oneself over to the dialectical movement of conversation which Gadamer identifies with Platonic dialogue (or those Platonic dialogues, at any rate, in which Socrates does not merely hold court amid a chorus of enthusiastic yeses). It requires as well (as Gadamer also points out) a measure of good will toward one's interlocutors, a recognition of their rationality and of the possibility of their being in the right.

In addition to Jaspers, Gadamer, and several other phenomenological and hermeneutical thinkers following in their wake,[12] Habermas, the most notable second generation member of the Frankfurt School of social criticism, has also defended a formulation of communicative rationality. A distinction fundamental to Habermas's social theory is that between instrumental/strategic and communicative action; the former being action that is oriented toward success in attaining personal ends and the latter being that which is oriented toward reaching an understanding or consensus concerning an object of investigation.[13] Both modes of action and utterance contain conceptions of rationality proper to them, yet the instrumental/strategic variety is parasitic upon the rationality implicit to communicative action. The latter mode of action and language use Habermas asserts to be the 'original' mode of which the strategic is derivative. Reaching an understanding through noncoercive means is the implicit *telos* of human language itself while strategic and instrumental modes of utterance represent departures from this original mode, ones in which the conditions of cooperation, freedom, and equality are suspended and replaced with egoistic calculations. Agreement, for Habermas, is the *telos* inherent in communicative action although it falls short of constituting a philosophical criterion of truth owing to the permanent threat of ideological distortion in social and discursive practices.

While Habermas's formulation of communicative rationality aligns itself closely with the doctrines of metaethical formalism and Piagetian-Kohlbergian evolutionary theory, the formulation of communicative reason that receives support here commits itself to neither of these doctrines but situates itself in the tradition of nonformalist ethics stemming from Aristotle. Communicative or dialogical reason, in the interpretation I propose, employs principles in its deliberations, yet it is distinguished categorically from the rule-governed rationality of both conventional (utilitarian and contractarian) liberalism and Habermasian social theory. This conception of rational discourse is not a technical rationality governed by formal methods and modelled on the applied sciences but a rationality that relies on the freedom and responsibility of the individual speaker. The scope of technique it delimits to specific areas of 'problem solving' while recognizing that not all moral and political discourse fits the problem-solving paradigm. It affords a central role to ordinary capacities of practical judgment, critical reflection and interpretation that do not conform to formalist models.

Communicative reason is the reason inherent to ordinary communication. It draws on the reflective competence of all interested discussants, including the practical judgment or *phronesis* which, because it does not employ formal decision procedures, does not permit expertise.

Much of practical reasoning – that which does not fit the problem-solving, utility-maximizing paradigm – is dependent on this ordinary and frequently misunderstood capacity. Practical judgment permits neither certainty nor expertise but depends on the perceptiveness and responsibility of the individual. It is neither a mode of demonstrative knowledge nor a privileged insight into deep moral truths, yet neither is it merely a feeling or an arbitrary act of decision. Rather it is a reflective act of reasoning capable of perceiving what is required and responding appropriately. It is a mode of interpreting and reasoning about particular cases with the aid of principles, a subsuming of particulars under universals in accordance with reasons (hence a mode of judgment), while falling outside the domain of deduction and induction. The appeal to practical judgment does not relieve one of the responsibility of justification but the kind of justification it produces does not compel the assent of an interlocutor or constitute a proof. The reasons it produces are constituted as reasons not on account of a general rule but on account of particular features of the case at hand. Practical reasoning is concerned with particulars, and it is particular features of a case that are appealed to in efforts at justification.[14]

Practical judgment is conceived as a hermeneutic skill in mediating between universal and particular without following rules. It detects the salient features of moral contexts and fashions an understanding of what justice requires by comprehending the particular case together with the relevant universal. Both universal and particular are mediated by the other; they are codetermined. The perception of a given case is mediated by a principle; it is interpreted as an issue of free speech, for instance, or as a violation of a human right, an act of friendship, of charity, etc. The particular is subsumed under a universal, and it is as an instance of this that the act is perceived. If the perception of a particular case is mediated by a principle, however, so too is the latter mediated by the former. The principle illuminates the individual case in the same hermeneutic act in which the latter illuminates (or determines the content of) the principle itself. This is a dialectical process of mutual illumination. Neither is immediately given in moral consciousness. Both universal and particular are determined in their being in the act of judging.

Practical judgment is the capacity that determines the manner in which this reciprocal illumination occurs. It is the skillful exercise of moving from universal to particular and back again, of determining both the principle to be applied and the manner of its application. As a skill,[15] it does not reach conclusions deductively but aims at reconciling universal and particular in a way that is suitable or reasonable given as comprehensive an understanding of the case as is possible. With Aristotle the vagueness of speaking of what is fitting, what is appropriate under the circumstances, or what the situation requires is ineluctable for the reason that there is no set of necessary and sufficient conditions governing the abstract content of these expressions nor a rule for determining the proper reconciliation of universal and particular. One applies normative principles not in the formalistic manner of the technician but in a manner that tailors them to the requirements of the individual case and with careful attention to extenuating factors which may cause a revision in judgment. Good judgment is an art that tailors a principle to the complexity of a particular case without criteria of appropriateness.

The capacities of critical reflection and judgment draw on tacit understandings of both ourselves and the traditions in which we are situated. A sense of the moral life of the community always informs our practices of reflection. Judgments are formed within a lifeworld and do not represent the exclusive concern of the individual. In determining the fit between universals and particulars, we bring our judgments into conversation with others and in the process of hermeneutic dialogue our perceptions are modified and refined. As the conversation continues, the pool of shared experience enlarges and practical judgments become less idiosyncratic and increasingly intersubjective. While consensus is not a formal criterion of truth in matters of morality, practical judgment endeavours to achieve as much intersubjective agreement as it can within the dialogical process and is ultimately inseparable from the practice of dialogue itself.

If rationality takes up neither the neutral perspective of formalist ethics nor the scientific standpoint of the nonparticipant observer, it must assume the finite perspective of real-world participants within the dialogical process. The rational agent is a situated agent whose distance from the practices and institutions which make up its lifeworld is never complete. No appeal to abstract technique enables it to attain the standpoint of unconditioned objectivity. It assumes a participatory perspective from which it is drawn into engagement with its lifeworld. Reason brings the individual into critical engagement with whatever matters are before it. This is a mode of engagement that is never without an element of distance, however limited.

Reason is properly understood in dialectical fashion as a critical engagement with one's lifeworld. As a mode of engagement it is contrasted with the habit of mind that takes all matters as settled and declines to enter into conversation for this reason. Communicative engagement is the turn of mind that refuses all reticence, which takes positions, provides accounts, entertains different points of view, and so on. Distance takes a backward step from such engagement and operates in a critical space wherein one perceives the contingency of human affairs and how what is could be otherwise. To the combativeness of communicative engagement, it contrasts a reflective and partial withdrawal into the realm of the abstract and theoretical. Communicative reason is comprised of these two complementary elements, each of which deteriorates into unreason when divorced from the other. Engagement without critical distance deteriorates into mere chatter. This is the chatter of the dogmatist whose unreflective naivety is a source of reassurance, who speaks only to enlighten or to pontificate, and who is largely content with conventional modes of thought and action. This is the irrationality of the unimaginative mind, the 'true believer' who refuses to look up from what is immediately before its eyes or to entertain the prospect that its cherished conventions are fundamentally in error. Distance without engagement also deteriorates into dogmatism, albeit a different kind. This is the dogmatism of the self-certain methodologist who, convinced of the soundness of his or her technique, sets about categorizing, mapping, explaining, and legislating the universe from an imagined transcendental standpoint. This is the irrationality or hyper-rationality of the Cartesian rationalist, the Hobbesian state of nature theorist, or the expertocratic mind which, having all its epistemic papers in order, pretends to operate entirely above the fray of ordinary communication. For such communication, which it dismisses with an air of superciliousness as mere rhetoric and gesticulation, it substitutes monological techniques which it sets up as the final court of appeal for all reasoned utterance.

Dialogical reason forswears both varieties of dogmatism by preserving and negotiating the tension between communicative engagement and theoretical distance. It escapes the narrowing of horizons associated with mere chatter as well as the rationalist excesses of methodologism. While it is never able to bracket entirely the passions, interests, particularities, and power relations endemic to ordinary communication, it insists on placing as many of these on the table as possible. The capacity of these factors to distort conversation stems primarily not from their mere presence in dialogue, as is often supposed, but their invisibility or their capacity to operate behind the back of discussants. Their presence in discursive practices has motivated philosophers since Plato to attempt to sanitize language by ridding it of 'sophistry,' 'rhetoric,' and 'ideology' in their multiple forms.[16] In modern times such efforts have largely been conducted with the assistance of formal methodology which pretends to abstract reason from all the contingencies, prejudices, particularities, uncertainties, passions, and relations of power endemic to ordinary dialogue while putting a safe distance between itself and all nonexpert and nontechnical discourses. Supposing each of these to be eliminable features of human language, philosophers have long sought their removal. Yet the possibilities, first, that these factors are not removable and, second, that they do not stand in need of removal, were this possible, warrant serious consideration. In different ways, nonfoundationalists, nonformalists, rhetoricians, phenomenologists, hermeneuticists, critical theorists, pragmatists, postmodernists, and others have begun to investigate the prospect of rational discourse that would not bracket these elements of ordinary communication but place them on the table alongside the ostensible object of investigation. On the premise that their power to distort and to conceal depends on their capacity to affect the course of inquiry by operating behind the backs of speakers, what is required of rational dialogue is not their total removal but their placement in full view of the participants. The hold they exercise on consciousness is not always dissolvable, yet when it is, it is not their elimination but their illumination that makes this possible. When it is not, holding these distorting factors in the open at the very least minimizes their capacity to persuade and dampens their appeal. Communicative reason involves less the suspension of interests, passions, and so on, from conversation than their illumination and confrontation with opposing interests and passions for the reason that it is in such open confrontation that their hold on dogmatic consciousness loosens and new possibilities of thought emerge. Advances in knowledge require (as J. S. Mill realized) an open space of ideas wherein novel utterances may emerge, an old consensus may be reaffirmed or dissolved in favour of a new consensus, or hypotheses may be tested and refined. They require a free market of ideas rather than a priori restrictions on what may be said, in what manner, and by whom.

The philosopher's disdain for the sophistry and petty interests which are so much a part of ordinary dialogue is certainly not misplaced, particularly when these masquerade (as they so often do) as objectivity and impartiality; yet they are not remedied by complete banishment from conversation but through detection and exposure within the dialogical process. Their remedy is not enforced silence but the shame that accompanies exposure. This is the commonplace phenomenon of the self-certain dogmatist or the posturing sophist being forced to admit that their premises are without justification, that their methods are patent falsehoods, and that their hypotheses are entirely at the disposal of the will to power. In this way conversational distortions are detected and set right rather than through rationalistic retreats into transcendental theorizing, formalist methodology, or an ideal speech situation. Human dialogue may never become as disinterested, power-free, sanitized, and well-orchestrated as the rationalist temper dreams it might, but it may be fostered by an undogmatic reasonableness which would offer accounts, entertain conflicting points of view, and in general strive to put as many ideas on the table as it can. It can encourage the conversational virtues of open-mindedness, freedom, civility, equality, recognition, tenacity, and in doing so remove the conditions that make for distortion. Although communicative reason may not legislate in advance the content of expression, it can demand that all the interests, passions, and power relations which make for conversational distortions account for themselves by providing reasoned justifications for the (usually special) status and rights they demand for themselves. It can detect the presence of such distortions, question their legitimacy, challenge all dogmatism and reticence, and prevent speakers from asserting a right to have the last word or to pull rank by virtue of privileged insight.

The conception of rational agency and discourse one adopts is not an apolitical choice, nor is it without implications for practice. Dialogical rationality is properly describable as a liberal theory since it is the same principles of individual responsibility, freedom, equality, civility, and recognition which liberal politics enshrines in law that are here placed at the centre of a conception of rational discourse and agency. A liberal order is the political counterpart and implication of communicative reason since its principal task is to uphold the liberty of all persons to speak and act in accordance with their individual judgment, to participate in the political process, and to due process of law. It is the institutional application of the conversational virtues and the notion of the human being as a rational agent.

From the inception of the tradition, the principal task of liberal doctrine has been to uphold the rights of individual agency against a succession of historical conditions making for tyranny in its several forms. At the present historical moment, as the forces of political authoritarianism appear in full retreat throughout the world – a phenomenon that, it is to be hoped, is not a temporary abberation – the new set of historical conditions with which liberal doctrine must find the resources to cope are the subtler forms of hegemony stemming from the regime of instrumentality itself. The conception of reason defended here is adequately suited to counter this uniquely modern set of conditions. It limits the jurisdiction of instrumentality and technique (including scientific rationality and the calculus of social utility) while ensuring priority of place for the capacities of critical reflection and judgment which alone limit the dominion of technique. The dialogical conception refuses all reductionism and views individual freedom and responsibility as belonging to the structure of reason itself. Furthermore, it does so in a manner that accommodates the hermeneutic richness of the concepts of reason and reasonableness, explaining in the process why the concept of reason constitutes the principal defining characteristic of human beings and the basis of dignity. The human being, in this conception, is possessed of capacities not only to get what it wants but to reflect and judge, to provide or withhold consent, and to participate with others in discursive practices oriented toward an understanding of justice and the good. The exercise of these capacities occupies much of its existence while their presence in the constitution of the self comprises its fundamental and distinctive mode of comportment and is the basis of its intrinsic worth and dignity. The dialogical conception of reason offers an account of such values that surpasses the instrumentalist paradigm, which by contrast would subordinate all values to the requirements of the technical apparatus, whatever their consequences for individual freedom and human rights generally.

The need for a countervailing mode of thought to the reigning paradigm of instrumentality has never been more pressing than at the present historical moment. That the meaning of reason exceeds that of instrumental rationality – that it connotes a wider set of dispositions, capacities, and virtues appropriate to the communicative process – and that it is precisely these nontechnical connotations which limit the scope of instrumental rationality by situating it within a broader conception of communicative reasonableness is a lesson that contemporary liberalism must at last learn. If liberal politics is to cope effectively with the configuration of conditions that increasingly threatens to circumscribe liberal values in order to suit the requirements of the instrumentalist order (an order that liberalism itself played a large role in establishing), it must refuse to subordinate the values and rights of individuality to the edicts of scientific knowledge and to the calculus of social utility. It must conceive of liberal principles as the political counterpart and implication of communicative reason, hence as rooted in the constitution of the self as a morally rational agent, rather than as derivations of utilitarian or contractarian methodology. While I shall make no effort to argue that liberal

principles cannot be formally derived from these conventional methods –
on this matter I take no position – insisting on the logical dependence of
these principles on such methods places liberal values on perilous ground.
It would accordingly be better to inquire whether alternative interpretations and justifications of liberalism are available, particularly in view of
the inadequacy of conventional liberal assumptions about the self as a
moral and rational agent.

With this in mind, I undertake in the following and final chapter to
articulate a conception of liberal politics that spells out the implications
of the philosophy of the self here described. What becomes of liberal
doctrine when conventional assumptions about the individual are transformed is the matter to which I now turn.

6

The Political Conditions of Agency

Since the Enlightenment, political thought has been torn between two conflicting impulses at the levels of both political ideology and social ontology. One views the constitution of the individual agent as the foundation of all political legitimacy. Its underlying moral passion lies with the freedom of the individual to fashion its life in accordance with its own choices as well as its liberation from all unchosen obligations. The principal function of government, in this view, is to secure the conditions that allow for the expression of individual natures. The second impulse favours collective mutuality and the ties that bind individuals into a recognizable community of belief, sentiment, and obligation. Its dominant passion concerns the pursuit of deeper forms of mutuality and solidarity, in which the state is enlisted as one of the means at the community's disposal. The former impulse finds expression in a politics of individuality – a politics of individual rights and freedoms, limited government, and equality of all persons before the law – while the latter is a politics of collectivity – a politics of community, collective identity and collective rights, solidarity, nationality, class, gender, or tradition. Both political conceptions have multiple forms including, in the first case, the several variants of liberalism and libertarianism and, in the second, communitarianism, socialism, conservatism, nationalism, feminism, and so on.

The first political impulse is rooted in an ontology which conceives of the social world as the site of individuals pursuing their ends either singly, in cooperation with others, or in competition with them. It conceives of the self as a rational being capable of standing out from its environment and fashioning its own existence through autonomous acts of reflection. Any social or political order that would subvert personal autonomy, it views as an affront to the self conceived as an individuated agent. The second view regards the social order as á more intimate union of persons, a community of selves dependent for their values and identity on the shared tradition in which they are embedded. The self is in the first instance not a sovereign chooser but a member of the social whole and, as such, an inheritor of a configuration of shared beliefs, ends, sentiments, language, identity, practices, and institutions. As a strongly social being, the self in this view is bound by obligations that it did not expressly choose but inherited by virtue of the tradition and collectivity within which it always already stands.

These two standpoints differ fundamentally with respect to methodological and ontological commitments to viewing social phenomena from the perspective of either the individual or the social whole. Differences of political principle frequently have their roots in competing ontologies and must, for this reason, be resolved within the province of the latter. Political philosophies are never without ontological presuppositions. The choice is not whether a theory of justice will contain such commitments but in what they will consist: how it will conceive of the self and its basic mode of comportment as a moral agent; in what sense the self is a social as well as a rational being; whether it possesses a mutable or immutable constitution; what model of community or social participation accords with this view. Political philosophers ignore these questions at their peril – if they are intent on persuading others with a fundamentally different orientation to their own view.

Liberalism would have us adopt the perspective of the individual self, not as an arbitrary decision, but for the reason that, at the most fundamental level of social and political analysis, individual human beings and their interactions are all there is. Community, society, nation, class, gender, and other collective notions are derived from the individuals of whom they are constituted. Except metaphorically, such collective entities possess no existence whatever apart from or prior to the concrete individual, the most basic unit of political analysis. Adopting the standpoint of the individual self, if it is adequately conceived philosophically, will take each of these collective categories into account in instances where they cast light on social phenomena. Yet to adopt as a basic methodological starting point the view of one or another collectivity (a move typically made not on the grounds that it affords a more comprehensive and illuminating perspective on human affairs but as a matter of political 'commitment') is to succumb to misplaced concreteness and to account for the less derivative in terms of the more derivative. Both the individual and the collectivity are derivative, yet the latter is contingent on the former in a way that is not reversible. The collectivity is composed entirely of individuals, along with certain properties they hold in common, while the individual is never a mere instantiation of the collective whole. Interpretive obfuscation arises, often with dangerous political consequences, when collective categories are taken as the most fundamental or important lenses through which to comprehend human affairs rather than as derivative perspectives useful only within a limited province.

Critics of liberalism have often fastened on its ontology and the untenable metaphysical assumptions to which it has been unfortunately wedded since the inception of the liberal tradition. In its utilitarian and contractarian formulations, liberalism has indeed presupposed an ahistorical, metaphysical, and untenable conception of human beings, one in which the self is in essence a strategic, instrumentally rational, socially unconditioned, sovereign, hedonistic, and egoistic seeker of gratification. Liberal individualism requires a relatively strong conception of individual agency and its critics have been correct in taking many of its proponents to task for the ways in which this conception has been articulated since the seventeenth century. The ontology of classical liberalism failed to comprehend the extent and nature of human embeddedness, and this failure produced distortions within its political methodology the legacy of which is with us still. The self is a being-in-the-world and a being-with-others. It is constituted by an array of social and historical conditions, language and culture, its view of the good, its capacities for reflection and action, and a rationality which is itself inseparable from intersubjectivity. The self possesses no deep metaphysical core of being, no inner citadel or occult entity safely removed from the vicissitudes of history and sociality. It is a joint product of its facticity and its freedom, and is properly articulated within the categories of lifeworld, practice, narrative, and self-creation.

The failure of conventional liberal ontology requires a renunciation of that ontology alone and not the political impulse to which it has been unhappily married. The latter's best option is permanent separation from Hobbes and his progeny, and a recoupling with a social ontology derived from phenomenological hermeneutics and pragmatism. This move provides liberal principles with a more adequate philosophical underpinning and a less metaphysical, more phenomenologically adequate, conception of the self as a moral agent. It provides a degree of moral depth to liberalism's basic unit of analysis and rescues liberalism from the metaphysical embarrassment from which it has suffered. It makes it possible to conceive of the self as belonging to a lifeworld while still possessing a capacity for self-creation, as bearing an identity which is an inheritance from tradition yet one subject to personal revision and choice, and as a social yet separate being. It comprehends, in short, the 'unsocial sociability' of human beings and the distance inherent in intersubjectivity. If the self is not a sovereign chooser in the sense dear to classical and neoclassical liberals, it can still be its own principal author, with reflective capacities by which it lives and which the state or other persons negate at the expense of its happiness and integrity as a rational being. Violations of its autonomy offend not the deep metaphysical essence of its nature but the capacity and right of self-authorship without which it could not become what it is – a communicatively rational, free, and individuated agent.

As I argued in Chapter 5, nothing is more needed at present than countervailing modes of thought to the regime of instrumental rationality which currently exercises such a powerful hold on virtually all aspects of modern culture. Within politics in particular what is called for is a better mode of understanding the sense in which reflection and choice – especially the nonstrategic varieties – give meaning to our lives and constitute us as the particular beings we are. The individual exercises its liberty in order not only to gratify its desires but to fashion an existence that is both meaningful and its own. Through self-authorized commitment it becomes what it is within a process that is never without struggle: against an 'iron cage' of instrumental rationality and scientific totalization, a mass society of inhuman scale, a legion of scientific and utilitarian planners anxious to act on its behalf, collectivities claiming its allegiance, or the drift toward inauthenticity. It must struggle to assert authority over its own existence. As Isaiah Berlin writes; '[It] is at least part of what I mean when I say that I am rational ... to be conscious of myself as a thinking, willing, active being, bearing responsibility for my choices and able to explain them by references to my own ideas and purposes. I feel free to the degree that I believe this to be true, and enslaved to the degree that I am made to realize that it is not.'[1] Because the self is a rational being constituted by its ends and commitments it must be at liberty to exercise choice in the maximum degree compatible with the liberty of all others to do the same.

What I have called the revisability thesis – that persons are able to revise and rationally critique their inheritance, their conception of the good, their identity, practices, institutions, etc. – is never without political conditions of possibility, and it is these conditions that a liberal order seeks to identify and secure. The purpose of this chapter is to outline the set of political conditions that best provides for the possibility of individual agency in the sense in which I have characterized it. Its thesis is that a particular interpretation of liberal principles satisfies these conditions and that adopting the perspective of the self sustains a suitable interpretation of the idea of a free society.

The Free Society: A Justification

Liberalism's virtue is that it analyses political affairs from the standpoint of the individual and prioritizes this interpretive perspective over those afforded by collective notions. Its shortcoming lies in the ways it has conventionally conceived the individual agent, a shortcoming that I have sought to document and remedy in this study. Liberals have too often taken the individual, rightly regarded as the foundation of political legitimacy, as a given – a metaphysical given but also as a being with a fixed mode of comportment in its ethical relations. What is now apparent is that the self is far from given, that its basic constitution is a social and historical contingency, a construction with a genealogy, and most importantly that it is made possible by social and political conditions conducive to the development of personal agency. The self that is communicatively rational, autonomous, and perhaps authentic can become or fail to become this in its ethical and political relations. It fails if the requisite conditions are not in place: if, for instance, it is without the liberty to exercise and develop its capacity for autonomy; or through ignorance and failure of imagination, its horizon remains so circumscribed as to be incapable of conceiving more than a small number of options for what it will do with its life; or through subordination to the authority of custom or expertise, it never attains independence of judgment. Mature selfhood is made possible by a set of social conditions, several of which are expressly political.

Foremost among the political conditions of individual agency is the existence of a free society. One cannot be the principal author of one's existence without political guarantees that one will not be forcibly prevented from living by one's own light. One's life does not become one's own if it is not a product of choices freely made and where the options among which one may choose are unduly circumscribed. One's life becomes one's own – one's 'moral property,' so to speak – in the degree to which the various constituents of one's being, including one's conduct, view of the good, beliefs, group membership, and personal commitments are self-chosen or, if inherited from tradition, freely appropriated and adapted to suit the character one wishes to be. What makes reflective authorization imperative is the fact that it is by this means that the self authors itself; it becomes what it is – an agent constituted by its ends and commitments – by selectively fashioning these constituents of its being. Far from it being the case that liberalism requires an asocial self not constituted by its ends or attachments, it is precisely because it is so constituted that it must assert its rights to determine what these will be: whether the tradition or community in which it is embedded will continue to enjoy its allegiance; whether its constitutive ends will retain its loyalty; and whether the practices and moral vocabulary which make up its moral identity will continue to do so into the future. In each instance the individual asserts a right to determine such matters independently since in doing so it is in fact choosing itself. In proportion to the freedom guaranteed it by law the individual may become both the principal character and author of its own narrative history, optimally to the maximum degree compatible with the freedom of all others to do the same. Deprived of liberty, the self is a mere character in a story of someone else's telling, whether this is a community, government, bureaucracy, body of experts, planners, regulators, church, union, or other entity presuming to choose on its behalf. Under this condition authenticity is a remote possibility for all but the rarest of individuals.

Pursuant to the discussion of Chapter 5, it is the primary condition of rational agency in the dialogical model that the individual is at liberty to express itself, with the usual qualification that it not infringe on the identical rights of others. The free society properly embodies the conditions inherent to the communicative process. Through its laws, practices, and institutions it guarantees individuals the freedom to participate fully in practices of rational dialogue. Such a polity in fact represents the full institutional embodiment of communicative rationality. It makes it possible for all persons to speak on their own behalf whether individually or collectively, articulate their opinions and aspirations, express their interests, or agitate for reform in conversation with other discussants. Communicative reason requires as a condition of possibility a free market of ideas and worldviews, a plurality and even a conflict of opinions since it is only through open confrontation of opposing views that the most adequate among them will be discovered and the least adequate exposed. Superior ideas are demonstrated as such only in conversation with rival conceptions and never arise in a conversational vacuum or in contexts in which the conditions of expression are many or prohibitive of novelty and difference.

Freedom, tolerance, civility, and the rest of the conversational virtues find adequate political expression only in a liberal order. It is only there that all persons are guaranteed the freedom to express their individual natures in both speech and action. Just as communicative reason does not legislate the content of expression but limits itself to ensuring the participation rights of all discussants, just as it welcomes difference and accepts the verdict of consensus without determining in advance of actual dialogue in what the truth consists, a free liberal society permits individuals to experiment with ideas and lifestyles which may be at odds with convention, to advocate whatever opinion they think true, and act on their choices. It respects individual autonomy while making it possible, indeed requiring, that persons take full responsibility for their choices. It neither deprives us of choice in the fashion of political authoritarianism nor rescues us in paternalist fashion from the consequence of our choice in the manner of egalitarian socialism. The free society throws the individual back on its resources, ensures it as wide a range of options as is practically feasible, educates its capacity to choose, and bids it to accept responsibility for the consequences of its choices. Its actions and inactions of whatever kind (including the economic) are matters of personal accountability in the sense both that they call for individual decision and justification and that their results are something with which the individual must live.

The rational agent is capable of being held to account both for its judgments and actions. Its antithesis is the self that deflects responsibility onto others either to account for its choices or shoulder their consequences. The irrational (also the inauthentic) self would have others do its thinking for it, act on its behalf, and cope with the fallout in order to spare it the burden of reflection and action. It dreads above all else freedom and the burdens that accompany it – those of reflection and choice, autonomy and responsibility, and in general being held to account for its existence. It seeks comfort in anything that will deliver it from such burdens and offer it security in exchange for the liberty it happily renounces. This is the security of collective belonging, religious consolation, scientific expertise, and economic equality, sources of security with which its culture readily provides it.

The free society is the political counterpart and embodiment of the virtues inherent in rational agency. It upholds the principles of individual autonomy and tolerance central to all rationality, placing these at the heart of its political doctrine and insisting on their inviolability and constitutional primacy. Its most basic commitments are to the rights and freedoms of the individual, principal of which is the liberty to speak and act according to its own judgment without the intervention of any who would coerce it into behaving as an instrument of another's will. A liberal order strictly delimits the legally acceptable sphere of coercion to not merely the expedient or the decision of the majority but to procedures protective of human rights. The latter it views not as strategically efficient means of securing the general utility but as inviolable constraints of the utility calculus itself, constraints protective of the integrity of all persons alike and not merely that of the majority. It recognizes that majorities are frequently disposed to impose their will as widely as they are able, no matter what coercion this may involve against minorities, and insists that the rule of collective opinion operate in a limited sphere. Any coercion that would constitute an affront to rational agency and the dignity which stems from it are censured in a free society on grounds not of collective preference but the conditions of human agency.

The principles and institutions that make up a free political order constitute a myriad of applications of the virtues of rational dialogue. Besides liberty itself, the conversational virtues of tolerance, plurality, civility, and individual responsibility find a thousand applications within the legal statutes and procedures, institutions and practices that define the contours of a free society. Their applications make it possible for persons with competing interests to coexist peacefully, not by concealing these behind a veil of ignorance but establishing procedures that allow persons differently constituted to coordinate their actions. Properly applied, the principles of liberal rationality give political expression to the 'unsocial sociability' of the self, recognizing that persons desire at once to ensure their individual separateness and independence while participating in larger forms of community life. The liberal order preserves and negotiates the tension between distance and belonging – the dialectic inherent to reason itself – by ensuring rights of participation and refusal in various collective associations.

The free society negotiates this tension in a manner that surpasses illiberal doctrines of both the left and the right. All forms of political authoritarianism subordinate individuality to the will of the state. No possibility of rational contest exists in a state where arbitrary authority exercises unlimited discretion in all matters. The illiberal politics of the left, in its democratic no less than its undemocratic forms, fails entirely to preserve and negotiate the tension between these two poles. It too prefers to sacrifice individual autonomy, if not to the ruler's arbitrary decrees than to its (the party's or the majority's) idea of social justice –

above all, to the ideal of material equality and the method of compulsory redistribution which alone brings it about. The idea that persons are separate beings to be treated as such rather than units of political calculation and manipulation by the state is lost in socialist politics, which is content to reduce all persons to the uniform condition of wards of the state so long as it brings about the material equality it prizes. In order to protect the individual in paternalist fashion from the consequences of its actions and choices (particularly within the marketplace, wherein it is presumed to be either incompetent or brutal), it is necessary to restrict its sphere of autonomy and responsibility to that within which it may be guaranteed material comfort and absolute security. Similarly all illiberal majoritarianism, utilitarianism, and communitarianism fail to do justice to the notion of rational individual agency. In refusing priority to individual rights over majority preferences or communal ends, these political doctrines negate the conditions that make authentic belonging no less than individual separateness and rational agency possible. In the case of all illiberal modes of thought commitment to a particular end (for socialism, equality of economic condition, for communitarianism, the continued flourishing of designated traditions, for majoritarianism, the preferences of the largest voting block, for nationalism, the glory of the nation-state, and for fascism, the personal vanity of the rulers) undermines the autonomy of not only individual dissenters but all persons, whose autonomy is restricted in the service of the state's dominant (substantive) commitment. The only question for the individual is whether it shares that commitment or not, whether it wins or loses in the contest for ideological preeminence, political power, and material goods. It is the intrinsic nature of all illiberal thought to 'reconcile' the values of individuality and sociality by subordinating the former to the latter rather than preserving and negotiating the tension between the two values and thus preserving both. Liberalism pursues the latter course not by rejecting communal ends – of which it permits the free pursuit – but ensuring that their pursuit will not involve any enlistment of individuals against their will or interference with their liberty.

A distinction key to the understanding and rationale of the free society is that between two fundamentally differing kinds of legislation. The first, arising from the dominant regime of instrumentality, sets about fashioning law with a particular set of ends in view as that which law is thought an efficient means of achieving. The desirability of an end – whether the elimination of certain social ills, the attainment of a particular pattern of economic distribution, or the satisfaction of a community's conception of the good – is thought sufficient justification for the use of coercion, if by this means it may be ensured that the desired state of affairs will come about. Obliging persons to act or forbear in ways that will bring about a given end, and introducing legal coercion to ensure that these obligations will be met, are frequently the quickest and most efficient means of providing for the satisfaction of that end. Coercion – usually masked beneath the epithets of rational organization, coordination, conscious direction, social planning, or even democratization – is cleansed of its unethical connotation by being seen as an efficient and, if possible, necessary means of ensuring the desired result. The aim sanctifies the means provided that the aim is approved by the majority and the means – coercion – can be argued to be necessary for its attainment. Governments employing this method seek to appease widely shared passions for certainty, guarantees, and conscious control while speaking the language of social justice, democracy, community, and rationality.

The second method of fashioning laws does not work to bring about particular ends conceived in advance and in abstract form but secures the legal conditions that make it possible for persons to pursue self-chosen ends. It adopts a vocabulary not of instrumentality but of conditions of possibility. This it carries through less by pronouncing on the desirability or undesirability of particular states of affairs – including patterns of economic distribution and the preservation of communal traditions – than by concerning itself with procedures that guarantee for persons an optimal configuration of options from which they may determine their ends. It does not regard the attainment of socially approved ends as sufficient justification for legal coercion but insists on stronger and specific grounds for this within the ambit of individual rights. It regards neither collective expediency nor the removal of dissatisfaction as criteria of justice but the preservation of individual integrity alone. This method of legislation guarantees an array of options from which persons may choose, and not that they will select any given option. It ensures an autonomous sphere in which persons are free to fashion their own lives, and not that their actions will accord with the general welfare or secure the greatest happiness of the greatest number. It does not reduce all political questions to technical problems resolvable by scientific knowledge or utilitarian calculation but carefully distinguishes the latter from issues of justice resolvable only on principled grounds. It regards the means of government action as no less problematic than the ends, and is prepared to abandon a socially desired end if the price of its attainment entails a significant loss of freedom for some. It is not prepared to sacrifice the freedom of some for the happiness of others, regardless of the numbers involved.

While the free society does not entirely abjure legislation of the first type, it places it in carefully defined limits and accentuates laws of the second type. It is a question of accent and priority rather than categorical choice. It is nonetheless imperative that their relative priority is resolved in this manner in order that the conditions of rational agency are secured and the satisfaction of utilitarian or communal ends not involve the violation of individual rights. As history reminds us, collectivities of all descriptions seldom hesitate to sacrifice individual rights, if it is believed to serve a higher purpose. Recognizing that injustice is as much the stuff of means as of ends, the free society seldom provides guarantees that particular ends of the kinds mentioned will be brought about since the provision of such guarantees normally requires a level of coercion that such a society does not sanction. It does not grant that ends justify means or that there is a higher court of appeal – community, shared values, the common welfare, or the requirements of rational organization – than the integrity of individual persons. It recognizes that taking the notion of individual agency seriously requires placing limits on the rule of collective opinion and that stronger grounds than illiberal politics admits are needed to justify legal coercion.

The Free Society: An Interpretation

If the individual is a rational agent whose basic mode of existence requires the free exercise of its capacities, no deeper affront is possible than to treat such a being as if it were not so constituted. To treat it as a mere means to an end, an instrument of another's will or of a community's purposes, or as an unwilling draftee into a social cause is to violate not only its happiness but more fundamentally the conditions that make it the being it is. In most of its forms coercion removes all agency and reason, and replaces them with servility. Whether autonomy is sacrificed for an end approved by political authority or violated by a more powerful individual, servility entirely negates the conditions of selfhood and in the degree that it is permitted to govern human lives reduces persons to the status of objects – nonagents bowing to the will of others, and on account not of the latter's moral authority but its power. The injustice of most forms of coercion has its origin here – that the coerced individual is an instrument of another's purposes. Whether the coercer is benevolent or monstrous in intent, public official or criminal, matters little to the coerced. Whether the end for which it is sacrificed is noble or base, approved by the community or decried by it, is a matter of indifference.

It is the nature of coercion not to remove all options from the agent but impose a particular configuration of these in such a fashion as to guarantee by the threat of force selection of that option favoured by the coercer.[2] The possibility of the individual acting as it wishes, or even maintaining the status quo, is entirely removed. The injustice of coercion in this form stems not from its violation of one's happiness or the deep metaphysical essence of one's being – one's noumenal self – but from the fact that it negates the possibility of agency. The free society must therefore carefully delimit the scope of legal coercion, limiting it primarily to the requirement to respect the rights of all persons. The basic principle governing the use of legal coercion is that it is utilized to the degree and in the manner that produces a condition of optimal respect for individual rights. This gives rise to a condition not of anarchy but the rule of impartial laws before which all are equal in liberty and obliged to practice the same recognition which they demand from others. While, of course, legal coercion is not itself an injustice, it readily becomes one when its use is a matter of arbitrary discretion rather than one governed by the principle of the primacy of justice.

Accordingly, the first requirement of a free society is the primacy of individual rights over all other political considerations. The formation of law requires that considerations of justice take priority over all collectively approved ends, including what is vaguely referred to as the common good (usually meaning economic security or a roughly egalitarian pattern of distribution), a set of ethical values approved by a majority, cultural traditions, or communal identities. While communitarian values may carry justificatory weight in the formation of public policy, the question of relative priority (an inescapable issue given the tendency of the right and the good to conflict) must be resolved in favour of individual rights. Their primacy allows for persons to live not only good lives but lives of their own making. As George Kateb expresses it:

> [U]nless rights come first they are not rights. They will tend to be sacrificed to some purpose deemed higher than the equal dignity of every individual. There will be little if any concept of the integrity or inviolability of each individual. The group or the majority or the good or the sacred or the vague future will be preferred. The beneficiaries will be victimized along with the victims because no one is being treated as a person who is irreplaceable and

beyond value. To make rights anything but primary, even though in the name of human dignity, is to injure human dignity.[3]

Beginning with liberty, then, a free society ensures that the rights of the individual constrain the ends of the majority or any other collectivity. Asserting the primacy of justice amounts to the claim that those ends which a community can bring about only by coercive means, first, do not warrant state protection and, second, would be better lost.

Nothing is more contrary to the spirit of a free society than the sort of tallying with human rights implicit to utilitarian morality. Rights are not mere utilities commensurable with interests and 'preferences' or convertible into a common currency with them, potentially one that could be maximized by sacrificing the rights of some for the greater utility of others. They are not utilities but constraints on utility. An agent cannot set about maximizing utility if the conditions of agency have not been secured. No more can it authentically belong to a community or promote the common good under this condition. It can do none of these things, but at best go through the motions in each case, conforming outwardly to ends not its own and preserving traditions experienced as the dead weight of the past and for which it offers itself up as a sacrifice. That tradition survives sometimes only in mummified form is something that the free society fully recognizes. It is, moreover, a recognition that introduces a note of suspicion into the reception of communitarian appeals to shared values and ways of life asserted to enjoy the allegiance of an ambiguous number of persons.

The free society guarantees neither the continued flourishing of communal traditions and ways of life nor any particular pattern of economic distribution. It promises neither material equality, personal happiness, nor indeed the attainment of any given end but that the political conditions necessary for their attainment will be secured. It provides for the protection of individual rights and freedoms primarily in the form of immunities against coercion. The basic civil and political rights traditionally upheld in the liberal tradition, including rights to life, liberty, property, due process, equal protection, free speech and association, etc. are best understood as conditions of this sort – not guarantees that one's ends will be attained but legal conditions necessary for their pursuit, primarily in the form of protection against coercive interference. Freedom does not entail the successful attainment of one's ends, nor should it be confused with any personal capacity to secure them. Confusion regarding the meaning of freedom has been widespread since T.H. Green modified the term to connote the 'positive' freedom or (better) power to achieve one's personal ends, provided that such ends be self-chosen and 'worthy.' The meaning of freedom has also been obscured through the efforts of socialist thinkers to enlist support for their cause by identifying true freedom with the condition of material equality, in effect identifying freedom with wealth. To be free does not mean to possess power, wealth, happiness, or all good things but to hold legal immunities against harmful interference. It is to enjoy specific liberties which make it legally possible to pursue one's values without threat of coercive interference. It is not necessary to enjoy the benefits of liberty, the particular utilities which its exercise may bring about, but to live in the knowledge that one's pursuit of the benefits of liberty will not be hampered by any persons or the state. To be free is to possess the right not to happiness or wealth but to their pursuit and also the responsibility for the consequences of their pursuit. As Friedrich A. Hayek remarks, 'Liberty and responsibility are inseparable. A free society will not function or maintain itself unless its members regard it as right that each individual occupy the position that results from his action and accept it as due to his own action.'[4] A political order is not properly free in which actions are divorced from their consequences and agents are not held accountable for both.

If freedom is bound analytically with the notion of noncoercion, it is made possible politically by ensuring that all persons possess what Lawrence Haworth terms a 'domain for autonomy.' This is a legally protected sphere or jurisdiction within which the individual is free to decide how it will act, and what it will believe. A domain for autonomy is defined by a person's rights, '[It is] the sphere of action the society delegates to that individual's decision, in which he is held responsible. A domain for autonomy thus forms an office or jurisdiction. The officeholder's rights and duties identify the work of the office; they mark out his sphere of responsibility.'[5] Much the same sentiment is expressed by Berlin:

> [T]here ought to exist a certain minimum area of personal freedom which must on no account be violated; for if it is overstepped, the individual will find himself in an area too narrow for even that minimum development of his natural faculties which alone makes it possible to pursue, and even to conceive, the various ends which men hold good or right or sacred. It follows that a frontier must be drawn between the area of private life and that of public authority.[6]

An idea deeply rooted in the liberal tradition, an individual's sphere of autonomy establishes inviolable constraints on the actions of persons and institutions, constraints limiting the effects of such action on the individual. This liberal idea is meant to give practical legal expression to individual integrity or inviolability, without which one's conduct would not be one's own, something for which one may legitimately be held to account.

It is customary for liberals, in speaking of an individual's sphere of autonomy, to either misdescribe it in asocial terms as a domain of 'self-regarding action,' in Mill's phrase, or suggest in the fashion of classical liberalism that freedom could be optimally achieved in a state of isolation or even anarchy. Both tendencies are mistaken. The domain of the self-regarding, as critics of Mill have rightly pointed out, is so small as to include trivial acts only, while it is only in Hobbes's exceedingly narrow and mechanistic definition of liberty as 'the absence of opposition' or of 'external impediments of motion,'[7] and as 'the silence of the law,'[8] that a condition of isolation or anarchy could be regarded as one of optimal freedom. The condition of freedom and autonomy is necessarily characterized by the rule of law and the presence of institutions guaranteeing one protection against harmful interference. It is not a sufficient condition of freedom that one not in fact be interfered with in pursuing an action. One must in addition hold a legal guarantee that one will not be interfered with or that in the event that one is, one may seek legal redress. This condition obtains only in a political order and optimally in one providing equal protection before the law together with a variety of institutions organized to make autonomous action possible. As Haworth writes, 'A person is not ensured a domain for autonomy by being left alone. The view that the only enemy of autonomy is government, and that to generate domains for autonomy it is sufficient to roll back government so that people confront fewer coercive laws, is highly simplistic.'[9]

The condition of autonomy is made possible by a combination of restrictions on individual action and state power and a system of laws, practices, and institutions whose function, broadly conceived, is to educate the capacity for reasoned choice. This latter point is frequently overlooked by libertarians whose focus (understandably) is the steady encroachment by government of many of our civil liberties, a process that restricts our sphere of autonomy within narrow confines as a means of accomplishing particular social purposes. The manner in which individuality is presently hemmed in by government regulators, planners, and administrative authorities easily tempts one into the view that autonomy could be maximized simply through wholesale deregulation and the elimination of state institutions. It is only partially correct that such means will secure the conditions of individual autonomy. Given the enormous size and scope of government in present-day democracies, deregulation in numerous areas of law combined with the rolling back or even elimination of some state institutions is indeed one way of increasing the autonomy of citizens within such democracies. It is, in my view, an advisable way as well. Yet equally important is the refashioning of many such institutions in order to better secure the conditions of freedom and autonomy.

If the free society ensures the individual a domain for autonomy as wide as is compatible with a similar domain for all persons, it also makes possible the attainment of authenticity. To avoid misunderstanding, it is important that the concept of authenticity and the manner in which liberal principles relate to this ideal are clarified. Authenticity is not an egoistic or hedonistic view of the good life; nor is it an expression of social atomism or, worse, moral laxity as its critics have supposed. It finds neither sole nor optimal expression within a life that is constantly reinventing itself or overturning convention. Rather, it is a mode of existence characterized by commitment to self-chosen ends. It is opposed to a life that is without a significant range of options, without knowledge of these options, devoid of the capacity to select intelligently among them, and also without the legal right to revise one's given ends or identity as one chooses. The authentic life is no less one of commitment to tradition and community than one of romantic self-invention, provided that such a commitment is of one's choosing; it is a life no less of strong social ties than of solitariness, provided that such ties are genuinely self-chosen; it is not a life that comes in one shape or size but a mode of existence characterized by reflection and choice. It recognizes that its commitments could have been otherwise, yet not in the sense that one could modify them wholesale, with equanimity, or without significantly modifying one's identity, but that one is the final judge of one's commitments, having both the capacity and right of revision.

There are several reasons why authenticity is frequently confused with simple egoism and moral laxity.[10] One is that its liberating potential rests in part on a 'negative' injunction against servility, and this negative moment is easily mistaken as its only moment, leaving the individual in an ethical vacuum in which it will usually act on whatever range of the moment passion it happens to experience; having been liberated, it follows the path of the newly liberated everywhere: the abuse of liberty. (Indeed were there iron-clad laws of history and human nature one would surely be that liberty newly acquired is either abused, chiefly by depriving others of their freedom, or surrendered anew to one of the many would-be authors of our existence with which our culture provides us. The responsible use of freedom presupposes a degree of moral education of which the newly liberated have often been deprived and must acquire only after the period of tutelage or servility ends. The ethnic hostility that swept across much of Eastern Europe immediately after the collapse of totalitarianism is a case in point, although examples of this phenomenon are vast in number and occur at both a macro and micro level.) A second reason for the confusion of authenticity with egoism and laxity is that unlike some ethical ideals, this one prescribes relatively little by way of outward conduct, limiting itself primarily to the recommendation that one follow a path of one's own choosing. Other moralities will often misinterpret this as laxity on the assumption that any path but the straight and narrow must lead to the devil. Moreover, since the neophyte of authenticity will often choose the path of least resistance, laxity does remain a possibility, and one for which there is no guaranteed means of escape. One liberates oneself from the deviant and superficial forms of authenticity in the course of reexamining previous choices, in a process of pragmatic refinement and experience. A third reason for the confusion lies in the relative difficulty of the task. Unlike moralities that offer decision procedures or determinate values, the ethics of authenticity throws the individual back upon its resources in a more thoroughgoing manner, determining neither what one is to choose nor how, but only who is to choose. The difficulty of the task is compounded by the element within the self, detected by Dostoyevsky and the philosophers of existence, that does not want freedom but servility and the security that it affords.

A further point of clarification concerns the relation of liberal principles to the ethics of authenticity. Liberalism is not a perfectionist theory whose principles of right are placed at the disposal of a particular conception of the good life. It does not presuppose that there is one way of life – the authentic life – uniquely worthy of state protection. Given that authenticity is a pluralistic notion which purposely refrains from prescribing substantive commitments, liberalism presupposes a multiplicity of ends from which persons may, and are presumed competent to, choose. What must be kept in mind with respect to the concept of authenticity is that it refers not to a particular set of substantive values but a way in which values are held; it connotes a mode of existence in which all ends, whatever they be, are autonomously self-chosen. The liberal state does not favour any given conception of the good but provides the conditions that allow persons to pursue the ends they favour and prevents the use of coercion in conscripting persons into the service of ends not of their choosing. Further, a liberal order does not guarantee that persons will in fact succeed in attaining an authentic or autonomous existence. Indeed they may fail altogether to do so. Yet when they fail, their failure must not be assisted by coercive agencies but instead be a product of their choices or (what comes to the same thing) refusals to choose. It is not the attainment but the pursuit of authenticity, autonomy, and happiness that a liberal society ensures by right.

The free society, accordingly, remains neutral with respect to competing values and ways of life. As mentioned in Chapter 3, the neutrality thesis has come to be regarded as one of liberalism's main defining principles and has been defended on several grounds including scepticism regarding the good, controversy about ends, the principles of tolerance and plurality, the practical requirements of accommodation, and the value of autonomy. The most compelling justification of neutrality, I have argued, stems from the premise that persons are able to revise their ends, critique traditions, modify inherited ways of life, and learn from different perspectives. In exercising these capacities there is no reason to believe that all persons will or ought to agree about the nature of the good life. Indeed it is the nature of rational discourse that, while it aims at securing agreement, there is absolutely no guarantee that it will achieve this aim and that, if it does not, we may not assume that rational procedures have broken down. Contest is an ineluctable feature of reasoned reflection, and should not be lamented but recognized as belonging to the human condition. Politically this entails that we should not expect to find in modern society the degree of solidarity over ends which communitarians claim to identify. Rather than continue the search for a substantive conception of the good which properly fits the description of 'our' way of life (that of all of us rather than some) or show favour for any particular community and their collective ends, the state in a free society remains neutral between competing views of the good. It refuses to become partisan when differences concerning lifestyles, religious beliefs, ideals of the good life, or communal ends arise between rival collectivities but rather regards such disagreement as the normal outcome of autonomous agency and rational reflection. It is a condition that requires not a political remedy but procedures of mutual accommodation.

State neutrality provides this procedure by extending the principle of tolerance, making it possible for persons and collectivities with incompatible conceptions of the good to arrive at political agreements in ways that do not involve coercion. The neutral state serves as referee rather than active participant in the search for the good life, limiting its role primarily to securing conditions of peaceful coexistence among persons pursuing, whether singly or collectively, their chosen ends. It declines the role of moral educator – a role that it is singularly unfit to assume – and in the same spirit forbids other would-be moral educators from imposing their individual or collective wills on the unconsenting. It practices neutrality in recognition of the controversy about moral ends, the inescapable and legitimate plurality of ideals and identities, and the capacity of the self to decide which among these it prefers. It assumes that persons are able to determine these matters for themselves without the 'benefit' of paternalistic coercion.

Neutrality does not presuppose, first, any strong form of ethical relativism, but insists that, from the point of view of the state, differences concerning ethical ideals are politically unresolvable. Second, it presupposes a view of tolerance and plurality not as moral ends in themselves but as means of political accommodation. As a political, rather than an ethical, thesis neutrality satisfies the need of free persons to fashion their own lives. As a principle of accommodation, it cares less about what ends an individual chooses than whether it is the individual who chooses them. Moreover, the neutrality principle need not presuppose either the possibility or desirability of perfect neutrality in the sense of a complete abstraction from all substantive commitments regarding the good, including any that may genuinely be shared not only by the majority of persons but by all competent and adult members of a nation or other political jurisdiction. Imperfect or relative neutrality suffices here – one that abstracts from controversial ideals or ends that are contested by persons not readily dismissable as pathological or morally obtuse.[11] Relative neutrality need not abstract from noncontroversial ends, although these may be few in number. Finally, liberal neutrality must not be misinterpreted as a doctrine of indifference toward the particularities which for political purposes it brackets. The communitarian charge of indifference misses the mark[12] since what neutrality enjoins is not that institutions overlook the importance of particularities – as if a person's particular ends, culture, identity, gender, religion, ethnicity, and so on, were a matter of indifference to that person – but that, for purposes of civil accommodation, governments must not view these considerations as legitimating grounds for public policy in instances where they generate disagreement. Neutrality imposes the same impartiality on legislators that requires judges to bracket the religion or ethnicity of a defendant from their deliberations. The requirement of impartiality certainly does not deny the reality and importance of particular constitutive features of the self. On the contrary, it is premised on the view that these features are often of the highest importance to individuals and precisely for this reason they must be at liberty to decide for themselves what their constitutive attachments and, as much as possible, what their constitutive traits will be. Indeed, it is on account of the importance to persons of many of their constitutive attachments that frequently they will not hesitate to impose these same attachments on others coercively. The principle of neutrality protects persons from such coercion and from governmental favouritism, and leaves as much space as possible for voluntary decision.

The free society refuses any public ranking of ethical ideals or ways of life by a communitarian or any other standard. It rejects as politically undecidable all perfectionist claims regarding the intrinsic superiority of any one conception of the good life. By the same token it reserves judgment in all criticism of allegedly inferior modes of life, preferring to leave individuals to determine these matters for themselves and presuming them competent to do so (or no less competent, at any rate, than the majority of voters or public officials). The neutral state recognizes that there are multiple ways in which an individual may fashion for itself a meaningful existence, a plurality of personal or shared ends, which from the standpoint of public policy must be regarded as equally legitimate. It further recognizes that freedom is never without a price, and that included in this price are the unwise choices that countless individuals make. Indeed the advocate of neutrality may grant that within the antiperfectionist state persons will often do things of which others morally disapprove; the neutralist will permit the flourishing of economic materialism, the shopping mall culture, the decline of traditions and ethical virtues, and a variety of other consequences which may be viewed with regret. Yet it will not permit the deterioration of civic virtues, the virtues of rational dialogue, which constitute not a comprehensive view of the good but principles of political right. The neutral state puts in place a system of checks and balances in which power limits power, interests check opposing interests, beliefs constrain beliefs, and communities limit other communities. In each instance constraints are sought to facilitate accommodation and limit coercion to what is necessary for the preservation of equal freedom.

The society that takes freedom seriously leaves the question of the good life to individuals and the associations to which they freely belong, and limits the role of government to the protection of human rights and the promotion of uncontroversial ends (if there are any[13]). It views the state's role as the pursuit of justice and the pursuit of happiness as the private concern of individuals. It shares Mill's belief that 'there is a limit to the legitimate interference of collective opinion with individual independence,'[14] and that identifying this limit is among the principal questions of a just order. The free society limits the scope of legal compulsion to the preservation of individual rights and views utilitarian projects of social engineering and 'rational' planning with the utmost caution in recognition of the tendency intrinsic to many such projects to resort to coercion (or something closely resembling it) in order to attain ends with optimal efficiency. It recognizes that once governments restrict the exercise of individual rights to what is believed conducive to the well-being of a community, no effective constraint on coercion exists and the protection of rights increasingly depends on collective expediency and the discretion of legislators. Since virtually any violation of individual rights can be described, with the help of a 'committed' audience and a little rhetoric, as contributing to the common welfare, a free society removes rights from the vicissitudes of the calculus of social utility and places renewed accent on the limits of state power.

Free societies also take a particular view of the principle of equality. As a principle with two meanings, equality in its original interpretation within liberal doctrine means the equality of all persons before the law (what is sometimes referred to as formal equality). A second meaning is equality of economic condition. The main problem concerning equality is that its two forms conflict when governments anxious to secure material equality impose unequal and potentially burdensome demands on some (the more economically successful) for the benefit of others (the less economically successful). (The distinction is indeed a quantitative one between the relatively more and the relatively less successful, not a qualitative one between the 'haves' and the 'have nots' or the rich and the poor, as economic egalitarians typically urge. Contemporary welfare states do not limit themselves to imposing redistributive burdens on the so-called rich for the benefit of the economically destitute, but distribute both the burdens and the benefits of welfare and related programs widely, a fact often concealed by the rhetoric of egalitarianism and socialism.) Given the propensity for conflict between the two senses of equality, it is important to establish their proper relation. In terms of relative priority, the free society subordinates the pursuit of material equality to the principle of equality before the law. It does so on the grounds that reversing this priority effectively undermines freedom to the degree that the pursuit of material equality overshadows equal treatment. To the extent that governments pursue a policy of material equality, the unequal treatment of individuals will be a predictable consequence since it is a necessary means of bringing this condition about – unequal both between the beneficiaries of redistributive schemes and those compelled to subsidize them, and unequal in the level of burden or benefit. Governments that act to ensure a particular pattern of distribution must treat persons in markedly different ways according to their degree of wealth and use coercive means to ensure this result. Such governments regard the desirability of the preferred pattern of distribution as sufficient justification for coercion in the form of mandatory contributions to welfare and other redistributive schemes benefitting some persons at the expense of others. The fundamental principle of equality before the law prevents such redistributive efforts from extending nearly as far as economic egalitarians desire, in recognition of the fact that discriminatory means are essential to the achievement of egalitarian ends. As Hayek writes:

> [W]hen the opinion of the community decides what different people shall receive, the same authority must also decide what they shall do. This conflict between the ideal of freedom and the desire to 'correct' the distribution of incomes so as to make it more 'just' is usually not clearly recognized. But those who pursue distributive justice will in practice find themselves obstructed at every move by the rule of law. They must, from the very nature of their aim, favor discriminatory and discretionary action.[15]

Hayek correctly observes that governments committed to an egalitarian distributive ideal must severely attenuate the equal treatment principle while states committed to equal treatment can offer no guarantees regarding distribution. To achieve material equality, governments must legislate all resource allocation and achieve optimal control over the economic and social environment generally; it must not permit economic agents to strike agreements without government surveillance, regulation, and control; above all it must not allow persons to bear the consequences of their economic actions or allow the successful to enjoy the fruits of their labours.

This raises the matter of a further condition indispensable to all free societies. This is economic freedom or the right broadly conceived to hold property and to exchange goods and services through uncoerced agreement with others under free market conditions. It is no accident of history that political liberty has never existed in nations that did not recognize economic liberty as well. States that forbid the spontaneous growth of free markets must assume broad powers of regulation, surveillance, micromanagement, taxation, and redistribution in order to direct the general course of economic life and to ensure a particular distributive outcome. That modern states have long assumed these powers as a matter of course, exercising them in varying manners and degrees, is something about which political philosophers, including many liberals, have appeared remarkably untroubled. A frequent assumption is that liberty, while important in some areas of our public and private lives, is dispensable in our economic lives, an assumption common among intellectuals with a supercilious disdain for what they regard as the vulgarity of economic affairs. Intellectuals often believe that having perceived values more elevated than the economic, they must defend only the liberty that is necessary for the attainment of higher ends and turn a blind eye to all but the most gross infringements of economic liberty provided that such infringements or 'restrictions' are in the service of a higher social purpose.

That freedom requires protection only in particular areas of human life, the areas of higher ends and major undertakings, while leaving the details for the state, is a danger which Tocqueville noted: 'It must not be forgotten that it is especially dangerous to enslave men in the minor details of life. For my own part, I should be inclined to think freedom less necessary in great things than in little ones, if it were possible to be secure of the one without possessing the other.'[16] It is not less dangerous but more so to consign economic affairs or the other 'minor details of life' to unconstrained government authority for the reason that this is the usual path followed in the renunciation of freedom. A free citizenry does not abandon its liberty in an explicit fashion but by a slow and unwitting process of gratification, the price of which it never perceives because it belongs to the minor details of life. Minor areas of concern and choice are dismissed as trifles until the cumulative effect of their renunciation becomes apparent, by which time the process is irreversible owing to the security that the renunciation has made possible.

It must also be borne in mind that no matter what distaste many feel toward the culture of consumerism, the rat race, or economic affairs generally, economic life is commonly regarded by persons in modern society as the most important of human concerns, the antithesis of the attitude prevalent among many intellectuals. So much of our day-to-day life is preoccupied by economic pursuits that it is grossly mistaken to hold that we may be a free people without being free in our capacity as economic agents to hold property, produce, consume, and form contracts with considerable autonomy. Political and civil liberty cannot exist without economic liberty because economic activity is a dominant preoccupation which extends into virtually all areas of human life. It is as important to autonomy as the pursuit of 'higher' ends. The principles of private property and free exchange, and in general the conditions for a free marketplace, are indispensable to a free society, and not merely as means of assuring civil and political liberty but as conditions of autonomous agency.

Amid the drive for utilitarian satisfaction, modern states have largely opted to constrain economic liberty to a high degree, promising in return a kind of security impossible under free market conditions. Economic security, shrewdly misnamed economic 'freedom,' along with employment security and other promised forms of stability, certainty, and predictability, highly valued by the regime of instrumentality, have largely replaced economic liberty as the governing principles of economic life. In exchange for the power to direct the economic activities of individuals and corporations alike with the omnipresent threat of coercion, and to tax and redistribute resources with unlimited discretion, the contemporary welfare state promises deliverance from the consequences of our economic actions. It institutes a vast network of regulations and obligations, governing bodies and administrative agencies of various descriptions the combined effect of which is a pervasive psychology of dependence on the state. From cradle to grave, we are all wards of the state now. We have chosen dependence on a massive administrative welfare state with an unlimited penchant for wielding authority in matters great and small – for determining an overall conception of social utility, identifying our needs, ascertaining optimally efficient means, and administering satisfaction in accordance with the requirements of collective expediency. The welfare state offers security at the cost of independence, a kind of material comfort which is the economic counterpart of the existential security prized by the inauthentic self. It is the kind of stability and certainty that can only be purchased at the price of independence and the autonomy to direct our own economic affairs and bear responsibility for the consequences. Fearing the consequences of personal autonomy, we have opted for collectivized dependence.

What we have gained for our renunciation is nothing resembling the 'Great Society' or even the full economic security sought by so many and as eagerly promised by the state, but a condition of insipid levelling and economic wardship. Incapable of creating full material equality except at a low level of prosperity, the modern welfare state levels downward toward a condition of declining fortunes, widespread dependence, and uncertain benefit. It produces an economy in which the wealth of some clearly recedes while the benefits for others are barely discernible. As Hayek writes, '[W]ho really benefits [from welfarist levelling]? Where does the real benefit lie? It is not a material benefit. It is an imaginary and sentimental one, and the fantasies and sentiments to which it appeals are of the basest sort: the satisfaction which this kind of equality affords me is the opportunity of feeling, if I am exposed to constraints and vexations, or am in an actual state of wretchedness, that my neighbor is in the same boat. A very negative satisfaction, it will be said.'[17] Tocqueville's diagnosis of conditions in nineteenth century America applies still more to the administrative welfare state of our own time:

> The first thing that strikes the observation is an innumerable multitude of men, all equal and alike, incessantly endeavoring to procure the petty and paltry pleasures with which they glut their lives.... Above this race of men stands an immense and tutelary power, which takes upon itself alone to secure their gratifications and to watch over their fate. That power is absolute, minute, regular, provident, and mild. It would be like the authority of a parent if, like that authority, its object was to prepare men for manhood; but it seeks, on the contrary, to keep them in perpetual childhood.... For their happiness such a government willingly labors, but it chooses to be the sole agent and the only arbiter of that happiness; it provides for their security, foresees and supplies their necessities, facilitates their pleasures, manages their principal concerns, directs their industry, regulates the descent of property, and subdivides their inheritances: what remains, but to spare them all the care of thinking and all the trouble of living? Thus it every day renders the exercise of the free agency of man less useful and less frequent; it circumscribes the will within a narrow range and gradually robs a man of all the uses of himself. The principle of equality has prepared men for these things; it has predisposed men to endure them and often to look on them as benefits.[18]

Tocqueville's remarks serve for contemporary purposes as one of the most eloquent characterizations of the welfare state – a century before its introduction – that has been offered.

The welfare state diminishes autonomous agency by divorcing economic actions from economic consequences. In paternalist fashion it relieves persons of responsibility for the consequences of their economic choices, and in doing so relieves them of their agency. It fails to realize that economic agency is an indispensable component of agency as such, that all agency is inseparable from action, that actions are inseparable (in their meaning and import) from their consequences, and therefore responsibility for the one cannot be had without responsibility for the other. Agency is constituted no less within the domain of the economic than in other fields of human practice. Indeed this area of practice consumes so much of the capacities and energies of persons that it may be said to represent one of the more significant areas of practice in which autonomous agents fashion their own lives (to the degree that the state permits). It is a field of human endeavour in which one can either exercise or fail to exercise one's capacity for autonomous agency and one which the welfare state deprives us of in direct proportion to the relative security it offers.

That we have opted largely for security over liberty in our economic practices may not be explained nor properly justified on the usual paternalist grounds of compassion. The culture of dependence, the levelling of fortunes, and the general enervation of initiative which the administrative welfare state brings about are a recipe not for compassion but for nonagency and organized tutelage. While creating benefits of a highly uncertain nature for some, the welfare state imposes a high level of burden on others. It considers no end of economic sacrifice excessive provided that those making the sacrifices are relatively successful economically and those reaping the rewards of the involuntary transaction are relatively less successful. It requires as well majority approval, which it typically receives since most wager they will be on the receiving end of the equation.

The society that takes freedom seriously distinguishes between two fundamentally different conceptions and rationales of welfare and related programs. The first views such programs as providing usually short-term relief for the economically destitute, unemployed, and unemployable. It aims at ensuring a modest level of income security for persons all of whom are subject to the vicissitudes of market forces and most all of whom enjoy less than absolute employment security. The second view aims at a more wholesale redistribution of capital as a requirement of what is called 'distributive justice.' It views material equality as a condition of justice and welfare programs as necessary means thereto. It cares little about the level of economic burden it imposes on some and the permanent, often intergenerational, dependence it all but guarantees for others provided that material equality is the result. The second view cares about ends, not means, and tolerates a level of coercion and dependence refused by the first conception. The first view is concerned equally with the means and aims of government action, recognizing that only certain means respect the requirements of personal agency. It recognizes that there is a limit to the level of obligation and tutelage that welfare programs may create and that this limit is defined by the conditions of autonomy.

While the second view insists on the state being the sole provider and guarantor of services deemed essential to the general welfare, the first is prepared to permit experimentation in competition between free market corporations which may see an advantage in the provision of such services. Experiments of the kind favoured by libertarians in private organizations (whether for-profit or not-for-profit) entering service areas currently monopolized by government would represent an important advance for a society that values liberty. At present it is impossible to predict whether experiments of this kind are practically feasible or improve the quality of service if market conditions were brought to bear on the provision of unemployment insurance, disability insurance, old-age pensions, or even welfare itself. Reforming some or all of these as private insurance schemes, in competition perhaps with conventional state programs, is a prospect many may find objectionable, yet a free society is committed to investigating its possibility. The fact that government provides service ineptly affords room for optimism that others with an economic incentive may provide superior service under conditions that respect rather than negate autonomy. No persuasive rationale exists for the exclusive provision of virtually any service by the state rather than private corporations or a combination thereof. A rule of thumb governing the provision of services, whether they are deemed essential or nonessential to the general welfare, is that those which the free market can render at the desired level of effectiveness ought to be rendered by it, while those which it cannot ought to be left to the state. Government's role would be the limited one of taking up slack left by free market institutions and setting minimum standards for service provision rather than the aggressively interventionist, paternalist, and monopolistic role government currently arrogates to itself. This principle would widen the scope of autonomy while potentially enhancing the quality of service available to all those requiring it.

Aside from welfare programs, many services which contemporary states provide could be provided by corporations on either a profit or nonprofit basis. Under conditions of state monopoly it is impossible to know how many of these services could be provided more effectively and under conditions more in keeping with economic liberty than current practice. The old idea, still professed by those on the left, that the free market is the road to inequality and other social ills has been displaced by the recognition that big government fouls almost everything it touches. We currently suffer less from the ill effects of the free market than from government ineptitude in providing for their relief. Yet what is most objectionable in the current practice of government service is not (or not primarily) that government has taken upon itself to provide such a vast number of services but its frequent insistence on monopoly status and refusal of competition with private sector corporations or experimentation along these lines. Entire generations raised on the belief that services important to the general welfare must be provided by state institutions have produced a mentality for which any mention of 'privatization' or 'deregulation' prompts a fearful reaction. Liberty becomes a bromide piously recited yet studiously avoided when material satisfactions or a thousand other utilities are at stake. The fashion prevalent among intellectuals and public officials has been to defend virtually any expansion of state power, and consequently to circumscribe further the domain for individual autonomy, provided that such measures are conducive to economic security and equality. The results are a state apparatus of overwhelming proportions, a virtual 'iron cage' of regulation and administrative authority, a widespread psychology of dependence, a massive tax burden, and a legacy of public debt ensuring that the folly and irresponsibility of one generation will be paid for by the next.[19]

A free society takes each of these problems seriously and views them not as incidental disutilities offset by a greater benefit but as symptomatic of the general devaluation of autonomous individuality which threatens in a manner hitherto unknown to undermine liberal values. Reversing the trend now generations in the making calls in the main for a reaffirmation of the several principles mentioned above as well as creative exploration of possible legislation widening the scope of personal autonomy beyond current limits. An example of this is privatization of some, or even many, services conventionally provided by government as a method of returning to individuals a measure of the economic freedom that they have surrendered. The overall size and scope of government could be reduced as could the degree of state intervention in economic life and a myriad other paternalist measures of 'rational' planning and utilitarian organization. Wherever possible, government ought to allow for the development of what Hayek calls 'spontaneous orders' not least of which is the free market, limiting its interventions therein to necessary correctives of a kind conducive to their spontaneous development, rather than aggressively transform these into utilitarian 'instrumental orders' designed to guarantee the efficient satisfaction of ends at a high cost to human freedom.

A more radical proposal is that governments permit individuals who object to specific government programs to opt out of both the obligation to subsidize them and the right to receive their benefits. As far as possible, those who object to certain public policies ought to reserve a right of nonparticipation. This could apply to policies and programs from unemployment insurance to old-age pensions, public health care and educational systems any of which may fail to gain the support of those subsidizing them, on civil libertarian or other ethical grounds or for reasons of nonuse or government incompetence. It would be an interesting experiment in democracy to allow individuals who do not share the commitments or priorities of their political rulers to have a greater say regarding how their tax contributions are to be allocated. This would go a long way in relieving widely experienced discontent with the manner in which government spends money and the associated sense of disempowerment and disenfranchisement, by allowing individuals to choose the programs and services they actually want.

Enlarging the domain of personal autonomy means strengthening rights of nonparticipation, opting out, and conscientious objection to collective undertakings which fail to gain one's support, while seeking to enlist it in coercive fashion. It entails the right of individuals to opt out of certain majority-approved decisions that have an adverse effect on liberty. It entails a right, for instance, to refuse participation in a labour union, including the payment of dues, if one objects to its activities. Allowing unions to compel unwilling persons to join and subsidize their organization is indeed an injustice, and while it may be one of small proportion, it bears repeating that when freedom is surrendered it is typically done so in a thousand small increments which combine to undermine the capacity for agency. By the same token, the right to participate in or opt out of various collectivities is a principle fundamental to any social order that calls itself free. Instead of governments deciding which communities or organizations are most valuable, individuals must hold a right to determine this for themselves.

Lest it be thought that a free society as described here simply refuses to grant political legitimacy to any communitarian considerations, or even those of a utilitarian nature, it must be carefully delimited what the just scope of both types of arguments are. Utilitarian considerations invariably play a large role in the fashioning of public policy, and this in itself is unobjectionable. Yet what must be insisted on amid the current reign of instrumentality are the limits of the utilitarian calculus. These limits are the rights of the individual. The latter are not merely so many utilities to be tallied alongside the various objects of desire and aversion but belong to an altogether different and more fundamental level of discourse, one concerned not merely with how we get what we want but how we become individuated, autonomous, rational, and responsible agents in social conditions that frequently conspire against this.

Similarly, considerations of collective identity, tradition, and other cultural particularities deserve to factor into the deliberations of legislators and may justify laws protective of each of them, laws that will primarily take the form of immunities rather than entitlements. Yet the same limits apply here as well. Taking these constraints seriously means that we must not expect strong forms of mutuality and fellowship within our political practices but must limit these to arrangements of peaceful accommodation in which only a limited form of 'recognition' is practiced – the recognition of another's autonomy to fashion its own existence. This is not the more thorough-going 'recognition' that has the effect of obliging participation in forms of community life to which one may or may not subscribe or outright conformity to collective ends not one's own, but is limited to the recognition of individual inviolability. Stronger forms of mutuality are properly sought in ethical, not political, relations for the reason that any strong mutualism at the political level invariably requires a sacrifice of individual rights. Strong human fellowship is not to be found in political institutions and laws but only at a more intimate level of intersubjectivity. That this could be otherwise – that the values of some could be imposed on all in the interests of solidarity, mutuality, and community – has always been the dream of tyrants.

The call for greater legal compulsion in the name of community or the common good only conceals real differences between persons with respect to ends and identity. A just social order must remain mindful of the separateness of persons and the distance that is a necessary part of all genuine belonging. It recognizes and negotiates the tension within the self between the requirements of sociability and unsociability, and it achieves this by ensuring for all persons a wide domain for autonomy.

In doing so, it fashions laws that seek accommodation and coexistence over stronger forms of emotional satisfaction and is permanently suspicious of law as a source of such satisfaction. It views the discourse of common purposes and shared aspirations with trepidation since it so commonly serves as a formula for legalized coercion and tyranny.

Yet at the same time, a liberal order recognizes that particularity is not an eliminable feature of political discourse and, in fact, is ultimately inseparable from universality. The rights and freedoms for which it demands universal recognition are never altogether separable from the particular contexts and applications in which they have their being. Individual rights are not comprehended in a cultural vacuum but depend for their practical significance on the particular circumstances and contexts in which they are applied. They are inseparable in their meaning from the forms of legislation in which they have their being, or from the actual ways in which they govern and limit human action. Yet the application of universal principles to particular cases is made possible by the capacity for reflective or practical judgment. Principles do not apply themselves but depend on practical judgment, the reflective capacity that mediates between universal and particular without recourse to further, second order, rules.

As Aristotle knew, practical judgment or *phronesis* is far from a mechanical procedure which may be divorced from particularities and historical contingencies. It is a skill informed by not only universals but above all particulars, by an understanding of particular features of actual cases. More important, practical judgment is a capacity that always operates within a lifeworld. It draws on a tacit understanding of ourselves and the historical tradition of which we are a part, on the shared experience, practices, and forms of life which comprise our historical situation. A sense of the moral life of the community always informs reflective judgment, as does the moral character and education of the speaker. This line of argument leads to a recognition of the inadequacy of any theory of right that conceives itself as a purely universalist (and formalist) theory devoid of communitarian elements. It points out the necessary limitations of a theory that awards priority to universal over particular considerations. Because the application of universal principles must rely on practical judgment that is always already historically situated, a universalist theory unmixed with local elements or values is incapable of practical implementation. A conception of justice that includes a place for universal principles must also include the various local particularities (practices, values, traditions, etc.) which invariably inform practical judgment and the reflective capacities in general. Both carry justificatory weight, even while the former takes priority over the latter.

What liberal doctrine insists on, then, is not the elimination of communitarian considerations from political discourse but their limitation. The values of a community, like the calculus of social utility, carry a degree of justificatory weight in the formation of public policy, yet both considerations violate the conditions of a just order when they are valued above or 'balanced' against the rights of the individual. The conditions of a free society and autonomous selfhood must be thus conceived.

Conclusion

Conceptions of moral selfhood in the liberal tradition have undergone periodic transformation in response to either political critiques (primarily from the left), advances in scientific knowledge, or developments in other areas of philosophy which bear on the notions of individuality, community, and rationality. Assumptions both metaphysical, ontological, psychological, sociological, economic, and moral regarding the constitution of the self as a moral and political agent on which the classical liberal problematic was originally premised were fundamentally reconceived in the decades of the late nineteenth and early twentieth centuries by Mill, Green, Hobhouse, Hobson, and Dewey. What each of these figures perceived was the need to modify, in one fashion or another, basic assumptions of liberal politics, particularly concerning the notion of the individual on which political individualism is premised. In keeping with scientific, philosophical, and political currents of that time, these liberal reformers sought in different ways to overcome aspects of the Hobbesian legacy, with mixed success. Each of these figures sought a new way of recognizing the fact and import of human sociability and incorporating this recognition into a political morality that had traditionally given priority to the rights of the individual as such. In doing so, liberal politics took a historic turn to the moderate left of the political spectrum, a partial accommodation to socialist and Marxist doctrine, believed to have comprehended the essentially social and embedded character of the self. Liberals charted a middle course between the older individualism and the fashionable politics of the left, establishing a new basis for a view of the state not as a necessary evil in the life of the individual but an expedient and vigorous promoter of human happiness. Welfare politics, the mixed economy, and the administrative megastate of contemporary lib-

eral societies were results in part of the recognition of human intercon-
nectedness and the obligations that this recognition seemed to entail.

It is the argument of this study that a satisfactory philosophical account of intersubjectivity does not entail, either directly or indirectly, any
strong mutuality or duties of mutual aid of the kind asserted by not only
several variants of illiberal politics but most liberals since the late nineteenth century. A proper recognition of human embeddedness, while an
essential step in overcoming the Hobbesian legacy, does not entail the
abandonment of political individualism, if by this term we intend the
primacy of individual rights and freedoms, state neutrality, limited government, and related principles. The failure of metaphysical conceptions
of individuality of the kind that informed the classical liberal problematic does not require an abandonment of the politics of individuality but
calls for an overhauled conception of rational moral agency which is
phenomenologically adequate and capable of recognizing the sense in
which the self is a social being.

By no logical route does sociality entail socialism, nor does a proper
recognition of the constitutive nature of community and tradition entail
a communitarian or traditionalist politics which would potentially erect
new obstacles to individual selfhood in the name of an allegedly higher
collective good. A politics of mutuality, solidarity, collectivity, and ultimately servility is not a logical consequence of a philosophy of the self
that properly accentuates its participation in lifeworld practices and
webs of intersubjectivity. A political morality of this kind, far from providing just conditions for sociability, effectively undermines authentic
belonging – now a matter of not only social but political obligation – no
less than authentic individuality. It fails to observe both the tension
within the self identified by Kant as its 'unsocial sociability' and the separateness of persons, a proper recognition of which undermines strong
appeals to solidarity and community. It subordinates all recalcitrant individuality to collective preferences in a fashion governed only by the
discretion of legislators rather than any principled constraint. Because
individual rights thrive only when they function as constraints on communitarian and utilitarian discourse rather than elements within it to be
'balanced' or 'tallied' alongside competing values, a political culture
committed to these rights places them beyond the vicissitudes of social
utility and collective preference.

While, for over a century, liberals have adopted something of a defensive posture regarding notions of sociability, embeddedness, and intersubjectivity, and have conceded political ground as a partial consequence

to socialist and communitarian politics, both the defensiveness and the concession are unwarranted. The defensiveness rests on the twin assumptions that political individualism is necessarily predicated on a socially unconditioned and absolutely sovereign individual antagonistically related to the social whole and that a socially embedded self is necessarily the inheritor of an assortment of unchosen obligations over which the state rightly presides – a cell within a greater and morally prior communal organism. That both assumptions are false may be seen by conceiving of the self as embedded in a lifeworld yet in a reflective and distanced fashion, as a socially constituted yet self-constituting agent, as belonging and participating within community life yet in a communicatively rational manner. By conceiving of the individual thus, we view it as having a capacity for agency that nonliberal politics typically overlooks or negates and for which political individualism expressly provides. The authentic integration of human sociability and unsociability – of inclinations of fellowship and detachment, public and private sentiment – is properly viewed as an achievement in the life of the individual, as is more generally the attainment of integration and coherence that is so much a part of human life. Individual agency is itself an achievement, one taking a myriad of forms and which is never without political conditions of possibility.

It is these conditions that liberal politics seeks to secure through the establishment of institutions protective of the right and capacity of self-authorship. Laws and institutions of this kind ensure that persons have the freedom to fashion their lives and to determine their ends without threat of coercion. They ensure that no persons will be consigned to a subordinate status within the larger social body, as means to the ends of a community or the state, or unwilling draftees into collective purposes not their own.

If suitably fashioned, liberal institutions protect the individual as well from the order of instrumentality for which the rights of the person are increasingly contingencies to be upheld when it suits a convenient purpose or sacrificed under the same condition and at the discretion of public officials and others in whom it places unlimited confidence. A political culture in which individuality is menaced by the very institutions charged with its cultivation, the regime of utilitarian instrumentalism presently serves as a negation of personal agency through countless measures of administering, regulating, facilitating, and micromanaging the affairs of the individual, conscripting it into a culture of organized dependence and docility. A liberal order limits the scope of the calculus of social utility just as it limits the power of communities and the state in the service of human freedom. The rights of the individual it limits only by the rights of other persons and in recognition of the equality of all before the law. It cultivates the freedom and responsibility of the individual and encourages pragmatic experimentation with deregulation and privatization of services currently provided by paternalistic government. It thus acts in recognition of the fact that autonomous agency is a contingent and ultimately fragile proposition, one that is made possible at the political level by laws and institutions protective of the rights of all and by securing for all persons a sphere of autonomy in which the cultivation of individuality may be practised.

Notes

1. The Classical Liberals

1 Michael Sandel puts this point rather well. As he expresses it, liberalism presupposes that 'certain things must be true of us. We must be creatures of a certain kind, related to human circumstance in a certain way. In particular, we must stand to our circumstance always at a certain distance, conditioned to be sure, but part of us always antecedent to any conditions. Only in this way can we view ourselves as subjects as well as objects of experience, as agents and not just instruments of the purposes we pursue.' (Michael J. Sandel, *Liberalism and the Limits of Justice* [Cambridge: Cambridge University Press, 1982], 10–11)

2 This is, of course, a standard assumption not only of early liberal thought, but of nearly all modern moral and political philosophy, and commonly referred to as foundationalism. The debate concerning foundationalism and antifoundationalism primarily turns on the issue of what kind of rational warrants are required in order for moral and political judgments to be considered justified. The most basic point of contention between foundationalists and nonfoundationalists is described by Evan Simpson as follows: 'Foundationalism and anti-foundationalism remain positions best understood by their relationship to epistemology. The one seeks, and the other dismisses the notion of, criteria defining conditions in which some beliefs are finally justified. Few deny that beliefs need foundations, that is, the more or less secure grounds which make the conclusions of argument as solid as they can be. Any pure foundationalism, however, supposes that genuine grounds for judgment are not merely confident assumptions but absolutely secure bases which are not subject to amendment, or are amenable only in the direction of greater accuracy. Only in this way could they serve as arbiters

of rational judgment. This is the notion of a single, over-arching, ahistorical standard against which any claim can be tested, so that it is possible in principle to decide between rival points of view.' (Evan Simpson, 'Colloquimur, ergo sumus' in *Anti-Foundationalism and Practical Reasoning: Conversations Between Hermeneutics and Analysis*, ed. Evan Simpson [Edmonton: Academic Printing and Publishing, 1987], 2–3)

3 See C.B. Macpherson, *The Political Theory of Possessive Individualism: Hobbes to Locke* (Oxford: Clarendon Press, 1962), 3.

4 Thomas Hobbes, *Leviathan* (Indianapolis: Hacket Publishing, 1994), 76.

5 One early liberal who held this view was Benjamin Constant. As he writes: 'The citizens possess individual rights independently of all social and political authority, and any authority which violates these rights becomes illegitimate. The rights of the citizen are individual freedom, religious freedom, freedom of opinion, which includes the freedom to express oneself openly, the enjoyment of property, a guarantee against all arbitrary power. No authority can call these rights into question without destroying its own credentials.' (Benjamin Constant, *Political Writings*, ed. and trans. Biancamaria Fontana [Cambridge: Cambridge University Press, 1988], 180)

6 Rousseau took issue with Locke on this point, maintaining that property rights cannot be derived from the state of nature. At most, goods may be held (in the physical sense of having them within one's grasp), but they may not strictly be owned in this state, according to Rousseau. Ownership of property, he pointed out, necessarily presupposes a positive title, and this is only to be had in civil society.

7 John Locke, *Two Treatises of Government*, ed. Peter Laslett (Cambridge: Cambridge University Press, 1988), 269.

8 Ibid, 350.

9 Kant went as far as to define justice itself as 'the restriction of each individual's freedom so that it harmonizes with the freedom of everyone else (in so far as this is possible within the terms of a general law).' (Immanuel Kant, *Political Writings*, ed. Hans Reiss [Cambridge: Cambridge University Press, 1991], 73)

10 Ibid, 74.

11 Hobbes, *The Elements of Law Natural and Politic*, ed. J.C.A. Gaskin (Oxford: Oxford University Press, 1994), 70.

12 Ibid, 71.

13 Ibid, 71.

14 Hobbes, *Leviathan*, 28–9.

15 Ibid, 22–3.

16 Hobbes, *The Elements of Law Natural and Politic*, 71.

17 Hobbes, *Leviathan*, 136.

18 Richard Peters and Henri Tajfel, 'Hobbes and Hull: Metaphysicians of Behavior,' in *Hobbes and Rousseau: A Collection of Critical Essays*, ed. Maurice Cranston and Richard S. Peters (Garden City, NY: Anchor Books, 1972), 180.
19 Locke, *Two Treatises of Government*, 318–19.
20 Locke, *An Essay Concerning Human Understanding*, ed. Peter H. Nidditch (Oxford: Clarendon Press, 1975), 283.
21 Ibid, 346–7.
22 The problem of classification is not one that I intend to belabour here. Certainly not all liberal theorists, classical or contemporary, hold an identical set of doctrines in common and are more likely related by means of Wittgensteinian family resemblances than with reference to a shared allegiance to a core doctrine. It is primarily on account of Rousseau's commitments to principles of civil liberty, moral autonomy, the social contract, governance according to the general will and related principles that I include this figure for discussion in the present chapter.
23 Jean-Jacques Rousseau, *Discourse on Political Economy*, trans. Christopher Betts (New York: Oxford University Press, 1994), 18.
24 As one commentator has pointed out, Rousseau held a realist view of the general will: 'The general will ... is not the policy decided upon in public deliberation, but rather the policy that *ought* to be decided upon in public deliberation. Rousseau himself sometimes obscures this distinction, by (carelessly) using the term "general will" to refer to the outcome of public deliberation. Nonetheless, he holds a realist conception of the general will, in the sense that he holds that its content is a matter of fact and this fact is independent of any actual procedure a society might use to determine its general will.' (Zev M. Trachtenberg, *Making Citizens: Rousseau's Political Theory of Culture* [New York: Routledge, 1993], 8)
25 Rousseau, 'A Discourse on the Origin of Inequality,' in *The Social Contract and Discourses*, trans. G. Cole (London: Everyman Library, 1993), 60.
26 Rousseau, *Discourse on Political Economy*, 6.
27 Rousseau, *The Social Contract*, trans. Christopher Betts (New York: Oxford University Press, 1994), 57.
28 Constant, *Political Writings*, 195.
29 Kant, *Groundwork of the Metaphysics of Morals*, trans. H.J. Paton (New York: Harper and Row, 1964), 114.
30 Kant, *Political Writings*, 44.
31 Ibid, 46.
32 Ibid, 46.
33 Kant, *Critique of Pure Reason*, trans. Norman Kemp Smith (New York: St Martin's Press, 1965), 312.

2. Utilitarian and New Liberals

1 Jeremy Bentham, *An Introduction to the Principles of Morals and Legislation*, ed. J.H. Burns and H.L.A. Hart (London: Athlone Press, 1970), 1.
2 John Stuart Mill, *Utilitarianism*, ed. George Sher (Indianapolis: Hacket Publishing Company, 1979), 34.
3 Thomas Hill Green, *Prolegomena to Ethics* (Oxford: Clarendon Press, 1906), 10.
4 Mill, *Utilitarianism*, 30.
5 Ibid, 31.
6 Leonard Trelawny Hobhouse, *Morals in Evolution: A Study in Comparative Ethics* (New York: Henry Holt and Company, 1923), 15.
7 Green, *The Political Theory of T.H. Green: Selected Writings*, ed. John R. Rodman (New York: Meredith Publishing Company, 1964), 51–2.
8 Bentham, *Bentham's Political Thought*, ed. Bhikhu Parekh (London: Croom Helm, 1973), 269–70.
9 Perhaps the most significant point of disagreement concerned the question of whether there may be thought to be a social will that transcends in nature and importance the sum of individual wills in the community. Is society a living organism possessing ends of its own to which individual rights are subordinate? Green and Hobhouse, as we shall see, both replied in the negative while Hobson and other left liberals replied in the affirmative.
10 Hobhouse, *Liberalism and Other Writings*, ed. James Meadowcroft (Cambridge: Cambridge University Press, 1994), 32.
11 John Atkinson Hobson, *Work and Wealth: A Human Valuation* (London: Macmillan, 1914), 304.
12 Bentham, *An Introduction to the Principles of Morals and Legislation*, 33.
13 Ibid, 33–4.
14 The Manuscripts of Jeremy Bentham, Dumont College, University of Geneva, Folder 33/1, 161.
15 The Manuscripts of Jeremy Bentham, University College, London, Box 15, Folder 19, 153.
16 Mill, *Utilitarianism*, 36.
17 Mill, *On the Logic of the Moral Sciences*, ed. Henry M. Magid (New York: Bobbs-Merrill, 1965), 10.
18 Albert William Levi, 'The Value of Freedom: Mill's Liberty' in *On Liberty*, John Stuart Mill (New York: W.W. Norton and Company, 1975), 197.
19 Mill, *On Liberty*, 57–8.
20 Ibid, 64.
21 Ibid, 7.
22 Green, *Prolegomena to Ethics*, 110.

23 Ibid, 207.
24 Ibid, 113.
25 Green, *Lectures on the Principles of Political Obligation* (New York: Longmans, Green and Company, 1950), 26.
26 Ibid, 110.
27 Ibid, 24.
28 Green, *Prolegomena to Ethics*, 117.
29 Ibid, 100.
30 Ibid, 120.
31 Green, *The Political Theory of T.H. Green*, 52.
32 Hobhouse, *The Elements of Social Justice* (New York: Henry Holt and Company, 1922), 56.
33 Ibid, 52–3.
34 Hobhouse, *Liberalism and Other Writings*, ed. James Meadowcroft (Cambridge: Cambridge University Press, 1994), 61.
35 Ibid, 62.
36 Hobhouse, *The Elements of Social Justice*, 122–3.
37 Hobhouse, *Liberalism*, 32.

3. Neoclassical Liberals and Communitarian Critics

1 I emphasize that the selection of these two figures for detailed discussion by no means suggests that their views of the self warrant more serious attention than those offered by other liberal writers. Indeed, I do not hold this view. As I argue in Chapter 4, the liberal philosopher of the twentieth century whose account of the self deserves to be taken most seriously is John Dewey. My discussion of Dewey's account is postponed for the following chapter because of its somewhat anomalous status in the context of twentieth-century liberal thought and the use to which I put it in developing my own theory of the self in the second part of this book.
2 Robert Nozick, *Anarchy, State, and Utopia* (New York: Basic Books, 1974), 33.
3 John Rawls, *A Theory of Justice* (Cambridge: Harvard University Press, 1971), 3.
4 Nozick, *Anarchy, State, and Utopia*, 29.
5 Ronald Dworkin, *Taking Rights Seriously* (Cambridge: Harvard University Press, 1977), xi.
6 Rawls, *A Theory of Justice*, 3–4.
7 Nozick, *Philosophical Explanations* (Cambridge: Harvard University Press, 1981), 522.
8 Rawls, *Political Liberalism* (New York: Columbia University Press, 1993), 51.
9 See Sandel, *Liberalism and the Limits of Justice*.

10 See Rawls, *Political Liberalism*, 27–9.

11 Ibid, 28.

12 Rawls, *A Theory of Justice*, 522.

13 Rawls, *Political Liberalism*, xxxi.

14 Rawls, *A Theory of Justice*, 137.

15 Ibid, 587.

16 Ibid, 255.

17 Rawls, 'Justice as Fairness: Political not Metaphysical,' in *Communitarianism and Individualism*, ed. Shlomo Avineri and Avner de-Shalit (Oxford: Oxford University Press, 1992), 198.

18 Rawls, *A Theory of Justice*, 560.

19 Ibid, 560.

20 Rawls, *Political Liberalism*, 380.

21 Like Rawls, Nozick is not concerned to elaborate in his political writings (notably *Anarchy, State, and Utopia*) a comprehensive philosophy of the self. Much of what is said or implied in these writings about moral agents has the status of assumptions. These assumptions, however, form a coherent picture, and when read in combination with some of Nozick's work published after *Anarchy, State, and Utopia* on ethics, politics, and metaphysics, the conception becomes more elaborate and philosophically interesting.

22 Nozick, *Philosophical Explanations*, 522.

23 Ibid, 110.

24 Nozick, *The Nature of Rationality* (Princeton: Princeton University Press, 1993), 133.

25 That such an assertion should be received in some philosophical circles as axiomatic should give us pause. The boldness of the claim is altogether lost on many readers for whom instrumental rationality is not one particular conception of human reason but the whole of it. An illuminating discussion of how this state of affairs came to pass and how it might be transcended is provided by Hans-Georg Gadamer in *Reason in the Age of Science* (trans. Frederick G. Lawrence [Cambridge: MIT Press], 1981).

26 Nozick, *The Nature of Rationality*, 134.

27 Another point deserving mention from Nozick's metaphysical writings is his view of the self as having a capacity for reflexive self-reference. The 'I' is synthesized in the act of referring to itself, and is reflexively present to itself. Conceived metaphysically, the self is nothing apart from the entity synthesized in the act of self-reference – thus no 'thing' at all.

28 Nozick, *Philosophical Explanations*, 291.

29 Ibid, 292. Nozick's treatment of the issue does arrive at a very halting and limited acceptance of the possibility of free will, however what is most striking

about his discussion is the extent of his reservation. The basis upon which Nozick apparently accepts this possibility is acknowledged by him as being not altogether satisfactory.

30 Ibid, 447.

31 Nozick, *Anarchy, State, and Utopia*, 95.

32 Nozick, *The Nature of Rationality*, 137.

33 In the more recent text, Nozick writes: 'The political philosophy presented in *Anarchy, State, and Utopia* ignored the importance to us of joint and official serious symbolic statement and expression of our social ties and concern and hence … is inadequate' (*The Nature of Rationality*, 32). All the same, it is doubtful that this modification of the earlier view pays proper heed to the idea of humanly significant meaning, much less to human sociability. Translating the hermeneutically rich concept of meaning or significance into the technical 'symbolic utility' – fully commensurable with other modes of utility and hence merely one more factor to be tallied, quantified, and scored in quasi-economic fashion – at best is a translation in which much is lost, and at worst flattens out the category of significance entirely. This rich notion is impoverished to the point of bankruptcy in being translated into the formal and technical vocabulary of decision theory.

34 Sandel, *Liberalism and the Limits of Justice*, 10–11.

35 Indeed, whether communitarianism lies within the ambit of the liberal tradition or falls outside it is a matter of some disagreement. Whether the debate between liberals and communitarians is construed as a family dispute or a dispute between rival paradigms is an issue of classification which need not be resolved here.

36 One would think there are several such exceptions, most or all of whom fall outside the main line of utilitarian and contractarian liberalism. Liberals such as T.H. Green, L.T. Hobhouse, and John Dewey suggest themselves as exceptions to the communitarian depiction of liberalism as an atomistic creed unmindful of the fact of human sociability. These theorists have little to learn from the communitarian critique, even if their ideas of the consequences of this recognition are not immune from criticism on other grounds.

37 Charles Taylor, *Sources of the Self: The Making of the Modern Identity* (Cambridge: Cambridge University Press, 1989), 27.

38 Taylor, 'Atomism,' in *Communitarianism and Individualism*, ed. Shlomo Avineri and Avner de-Shalit, 30.

39 Sandel, *Democracy's Discontent: America in Search of a Public Philosophy* (Cambridge: Harvard University Press, 1996), 13.

40 Alasdair MacIntyre, *After Virtue: A Study in Moral Theory*, 2nd ed. (Notre Dame: University of Notre Dame Press, 1984), 263.

41 Broad characterizations of this kind are destined to be flawed, and this one is no exception. To be sure, not all communitarians favour a sizeable turn to the left just as not all twentieth-century liberals favour a more moderate form of welfare politics. In the United States in particular, there is a formidable communitarianism of the right: the so-called moral-majority or family-values faction of the Republican Party. Some philosophers, such as Richard Rorty and Joseph Raz, employ communitarian arguments in reaching liberal conclusions. Other exceptions undoubtedly exist.

42 MacIntyre, *After Virtue*, 221.

43 Will Kymlicka, *Liberalism, Community, and Culture* (Oxford: Clarendon Press, 1989), 52.

44 David Gauthier, *Morals by Agreement* (Oxford: Clarendon Press, 1986), 350.

45 Sandel, *Liberalism and the Limits of Justice*, 179.

46 Ibid, 179.

47 Taylor, *Sources of the Self*, 37.

48 Amy Gutmann, 'Communitarian Critics of Liberalism,' in *Communitarianism and Individualism*, ed. Shlomo Avineri and Avner de-Shalit, 132.

49 Kymlicka, 'Liberal Individualism and Liberal Neutrality,' in *Communitarianism and Individualism*, ed. Shlomo Avineri and Avner de-Shalit, 178.

50 As Irving Kristol has stated: 'The liberty of a liberal society derives from a prevalent skepticism as to anyone's ability to know the "common good" with certainty, and from the conviction that the authorities should not try to define this "common good" in any but a minimal way.' (Irving Kristol, *Two Cheers for Capitalism* [New York: Mentor Books, 1979], 178)

4. Changing the Subject: Refashioning the Liberal Self

1 Friedrich Nietzsche, *The Will to Power*, trans. Walter Kaufmann and R.J. Hollingdale (New York: Vintage Books, 1968), sec. 561.

2 Anthony Paul Kerby, *Narrative and the Self* (Bloomington: Indiana University Press, 1991), 110.

3 Ibid, 5.

4 Emile Benveniste expresses a view of the subject as a linguistic construct in the following terms: 'It is in and through language that man constitutes himself as a *subject*, because language alone establishes the concept of "ego" in reality, in *its* reality which is that of the being. The "subjectivity" we are discussing here is the capacity of the speaker to posit himself as "subject." It is defined not by the feeling which everyone experiences of being himself (this feeling, to the degree that it can be taken note of, is only a reflection) but as the psychic unity that transcends the totality of the actual experiences

it assembles and that makes the permanence of the consciousness. Now we hold that "subjectivity," whether it is placed in phenomenology or in psychology, as one may wish, is only the emergence in the being of a fundamental property of language. "Ego" is he who *says* "ego." This is where we see the foundation of "subjectivity," which is determined by the linguistic status of "person."' (Emile Benveniste, *Problems in General Linguistics*, trans. Mary Meek [Coral Gables, FL: University of Miami Press, 1971], 224)

5 Theodore R. Sarbin, 'The Narrative as a Root Metaphor for Psychology,' in *Narrative Psychology: The Storied Nature of Human Conduct*, ed. Theodore R. Sarbin (New York: Praeger, 1986), 8.

6 Paul Ricoeur, *Time and Narrative*, vol. 1, trans. Kathleen McLaughlin and David Pellauer (Chicago: University of Chicago Press, 1984), 3.

7 Ricoeur, *Oneself as Another*, trans. Kathleen Blamey (Chicago: University of Chicago Press, 1992), 161.

8 Ricoeur, 'On Interpretation,' in *Philosophy in France Today*, ed. Alan Montefiore (Cambridge: Cambridge University Press, 1983), 170.

9 William Lowell Randall, *The Stories We Are: An Essay on Self-Creation* (Toronto: University of Toronto Press, 1995), 138.

10 Ricoeur, 'History as Narrative and Practice,' *Philosophy Today* 29 (1979), 214.

11 Kerby, *Narrative and the Self*, 4.

12 Randall, *The Stories We Are*, 111.

13 Nietzsche, *Beyond Good and Evil: Prelude to a Philosophy of the Future*, trans. Walter Kaufmann (New York, Vintage Books, 1989), sec. 62.

14 David Carr, *Time, Narrative, and History* (Bloomington: Indiana University Press, 1986), 89–90.

15 John Dewey, *Theory of the Moral Life* (New York: Irvington Publishers, 1980), 151.

16 Ibid, 149.

17 Dewey, *Human Nature and Conduct* (Carbondale: Southern Illinois University Press, 1988), 150.

18 G.W.F. Hegel, *Elements of the Philosophy of Right*, trans. H.B. Nisbet (Cambridge: Cambridge University Press, 1991), 124.

19 Gary Madison, in a discussion of Ricoeur, makes this observation: '[I]f "man," the human subject, is, as the Greeks said, the "speaking animal," it is equally true that he is the "acting animal," *animal agens*. If language is, as Heidegger would say, an *existentiale*, an essential characteristic of human being, so likewise is action. Action is co-primordial with language; human existence is inconceivable apart from it.' (Gary Madison, 'Ricoeur and the Hermeneutics of the Subject,' in *The Philosophy of Paul Ricoeur: The Library of Living Philosophers*, vol. 22, ed. Lewis Edwin Hahn [Chicago: Open Court, 1995], 82).

20 Mark Johnson, taking a cognitive scientific approach on this issue, defends a similar view in his *Moral Imagination: Implications of Cognitive Science for Ethics* (Chicago: University of Chicago Press, 1993). See especially Chapter 7, 'The Narrative Context of Self and Action.'

21 Nietzsche, *On the Genealogy of Morals*, trans. Walter Kaufmann and R.J. Hollingdale (New York: Vintage Books, 1969), I, sec 13.

22 MacIntyre, *After Virtue*, 213.

23 Nietzsche, *Beyond Good and Evil*, sec 97.

24 Ricoeur, *Oneself as Another*, 162.

25 Randall, *The Stories We Are*, 41.

26 Dewey, *Theory of the Moral Life*, 172.

27 See Ibid, 15.

28 Ibid, 11.

29 See especially *After Virtue*, chapt. 15.

30 Nietzsche, *The Gay Science*, trans. Walter Kaufmann (New York: Vintage Books, 1974), sec 290.

31 Carr, *Time, Narrative, and History*, 83.

32 The Heideggerian view ought to be clearly distinguished from Sartre's radically voluntaristic conception of existential authenticity according to which the human subject is a radically free agent capable of constituting itself seemingly out of nothing. The Heideggerian notion of authenticity, unlike Sartre's, is fully mindful of the extent to which the self as a being-in-the-world has already been constituted through its involvements in a network of practices, relationships, language, and preunderstandings. Authenticity for Heidegger is not a question of the self choosing itself in a perfectly unconditioned fashion or *ex nihilo*, an illusion of the modern metaphysics of individuality.

33 Ricoeur, *Oneself as Another*, 171.

34 Karl Jaspers, *Man in the Modern Age*, trans. Eden and Cedar Paul (Garden City, NY: Doubleday Anchor Books, 1957), 221.

35 José Ortega y Gasset, *The Revolt of the Masses* (New York: W.W. Norton and Co., 1957), 47–8.

36 Carr, *Time, Narrative, and History*, 96.

37 René J. Muller, *The Marginal Self: An Existential Inquiry into Narcissism* (Atlantic Highlands, NJ: Humanities Press, 1987), 103.

38 Nietzsche, *Thus Spoke Zarathustra: A Book for Everyone and No One*, trans. R.J. Hollingdale (New York: Penguin Books, 1985), 213.

39 'Freedom,' as Pierre Manent points out, 'is less doing what I want than being able not to do what you want me to.' (Pierre Manent, *An Intellectual History of Liberalism*, trans. Rebecca Balinski [Princeton: Princeton University Press, 1994], 62)

40 Jaspers, *Man in the Modern Age*, 14.
41 Gabriel Marcel, *Man Against Mass Society*, trans. G.S. Fraser (South Bend, Indiana: Gateway Editions, 1952), 59.

5. Rational Agency

1 Max Horkheimer and Theodor W. Adorno, *Dialectic of Enlightenment*, trans. John Cumming (New York: Continuum, 1991), 25.
2 See especially 'The Question Concerning Technology' and 'The Age of the World Picture' in Martin Heidegger, *The Question Concerning Technology and Other Essays*, trans. William Lovitt (New York: Harper & Row, 1977); see also *The Principle of Reason*, trans. Reginald Lilly (Bloomington: Indiana University Press, 1991).
3 See especially Hans-Georg Gadamer, *Truth and Method*, trans. Joel Weinsheimer and Donald G. Marshall (New York: Crossroad, 1989).
4 William Barrett, *The Illusion of Technique: A Search for Meaning in a Technological Civilization*. (Garden City, NY: Anchor Books, 1976), 27.
5 Gadamer, *Reason in the Age of Science*, trans. Frederick G. Lawrence (Cambridge: MIT Press, 1989), 73.
6 Heidegger, *The Question Concerning Technology and Other Essays*, 17.
7 Karl Jaspers, *The Future of Mankind*, trans. E.B. Ashton (Chicago: University of Chicago Press, 1961), 221.
8 Jaspers, *Reason and Anti-Reason in Our Time*, trans. Stanley Godman (London: SCM Press, 1952), 42.
9 Ibid, 39.
10 Ibid.
11 Gary Madison also notes that the 'voluntary renunciation of force' necessarily presupposed by communicative reason takes two forms: 'Communicative reason knows no absolute other than the will to communicate, to resolve differences, and to seek mutual, uncoerced agreement. The only condition for its taking place is a voluntary renunciation of force on the part of the discussants and any attempt on their part to coerce agreement, be it by brute force or "irrefutable" logical argumentation (of a theoretical or ideological sort).' (Gary Madison, *The Logic of Liberty* [New York: Greenwood Press, 1986], 218)
12 Some of the more notable of these include Richard Bernstein (see especially *Beyond Objectivism and Relativism: Science, Hermeneutics, and Praxis* [Philadelphia: University of Pennsylvania Press, 1985] and *The New Constellation: The Ethical-Political Horizons of Modernity/Postmodernity* [Cambridge: MIT Press, 1992]), Gary Madison (*The Logic of Liberty*), Richard Rorty (*Contingency, Irony,*

and Solidarity [Cambridge: Cambridge University Press, 1989]), Georgia Warnke (*Justice and Interpretation* [Cambridge: MIT Press, 1993]), P. Christopher Smith (*Hermeneutics and Human Finitude: Toward a Theory of Ethical Understanding* [New York: Fordham University Press, 1991]), and Roberto Alejandro (*Hermeneutics, Citizenship, and the Public Sphere* [Albany: State University of New York Press, 1995]). Also see an important collection of essays in *Rationality Today*, ed. Theodore F. Geraets (Ottawa, ON: University of Ottawa Press, 1979).

13 See especially Habermas's two-volume *The Theory of Communicative Action. Volume 1: Reason and the Rationalization of Society* and *Volume 2: Lifeworld and System: A Critique of Functionalist Reason*, trans. Thomas McCarthy (Boston: Beacon Press, 1984 and 1987).

14 As Charles Larmore writes: 'But if moral judgment is not thoroughly rule-governed, it is not arbitrary either. Judgment certainly involves risk. Yet it does not resemble the flipping of a coin or a decisionistic leap of faith. Judgment we do not exercise blindly, but rather by responding with reasons to the particularity of a given situation. The fact that we are struggling to comprehend is that our perception of these reasons as indeed reasons and the response that they motivate go beyond what the general rules given in advance (as well as characteristic sentiments and training) could alone make of the situation.' (Charles Larmore, *Patterns of Moral Complexity* [Cambridge: Cambridge University Press, 1988], 20)

15 Gadamer and Harold I. Brown have both likened judgment to skilful behaviour. See Gadamer, *Truth and Method*, 31; and Brown, *Rationality* (New York: Routledge, 1988), 165.

16 One recent manifestation of this is the political correctness movement. This assortment of enthusiasts would have language cleansed of all expressions that could possibly cause offence, at the cost not only of liberty but of a new linguistic conformism reminiscent of Orwellian newspeak. Ostensibly designed to rid language of all vestiges of power, it succeeds only in substituting one form of the will to power for another.

6. The Political Conditions of Agency

1 Isaiah Berlin, *Four Essays on Liberty* (Oxford: Oxford University Press, 1969), 131.

2 Friedrich A. Hayek expresses this as follows: 'Though the coerced still chooses, the alternatives are determined for him by the coercer so that he will choose what the coercer wants. He is not altogether deprived of the use of his capacities; but he is deprived of the possibility of using his knowledge for his own aims.' (Friedrich Hayek, *The Constitution of Liberty* [Chicago: University of Chicago Press, 1960], 134)

3 George Kateb, *The Inner Ocean: Individualism and Democratic Culture* (Ithaca: Cornell University Press, 1992), 5.

4 Hayek, *The Constitution of Liberty*, 71.

5 Lawrence Haworth, *Autonomy: An Essay in Philosophical Psychology and Ethics* (New Haven: Yale Universiy Press, 1986), 126.

6 Berlin, 124.

7 Hobbes, *Leviathan*, 136.

8 Ibid, 143.

9 Haworth, *Autonomy*, 119.

10 Charles Taylor correctly observes that this common confusion requires explanation. He writes: 'The culture of narcissism lives an ideal that it is systematically falling below. But if I'm right, then this fact needs an explanation. Why does it fall below its ideal? What makes the ethic of authenticity prone to this kind of deviation into the trivial?' (Taylor, *The Malaise of Modernity* [Concord, ON.: Anansi Press, 1991], 57)

11 On this point I am in agreement with Stephen Holmes, who writes: 'Yes, perfect neutrality is impossible; but relative neutrality is well within human powers.' (Stephen Holmes, 'The Permanent Structure of Anti-Liberal Thought,' in *Liberalism and the Moral Life*, ed. Nancy L. Rosenblum [Cambridge: Harvard University Press, 1989], 245)

12 Taylor makes this charge in the following passage, one representative of the communitarian sentiment regarding neutrality: 'A society like Quebec cannot but be dedicated to the defense and promotion of French culture and language, even if this involves some restriction on individual freedoms. It cannot make cultural-linguistic orientation a matter of indifference.' (Taylor, 'Cross-Purposes: The Liberal-Communitarian Debate,' in *Liberalism and the Moral Life*, ed. Nancy L. Rosenblum, 182)

13 The qualification is important and troubling since in mass societies universal agreement on virtually any end or law is often beyond reach. The anarchist may oppose on principle any act of government whatever, while in the less extreme case opposition, if only on a small scale, seems an omnipresent feature of modern political culture. Even the imperfectly or relatively neutral state may find the scope of genuinely shared ends exceedingly narrow or even nonexistent.

14 Mill, *On Liberty*, 6.

15 Hayek, *The Constitution of Liberty*, 232.

16 Alexis de Tocqueville, *Democracy in America.*, vol. 2 (New York: Vintage Books, 1972), 320.

17 Hayek, *The Constitution of Liberty*, 258.

18 Tocqueville, *Democracy in America.*, vol. 2, 318–19.

19 Theorists concerned with distributive justice and also intergenerational ethics
may want to consider the question, now an ethical one, of whether the
habitual practice of passing down massive government debt from generation
to generation might not conflict with an obligation to future generations to bear
full economic responsibility for state programs of which present generations
are the 'beneficiaries.' The distributive question no longer concerns solely who,
among those presently alive and earning incomes, should pay the cost of
various redistributive measures but more problematically which generations
will subsidize which others. The question has become one of some urgency
as the size of government debt increases in many nations at an alarming rate.

Bibliography

Ackerman, Bruce. *Social Justice in the Liberal State*. New Haven: Yale University Press, 1980.

Adorno, Theodor W. *The Jargon of Authenticity*. Trans. Knut Tarnowski and Frederick Will. Evanston, IL: Northwestern University Press, 1973.

Alejandro, Roberto. *Hermeneutics, Citizenship, and the Public Sphere*. Albany: State University of New York Press, 1993.

Apel, Karl-Otto. *Towards a Transformation of Philosophy*. Trans. Glyn Adey and Davis Frisby. Boston: Routledge and Kegan Paul, 1980.

Arblaster, Anthony. *The Rise and Decline of Western Liberalism*. Oxford: Blackwell, 1984.

Arendt, Hannah. 'Freedom and Politics.' In *Freedom and Serfdom: An Anthology of Western Thought*. Ed. Albert Hunold. Dordrecht: D. Reidel Publishing Co., 1961.

– *The Human Condition*. Chicago: University of Chicago Press, 1958.

– *The Origins of Totalitarianism*. New York: Harcourt Brace Jovanovich, 1973.

Avineri, Shlomo, Avner de-Shalit, eds. *Communitarianism and Individualism*. Oxford: Oxford University Press, 1992.

Barrett, William. *The Illusion of Technique: A Search for Meaning in a Technological Civilization*. Garden City, NY: Anchor Books, 1976.

Barry, Brian. *The Liberal Theory of Justice*. Oxford: Oxford University Press, 1973.

Beiner, Ronald. 'Do We Need a Philosophical Ethics? Theory, Prudence, and the Primacy of Ethos.' *Philosophical Forum* 20, no. 3.

– *Political Judgment*. Chicago: University of Chicago Press, 1983.

– *What's the Matter with Liberalism?* Los Angeles: University of California Press, 1992.

Bellamy, Richard. *Liberalism and Modern Society: A Historical Argument*. University Park, PA: Pennsylvania State University Press, 1992.

Bellamy, Richard, and Martin Hollis. 'Liberal Justice: Political and Metaphysical.' *The Philosophical Quarterly* 45, no. 178 (January 1995).

Benhabib, Seyla. *Critique, Norm, and Utopia: A Study of the Foundations of Critical Theory*. New York: Columbia University Press, 1986.

Benhabib, Seyla, and Fred Dallmayr, eds. *The Communicative Ethics Controversy*. Cambridge: MIT Press, 1990.

– *Situating the Self*. New York: Routledge, 1992.

Benn, Stanley I. *A Theory of Freedom*. Cambridge: Cambridge University Press, 1988.

Bentham, Jeremy. *Bentham's Political Thought*. Ed. Bhikhu Parekh. London: Croom Helm, 1973.

– *Deontology, A Table of the Springs of Action, and Article on Utilitarianism*. Ed. Amnon Goldworth. Oxford: Clarendon Press, 1984.

– *A Fragment on Government*. Cambridge: Cambridge University Press, 1988.

– *An Introduction to the Principles of Morals and Legislation*. Ed. J.H. Burns and H.L.A. Hart. London: Athlone Press, 1970.

– *The Theory of Legislation*. Ed. C.K. Ogden. London: Kegan Paul, 1931.

Benveniste, Emile. *Problems in General Linguistics*. Trans. Mary Meek. Coral Gables, FL: University of Miami Press, 1971.

Berlin, Isaiah. *Four Essays on Liberty*. Oxford: Oxford University Press, 1969.

Bernstein, Richard J. *Beyond Objectivism and Relativism: Science, Hermeneutics, and Praxis*. Philadelphia: University of Pennsylvania Press, 1985.

– 'From Hermeneutics to Praxis.' *Review of Metaphysics*, no. 140.

– *The New Constellation: The Ethical-Political Horizons of Modernity/Postmodernity*. Cambridge: MIT Press, 1992.

– 'Philosophy in the Conversation of Mankind.' *Review of Metaphysics*, no. 132.

Bobbio, Norberto. *Left and Right: The Significance of a Political Distinction*. Trans. Allan Cameron. Chicago: University of Chicago Press, 1996.

Brenkert, George G. *Political Freedom*. New York: Routledge, 1991.

Britton, Bruce K., and Anthony D. Pellegrini, eds. *Narrative Thought and Narrative Language*. Hillsdale, NJ: Lawrence Erlbaum Associates, 1990.

Brown, Harold I. *Rationality*. New York: Routledge, 1988.

Buchanan, James M. *The Limits of Liberty: Between Anarchy and Leviathan*. Chicago: University of Chicago Press, 1975.

Carr, David. 'Life and the Narrator's Art.' In *Hermeneutics and Deconstruction*, ed. Hugh J. Silverman and Don Ihde. Albany: State University of New York Press, 1985.

– *Time, Narrative, and History*. Bloomington: Indiana University Press, 1986.

Champigny, Robert. *The Ontology of Narrative: An Analysis*. The Hague: Mouton, 1972.

Coleman, J., and T. Fararo, eds. *Rational Choice Theory: Advocacy and Critique.* Los Angeles: Sage, 1992.

Constant, Benjamin. *Political Writings.* Ed. and trans. Biancamaria Fontana. Cambridge: Cambridge University Press, 1988.

Corngold, Stanley. *The Fate of the Self: German Writers and French Theory.* Durham: Duke University Press, 1994.

Cranston, Maurice. *Freedom: A New Social Analysis.* London: Longmans, 1967.

Cranston, Maurice, and Richard S. Peters, eds. *Hobbes and Rousseau: A Collection of Critical Essays.* Garden City, NY: Anchor Books, 1972.

Crites, Stephen. 'The Narrative Quality of Experience.' *Journal of the American Academy of Religion.* 39, no. 3 (Sept. 1971).

Cumming, R.D. *Human Nature and History: A Study of the Development of Liberal Political Thought.* Chicago: University of Chicago Press, 1969.

Daly, M., ed. *Communitarianism: A New Public Ethics.* Belmont, CA: Wadsworth, 1994.

Danto, Arthur. *Narration and Knowledge.* New York: Columbia University Press, 1985.

Dewey, John. *Freedom and Culture.* Buffalo: Prometheus Books, 1989.

– *Human Nature and Conduct.* The Middle Works, vol. 14: 1922. Ed. Jo Ann Boydston. Carbondale: Southern Illinois University Press, 1988.

– *Individualism: Old and New.* New York: Capricorn, 1962.

– *Liberalism and Social Action.* New York: Capricorn Books, 1963.

– *Theory of the Moral Life.* New York: Irvington Publishers, 1980.

Dietze, Gottfried. *Liberalism Proper and Proper Liberalism.* London: Johns Hopkins University Press, 1985.

Digeser, Peter. *Our Politics, Our Selves?* Princeton: Princeton University Press, 1995.

Douglas, Jack D. *The Myth of the Welfare State.* New Brunswick: Transaction Publishers, 1989.

Dumont, Louis. *Essays on Individualism: Modern Ideology in Anthropological Perspective.* Chicago: University of Chicago Press, 1986.

Dworkin, Ronald. 'Liberal Community.' *California Law Review* 77 (1989).

– *Taking Rights Seriously.* Cambridge: Harvard University Press, 1977.

Ellul, Jacques. *The Betrayal of the West.* New York: Seabury Press, 1978.

Esquith, Stephen L. *Intimacy and Spectacle: Liberal Theory as a Political Education.* Ithaca: Cornell University Press, 1994.

Ewin, R.E. *Liberty, Community, and Justice.* Totowa, NJ: Rowman and Littlefield, 1987.

Foster, Matthew. *Gadamer and Practical Philosophy: The Hermeneutics of Moral Confidence.* Atlanta: Scholars Press, 1991.

Foucault, Michel. *Politics, Philosophy, Culture: Interviews and Other Writings, 1977–1984*. Ed. Lawrence D. Kritzman. Trans. Alan Sheridan and others. New York: Routledge, 1988.

– *Power/Knowledge: Selected Interviews and Other Writings, 1972–1977*. Ed. Colin Gordon. Trans. Colin Gordon, Leo Marshall, John Mepham, and Kate Soper. New York: Pantheon Books, 1972.

– *Remarks on Marx*. Trans. James Goldstein and James Cascaito. New York: Semiotext(e), 1991.

Freeden, Michael, ed. *J.A. Hobson: A Reader*. London: Unwin Hyman, 1988.

– *The New Liberalism: An Ideology of Social Reform*. Oxford: Clarendon Press, 1978.

Gadamer, Hans-Georg. *The Idea of the Good in Platonic-Aristotelian Philosophy*. Trans. P. Christopher Smith. New Haven: Yale University Press, 1986.

– 'The Power of Reason.' *Man and World* 3, no. 1.

– 'The Problem of Historical Consciousness.' In *Interpretive Social Science: A Second Look*. Ed. Paul Rabinow and William M. Sullivan. Los Angeles: University of California Press, 1987.

– *Reason in the Age of Science*. Trans. Frederick G. Lawrence. Cambridge: MIT Press, 1982.

– 'Theory, Technology, Practice: The Task of the Science of Man.' *Social Research* 44, no. 3.

– *Truth and Method*. 2nd rev. ed. Trans. Joel Weinsheimer and Donald Marshall. New York: Crossroad, 1989.

Galston, William A. *Liberal Purposes: Goods, Virtues, and Diversity in the Liberal State*. Cambridge: Cambridge University Press, 1991.

Garvey, John H. *What Are Freedoms For?* Cambridge: Harvard University Press, 1996.

Gaus, Gerald F. *Justificatory Liberalism: An Essay on Epistemology and Political Theory*. Oxford: Oxford University Press, 1996.

– *The Modern Liberal Theory of Man*. New York: St Martin's Press, 1983.

Gauthier, David. *Moral Dealing: Contract, Ethics, and Reason*. Ithaca: Cornell University Press, 1990.

– *Morals by Agreement*. Oxford: Clarendon Press, 1986.

Geraets, Theodore F., ed. *Rationality Today*. Ottawa: University of Ottawa Press, 1979.

Goodin, Robert E. *Utilitarianism as a Public Philosophy*. Cambridge: Cambridge University Press, 1995.

Goodin, Robert E., and Andrew Reeve, eds. *Liberal Neutrality*. New York: Routledge, 1989.

Gray, John. *Liberalism*. Milton Keynes: Open University Press, 1986.

Gray, Tim. *Freedom*. Atlantic Highlands, NJ: Humanities Press, 1991.

Green, Thomas Hill. *Lectures on the Principles of Political Obligation*. New York: Longmans, Green & Co., 1950.

– *The Political Theory of T.H. Green: Selected Writings*. Ed. John R. Rodman. New York: Meredith Publishing Company, 1964.

– *Prolegomena to Ethics*. Oxford: Clarendon Press, 1906.

Griffiths, Morwenna. *Feminisms and the Self: The Web of Identity*. New York: Routledge, 1995.

Gutman, Amy. 'Communitarian Critics of Liberalism.' *Philosophy and Public Affairs* 14, (1985).

– *Liberal Equality*. Cambridge: Cambridge University Press, 1980.

Habermas, Jürgen. *The Inclusion of the Other: Studies in Political Theory*. Ed. Ciaran Cronin and Pable De Greiff. Trans. Ciaran Cronin. Cambridge: MIT Press, 1998.

– *Justification and Application: Remarks on Discourse Ethics*. Trans. Ciaran P. Cronin. Cambridge: MIT Press, 1993.

– 'On Systematically Distorted Communication.' *Inquiry* Vol. 13.

– *Moral Consciousness and Communicative Action*. Trans. Christian Lenhardt and Shierry Weber Nicholsen. Cambridge: MIT Press, 1990.

– *The Philosophical Discourse of Modernity: Twelve Lectures*. Trans. Frederick G. Lawrence. Cambridge: MIT Press, 1987.

– *The Structural Transformation of the Public Sphere: An Inquiry into a Category of Bourgeois Society*. Trans. Thomas Burger and Frederick Lawrence. Cambridge: MIT Press, 1991.

– *The Theory of Communicative Action*. Vol. 1: *Reason and the Rationalization of Society*. Trans. Thomas McCarthy. Boston: Beacon Press, 1984.

Hahn, Lewis Edwin, ed. *The Philosophy of Paul Ricoeur*. The Library of Living Philosophers, vol. 22. Chicago: Open Court, 1995.

Hall, John A. *Liberalism*. London: Paladin, 1987.

Halton, Eugene. *Bereft of Reason: On the Decline of Social Thought and Prospects for Its Renewal*. Chicago: University of Chicago Press, 1995.

Hampshire, Stuart. *Morality and Conflict*. Cambridge: Harvard University Press, 1983.

– ed. *Public and Private Morality*. Cambridge: Cambridge University Press, 1978.

Haworth, Lawrence. *Autonomy: An Essay in Philosophical Psychology and Ethics*. New Haven: Yale University Press, 1986.

Hayek, Friedrich A. *The Constitution of Liberty*. Chicago: University of Chicago Press, 1960.

– *Law, Legislation, and Liberty*. Vol. 1: *Rules and Order*. Chicago: University of Chicago Press, 1973.

- *Law, Legislation, and Liberty*. Vol. 2: *The Mirage of Social Justice*. Chicago: University of Chicago Press, 1976.
- *Law, Legislation, and Liberty*. Vol. 3: *The Political Order of a Free People*. Chicago: University of Chicago Press, 1979.
- *The Road to Serfdom*. Chicago: University of Chicago Press, 1944.

Healy, Paul. 'Situated Rationality and Hermeneutic Understanding: A Gadamerian Approach to Rationality.' *International Philosophical Quarterly*. 36, no. 2 (June 1996).

Hegel, G.W.F. *Elements of the Philosophy of Right*. Trans. H.B. Nisbet. Cambridge: Cambridge University Press, 1991.

Heidegger, Martin. *Being and Time*. Trans. John Macquarrie and Edward Robinson. New York: Harper and Row, 1962.
- *The Principle of Reason*. Trans. Reginald Lilly. Bloomington: Indiana University Press, 1991.
- *The Question Concerning Technology and Other Essays*. Trans. William Lovitt. New York: Harper and Row, 1977.

Held, David. *Introduction to Critical Theory: Horkheimer to Habermas*. Los Angeles: University of California Press, 1980.

Hobbes, Thomas. *The Elements of Law Natural and Politic*. Ed. J.C.A. Gaskin. Oxford: Oxford University Press, 1994.
- *Leviathan*. Ed. Edwin Curley. Indianapolis: Hacket Publishing, 1994.

Hobhouse, Leonard Trelawny. *The Elements of Social Justice*. New York: Henry Holt & Co., 1922.
- *Liberalism and Other Writings*. Ed. James Meadowcroft. Cambridge: Cambridge University Press, 1994.
- *Morals in Evolution: A Study in Comparative Ethics*. New York: Henry Holt & Co., 1923.
- *Social Evolution and Political Theory*. New York: Columbia University Press, 1928.

Hollinger, Robert, ed. *Hermeneutics and Praxis*. Notre Dame: University of Notre Dame Press, 1985.

Holmes, Stephen. *Passions and Constraint: On the Theory of Liberal Democracy*. Chicago: University of Chicago Press, 1995.

Horkheimer, Max. *Critical Theory: Selected Essays*. Trans. Matthew O'Connell. New York: Herder and Herder, 1972.
- *Critique of Instrumental Reason*. Trans. Matthew J. O'Connell and others. New York: Continuum, 1994.

Horkheimer, Max, and Theodor W. Adorno. *Dialectic of Enlightenment*. Trans. John Cumming. New York: Continuum, 1991.

Hospers, John. *Libertarianism: A Political Philosophy for Tomorrow*. Los Angeles: Nash Publishing, 1971.

Humbolt, William von. *The Limits of State Action*. Ed. J.W. Burrow. Indianapolis: Liberty Fund, 1993.

Ingram, David. *Reason, History, and Politics: The Communitarian Grounds of Legitimation in the Modern Age*. Albany: State University of New York Press, 1995.

Jaspers, Karl. *The Future of Mankind*. Trans. E.B. Ashton. Chicago: University of Chicago Press, 1961.

– *Man in the Modern Age*. Trans. Eden and Cedar Paul. Garden City, NY: Doubleday Anchor Books, 1957.

– *Reason and Anti-Reason in Our Time*. Trans. Stanley Godman. London: SCM Press, 1952.

– *Reason and Existence*. Trans. William Earle. London: Routledge and Kegan Paul, 1956.

Johnson, Mark. *Moral Imagination: Implications of Cognitive Science for Ethics*. Chicago: University of Chicago Press, 1993.

Kant, Immanuel. *Critique of Practical Reason*. Trans. Lewis White Beck. New York: Macmillan Publishing, 1956.

– *Critique of Pure Reason*. Trans. Norman Kemp Smith. New York: St Martin's Press, 1965.

– *Groundwork for the Metaphysics of Morals*. Trans. James W. Ellington. Indianapolis: Hacket Publishing, 1981.

– *Political Writings*. Ed. Hans Reiss. Trans. H.B. Nisbet. Cambridge: Cambridge University Press, 1991.

Kateb, George. *The Inner Ocean: Individualism and Democratic Culture*. Ithaca: Cornell University Press, 1992.

Kelly, Michael, ed. *Hermeneutics and Critical Theory in Ethics and Politics*. Cambridge: MIT Press, 1990.

Kemp, T. Peter, and David Rasmussen, eds. *The Narrative Path: The Later Works of Paul Ricoeur*. Cambridge: MIT Press, 1989.

Kerby, Anthony Paul. *Narrative and the Self*. Bloomington: Indiana University Press, 1991.

Koerner, Kirk F. *Liberalism and Its Critics*. London: Croom Helm, 1985.

Kögler, Hans Herbert. *The Power of Dialogue: Critical Hermeneutics after Gadamer and Foucault*. Trans. Paul Hendrickson. Cambridge: MIT Press, 1996.

Knight, Frank H. *Freedom and Reform*. Indianapolis: Liberty Press, 1982.

Kristol, Irving. *Two Cheers for Capitalism*. New York: Mentor Books, 1979.

Kymlicka, Will. *Liberalism, Community, and Culture*. Oxford: Clarendon Press, 1989.

Larmore, Charles E. *Patterns of Moral Complexity*. Cambridge: Cambridge University Press, 1987.

– *The Romantic Legacy*. New York: Columbia University Press, 1996.

Leonard, Stephen. *Critical Theory in Political Practice*. Princeton: Princeton University Press, 1990.

Locke, John. *An Essay Concerning Human Understanding*. Ed. Peter H. Nidditch. Oxford: Clarendon Press, 1975.

– *A Letter Concerning Toleration*. Ed. John Horton and Susan Mendus. New York: Routledge, 1991.

– *Two Treatises of Government*. Ed. Peter Laslett. Cambridge: Cambridge University Press, 1988.

Lomasky, L. *Persons, Rights, and the Moral Community*. Oxford: Oxford University Press, 1987.

Lyotard, Jean-François. *The Postmodern Condition: A Report on Knowledge*. Trans. Geoff Bennington and Brian Massumi. Minneapolis: University of Minnesota Press, 1979.

Lyotard, Jean-François, and Jean-Loup Thebaud. *Just Gaming*. Trans. Wlad Godzich. Minneapolis: University of Minnesota Press, 1985.

Machan, Tibor, ed. *The Libertarian Reader*. Totowa, NJ: Rowman and Littlefield, 1982.

– *Private Rights and Public Illusions*. New Brunswick: Transaction Publishers, 1995.

Machiavelli, Niccolò. *The Discourses*. Ed. Bernard Crick. Trans. Leslie J. Walker. New York: Penguin Books, 1970.

– *The Prince*. Ed. Quentin Skinner and Russell Price. Trans. Russell Price. Cambridge: Cambridge University Press, 1994.

MacIntyre, Alasdair. *After Virtue: A Study in Moral Theory*. Notre Dame: University of Notre Dame Press, 1984.

– *Whose Justice? Which Rationality?* Notre Dame: University of Notre Dame Press, 1988.

MacLean, Douglas, and Claudia Mills, eds. *Liberalism Reconsidered*. Totowa, NJ: Rowman and Allanheld, 1983.

Macmurray, John. *The Self as Agent*. London: Faber and Faber, 1953.

Macpherson, C.B. *The Political Theory of Possessive Individualism: Hobbes to Locke*. Oxford: Clarendon Press, 1962.

Macquarrie, John. *Existentialism: An Introduction, Guide and Assessment*. New York: Penguin, 1972.

Madison, Gary B. 'The Hermeneutics of (Inter)subjectivity, or: The Mind/Body Problem Deconstructed.' *Man and World* 21 (1988).

– *The Logic of Liberty*. New York: Greenwood Press, 1986.

– *The Political Economy of Civil Society and Human Rights*. London: Routledge, 1998.

– 'The Practice of Theory, The Theory of Practice.' *Critical Review* 5, no. 2.

- 'Ricoeur and the Hermeneutics of the Subject.' In *The Philosophy of Paul Ricoeur*. Vol. 22 of *The Library of Living Philosophers*, ed. Lewis Edwin Hahn. Chicago: Open Court, 1995.
Madison, James, Alexander Hamilton, and John Jay. *The Federalist Papers*. Ed. Isaac Kramnick. New York: Penguin Books, 1987.
Manent, Pierre. *An Intellectual History of Liberalism*. Trans. Rebecca Balinski. Princeton: Princeton University Press, 1994.
Mansfield, Harvey C. *The Spirit of Liberalism*. Cambridge: Harvard University Press, 1978.
Marcel, Gabriel. *The Existential Background of Human Dignity*. Cambridge: Harvard University Press, 1963.
- *Man Against Mass Society*. Trans. G.S. Fraser. South Bend, IN: Gateway Editions, 1952.
- *The Philosophy of Existentialism*. Trans. Manya Harari. New York: Citadel Press, 1995.
Marx, Karl. *Karl Marx: A Reader*. Ed. Jon Elster. Cambridge: Cambridge University Press, 1995.
May, Rollo. *The Discovery of Being: Writings in Existential Psychology*. New York: W.W. Norton, 1983.
Merquior, J.G. *Liberalism Old and New*. Boston: Twayne Publishers, 1991.
Mill, James. *Political Writings*. Ed. Terence Ball. Cambridge: Cambridge University Press, 1992.
Mill, John Stuart. 'Bentham.' In *Utilitarianism and Other Writings*, ed. Mary Warnock. New York: Meridian Books, 1962.
- *Considerations on Representative Government*. Indianapolis: Bobbs-Merrill, 1975.
- *On Liberty*. Ed. David Spitz. New York: W.W. Norton and Company, 1975.
- *On the Logic of the Moral Sciences*. Ed. Henry M. Magid. New York: Bobbs-Merrill, 1965.
- *Utilitarianism*. Ed. George Sher. Indianapolis: Hacket Publishing Company, 1979.
Mises, Ludwig von. *Liberalism: A Socio-Economic Exposition*. Kansas City: Sheed, Andrews, and McMeel, 1978.
Mitchell, W.J.T., ed. *On Narrative*. Chicago: University of Chicago Press, 1981.
Montesquieu, Baron de. *Selected Political Writings*. Ed. and trans. Melvin Richter. Indianapolis: Hacket Publishing Company, 1990.
Muller, René J. *The Marginal Self: An Existential Inquiry into Narcissism*. Atlantic Highlands, NJ: Humanities Press, 1987.
Murray, Charles. *What It Means to Be a Libertarian: A Personal Interpretation*. New York: Broadway Books, 1997.

Nagele, Rainer. 'Real and Ideal Discourses: Freud, Habermas and the Dialectic of Enlightenment.' *New German Critique*, no. 22.

Narveson, Jan. *The Libertarian Idea*. Philadelphia: Temple University Press, 1988.

Nietzsche, Friedrich. *Beyond Good and Evil: Prelude to a Philosophy of the Future*. Trans. Walter Kaufmann. New York: Vintage Books, 1989.

– *On the Genealogy of Morals and Ecce Homo*. Ed. Walter Kaufmann. Trans. Walter Kaufmann and R.J. Hollingdale. New York: Vintage Books, 1969.

– *Thus Spoke Zarathustra: A Book for Everyone and No One*. Trans. R.J. Hollingdale. Middlesex: Penguin Books, 1961.

– *The Will to Power*. Ed. Walter Kaufmann. Trans. Walter Kaufmann and R.J. Hollingdale. New York: Vintage Books, 1968.

Nozick, Robert. *Anarchy, State, and Utopia*. New York: Basic Books, 1974.

– *The Examined Life: Philosophical Meditations*. New York: Simon and Schuster, 1989.

– *The Nature of Rationality*. Princeton: Princeton University Press, 1993.

– *Philosophical Explanations*. Cambridge: Harvard University Press, 1981.

Olafson, Frederick A. *What Is a Human Being? A Heideggerian View*. Cambridge: Cambridge University Press, 1995.

Olney, James. *Metaphors of Self: The Meaning of Autobiography*. Princeton: Princeton University Press, 1981.

Ortega y Gasset, José. *The Revolt of the Masses*. New York: W.W. Norton and Co., 1957.

Paine, Thomas. *Political Writings*. Ed. Bruce Kuklick. Cambridge: Cambridge University Press, 1989.

Polkinghorne, Donald. *Narrative Knowing and the Human Sciences*. Albany: State University of New York Press, 1988.

Pollock, Lansing. *The Free Society*. Boulder: Westview Press, 1996.

Popper, Karl R. *The Open Society and Its Enemies*. Vol. 1: *The Spell of Plato*. Princeton: Princeton University Press, 1962.

– *The Open Society and Its Enemies*. Vol. 2: *The High Tide of Prophecy: Hegel, Marx, and the Aftermath*. Princeton: Princeton University Press, 1962.

Randall, William Lowell. *The Stories We Are: An Essay on Self-Creation*. Toronto: University of Toronto Press, 1995.

Rasmussen, David M., ed. *Universalism vs. Communitarianism: Contemporary Debates in Ethics*. Cambridge: MIT Press, 1990.

Rawls, John. 'Justice as Fairness: Political not Metaphysical.' In *Communitarianism and Individualism*. Ed. Shlomo Avineri and Avner de-Shalit. Oxford: Oxford University Press, 1992.

– *Political Liberalism*. New York: Columbia University Press, 1993.

– *A Theory of Justice*. Cambridge: Harvard University Press, 1971.

Raz, Joseph. *The Morality of Freedom*. Oxford: Clarendon Press, 1986.

Reich, Robert B. *The Resurgent Liberal and Other Unfashionable Prophesies*. New York: Random House, 1989.

Reiman, Jeffrey. *Critical Moral Liberalism: Theory and Practice*. New York: Rowman and Littlefield, 1997.

Ricoeur, Paul. *Hermeneutics and the Human Sciences: Essays on Language, Action and Interpretation*. Trans. John B. Thompson. Cambridge: Cambridge University Press, 1983.

– 'History as Narrative and Practice.' *Philosophy Today* 29.

– *Oneself as Another*. Trans. Kathleen Blamey. Chicago: University of Chicago Press, 1992.

– 'On Interpretation.' In *Philosophy in France Today*, ed. Alan Montefiore. Cambridge: Cambridge University Press, 1983.

– *Time and Narrative*. Vol. 1. Trans. Kathleen McLaughlin and David Pellauer. Chicago: University of Chicago Press, 1984.

Rorty, Richard. *Contingency, Irony, and Solidarity*. Cambridge: Cambridge University Press, 1989.

– *Essays on Heidegger and Others*. Cambridge: Cambridge University Press, 1991.

– *Objectivity, Relativism, and Truth*. Cambridge: Cambridge University Press, 1991.

Rosenblum, Nancy. *Another Liberalism: Romanticism and the Reconstruction of Liberal Thought*. Cambridge: Harvard University Press, 1987.

– ed. *Liberalism and the Moral Life*. Cambridge: Harvard University Press, 1989.

Rosenwald, George C., and Richard L. Ochberg, eds. *Storied Lives: The Cultural Politics of Self-Understanding*. New Haven: Yale University Press, 1992.

Rothbard, Murray N. *The Ethics of Liberty*. Atlantic Highlands, NJ: Humanities Press, 1982.

– *Man, Economy and State*. Menlo Park, CA: Institute for Humane Studies, 1970.

Rousseau, Jean-Jacques. *Discourse on Political Economy and The Social Contract*. Trans. Christopher Betts. New York: Oxford University Press, 1994.

– *The Social Contract and Discourses*. Trans. G. Cole. London: Everyman Library, 1993.

Ruggiero, Guido de. *The History of European Liberalism*. Trans. R.G. Collingwood. Gloucester, MA: Peter Smith, 1981.

Salvadori, Massimo. *The Liberal Heresy: Origins and Historical Development*. London: Macmillan, 1977.

Sandel, Michael J. *Democracy's Discontent: America in Search of a Public Philosophy*. Cambridge: Harvard University Press, 1996.

– ed. *Liberalism and Its Critics*. New York: New York University Press, 1984.

– *Liberalism and the Limits of Justice*. Cambridge: Cambridge University Press, 1982.

Sarbin, Theodore R., ed *Narrative Psychology: The Storied Nature of Human Conduct.* New York: Praeger, 1986.

Sartre, Jean-Paul. *Being and Nothingness: An Essay on Phenomenological Ontology.* Trans. Hazel E. Barnes. New York: Philosophical Library, 1956.

Schafer, Roy. *Retelling a Life: Narration and Dialogue in Psychoanalysis.* New York: Basic Books, 1992.

Schapiro, J. Salwyn. *Liberalism: Its Meaning and History.* New York: Van Nostrand, 1965.

Schrag, Calvin O. *Communicative Praxis and the Space of Subjectivity.* Bloomington: Indiana University Press, 1986.

- *The Resources of Rationality: A Response to the Postmodern Challenge.* Bloomington: Indiana University Press, 1992.

Sidorsky, David, ed. *The Liberal Tradition in European Thought.* New York: Capricorn Books, 1970.

Simpson, Evan, ed. *Anti-Foundationalism and Practical Reasoning: Conversations Between Hermeneutics and Analysis.* Edmonton: Academic Printing and Publishing, 1987.

Simpson, Evan, and Stanley Clarke, eds. *Anti-Theory in Ethics and Moral Conservatism.* Albany: State University of New York Press, 1989.

- 'Principles and Customs in Moral Philosophy.' *Metaphilosophy* 24, nos. 1 & 2.

Smith, Adam. *An Inquiry into the Nature and Causes of the Wealth of Nations.* Vols. 1 & 2. Indianapolis: Liberty Classics, 1981.

Smith, P. Christopher. *Hermeneutics and Human Finitude: Toward a Theory of Ethical Understanding.* New York: Fordham University Press, 1991.

Taylor, Charles. *Human Agency and Language: Philosophical Papers I.* Cambridge: Cambridge University Press, 1985.

- *The Malaise of Modernity.* Concord, ON: Anansi Press, 1991.

- *Sources of the Self: The Making of the Modern Identity.* Cambridge: Harvard University Press, 1989.

Theunissen, Michael. *The Other: Studies in the Social Ontology of Husserl, Heidegger, Sartre, and Buber.* Trans. Christopher Macann. Cambridge: MIT Press, 1986.

Tillich, Paul. *The Courage to Be.* New Haven: Yale University Press, 1952.

Tocqueville, Alexis de. *Democracy in America.* Vols. 1 & 2. Ed. Phillips Bradley. Trans. Henry Reeve. New York: Vintage Books, 1990.

Trachtenberg, Zev M. *Making Citizens: Rousseau's Political Theory of Culture.* New York: Routledge, 1992.

Unger, Roberto Mangabeira. *Knowledge and Politics.* New York: Free Press, 1975.

Wallerstein, Immanuel. *After Liberalism.* New York: New Press, 1995.

Walzer, Michael. 'The Communitarian Critique of Liberalism.' *Political Theory* 18, no. 1 (1990).

– *Spheres of Justice: A Defense of Pluralism and Equality.* New York: Basic Books, 1983.

Warnke, Georgia. *Justice and Interpretation.* Cambridge: MIT Press, 1993.

Watson, George. *The Idea of Liberalism: Studies for a New Map of Politics.* London: Macmillan, 1985.

Weber, Max. *The Protestant Ethic and the Spirit of Capitalism.* Trans. Talcott Parsons. New York: Routledge, 1992.

Weithman, Paul H. 'Contractualist Liberalism and Deliberative Democracy.' *Philosophy and Public Affairs* 24, no. 4 (Fall 1995).

Wolff, Robert Paul. *The Poverty of Liberalism.* Boston: Beacon Press, 1968.

Young, James P. *Reconsidering American Liberalism: The Troubled Odyssey of the Liberal Idea.* Boulder: Westview Press, 1996.

Zvesper, John. *Nature and Liberty.* New York: Routledge, 1993.

Index